ENCOUNTERS

TRY NOT TO SMILE

Wild Encounters

TRY NOT TO SMILE

WRITTEN & ILLUSTRATED BY

NICOLETTE SCOURSE

Published under licence by Brown Dog Books and
The Self-Publishing Partnership, 7 Green Park Station, Bath BA1 1JB

www.selfpublishingpartnership.co.uk

ISBN printed book: 978-1-78545-133-1
ISBN e-book: 978-1-78545-134-8

Cover design by Kevin Rylands
Internal design by Andrew Easton

Printed and bound by CPI Group (UK) Ltd, Croydon CR0 4YY

For Alfie, born 29.01.15

…and his generation, who will inherit the wild shores.

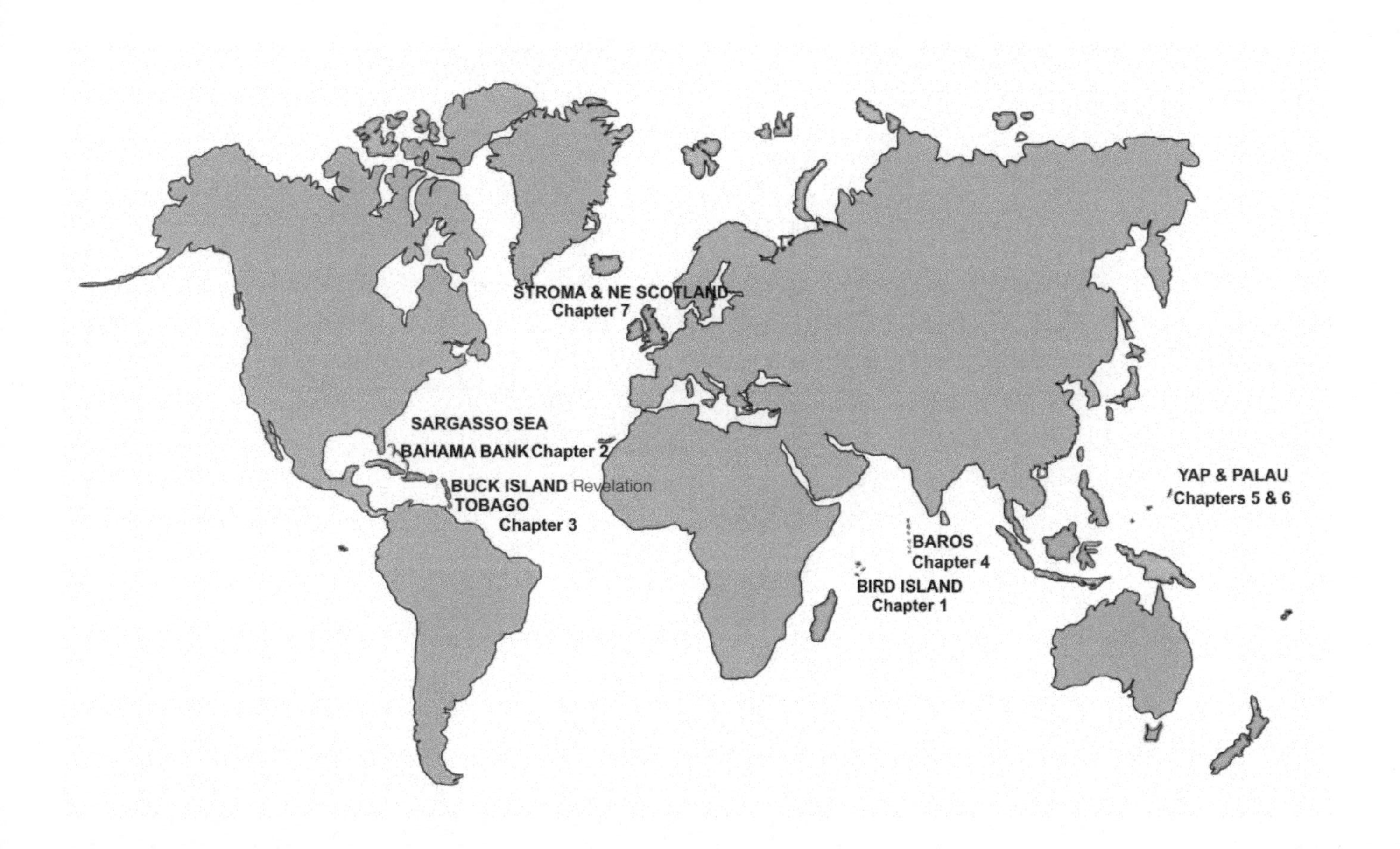
STROMA & NE SCOTLAND
Chapter 7
SARGASSO SEA
BAHAMA BANK Chapter 2
BUCK ISLAND Revelation
TOBAGO
Chapter 3
BAROS
Chapter 4
BIRD ISLAND
Chapter 1
YAP & PALAU
Chapters 5 & 6

Contents

Revelation

BUCK ISLAND, VIRGIN ISLES

As the bubbles cleared, I became aware of sudden weightlessness, dangling as if in the silent sky of another world. Below, and into the mid-turquoise distance, were orange-coloured 'tree tops' of Elkhorn Coral – groves of wide flat-ended branches, flaky layered like Cedars of Lebanon intermingled with spreading gnarled old oak forms. Coming in from above, it was like descending into a forest then suddenly being enclosed by its branches. In between there were 'glades' with isolated 'trees' – tall sea whips – waving gently and rhythmically with the ebb and flow, their lean simplicity resembling fantastical poplars. In contrast, the wafting wide sea fans of the shallows were like exotic tracery screens from an oriental palace – richly embroidered filigrees in bright pinks and purples obscuring shadowy gliding figures behind – sometimes shapes, recognisably fish, sometimes just a movement. Scattered in between were statuesque boulders: clumps of pinkish domed brain corals, intricately etched with tight maze crenellations and undulations.

Life was smoothly gliding and slow. A lobster teetered deeper into the shadows, its shades of blues and dark Prussian blue intricately patterned with earthy ochres and browns. A French Angelfish, spotted with tiny gold flecks, swivelled its eyes as its slim body curved and turned away; its colour changed as it twisted… was it vibrant violet, navy or dark blue? Light and movement created transient colours and volatile patterns, inseparable from the perpetual drifting, moving nature of life underwater. These were the pure hues of medieval stained glass in bright sunlight, intermingled with unexpected contrasts of dark shade. It was an ephemeral place.

I had come from a world of snatched sightings and inadequate images. Beyond fishing from a pier with a hand-held line, my experience of sea creatures seen from above amounted to the delight of a Fairy Penguin surfacing by the wall in Sydney Harbour, a freshly killed shark with the arm of a lone swimmer in its belly and the bizarre vision of turtle hatchlings in the bath of an otherwise orthodox bathroom. My underwater revelations had also been dry. I had never touched a snorkel – I remembered them as something vaguely resembling a shower tube with a caged ping pong ball at one end – with a warning it could cause drowning in very little water. The excitement of animal worlds came from text book diagrams and museum specimens lightened by films now looking like vintage caricatures in diffuse monochrome. This had been a world without digital photography or David Attenborough's natural histories and with no internet as a universal wallpaper of life. Impact comes from one's starting point. I had started from nowhere.

My practical instructions had been brief: 'Just hold the two small lumps between your teeth – not too hard, you don't want to swallow them – and breathe through your mouth… oh… and try not to smile…'

I smiled incessantly – at every fish that looked at me. My mask contorted accordingly. I rapidly achieved a liberal intake of water via the snorkel; my nostrils were enclosed in water rather than air. Vision was made hazy through a mounting level of sea in front of salt smarting eyes. Spluttering and coughing, I surfaced, shed quantities of water from mask and snorkel and tried hard not to smile.

The impact was intense... I was as hooked as a fish. Those glorious few hours had been of an intensity to change one's perception of living things, and life. An odyssey to encounter animals, people, beaches and seas in wild places had begun.

Chapter 1

A PARADISE FOR TURTLES AND BIRDS

Bird Island, Seychelles

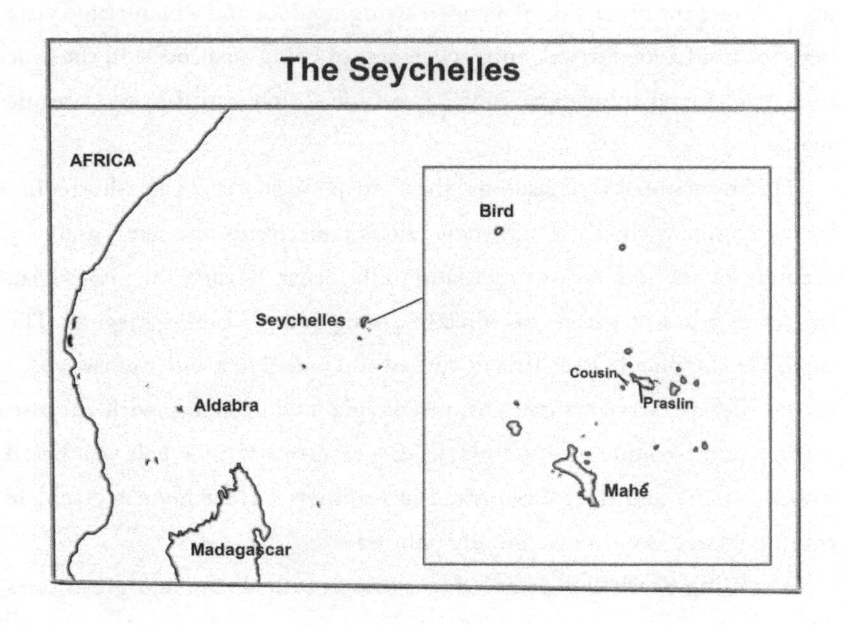

AN ISLAND APART

BACKDROP

The buoyant bounce of rubber wheels on grass lifted the soul, although I was not sure how much it really was so, or if it was just relief at having arrived safely. We had boarded the little aircraft bent double to better fit the headroom so could not fail to notice the old tubular frame seats and patched covers – a flashback to battered school buses of the 1950s. This aura of 'make do and mend' was not the 'look' to which modern travellers are accustomed: nor was the proximity of the pilot's hand clasping the joystick just the other side of an open swinging door and a blank blue vista beyond. It all added to a definite awareness of being suspended in the blue in a small metal tube above more, vast blue – rich with life and oceanic sharks.

The bouncing did not last long: the airstrip was short... in fact shortening by the season as the tides and trade winds redistribute the sand, grain by grain, from one end of this tiny island to the other. Beyond the pilot's head the lower band of green was already giving way to blue sea again. The small De Havilland Otter aircraft turned and taxied to a wider grassy space to the support services: two antique 'Fergie' style tractors with exposed engines and a couple of wood planks as a seat, one with a well weathered wooden trailer and the other parked in readiness – the emergency vehicle trailing a large water tank roughly painted red.

A smiling Seychellois lady led us through lush shrubs and green trees which had shed vivid orange Cordia blossoms across the dusty path. Matching Madagascar Fodies, fiery red and perky, hopped about in between more earthbound brown Barred Ground Doves and jaunty gawky Common Mynas, cavorting like clumsy clowns. Unperturbed by our proximity of only an arm's length, Lesser Noddy Terns and Fairy Terns (White Terns) alighted on branches and dishevelled leaf heaps, greeting, bickering, flexing their wings and going about their daily affairs. We skirted round an outsized tortoise. High overhead a flock of Frigate Birds hung motionless like tethered kites in a clear bright sky. A pair of White-tailed Tropicbirds flew in tandem into the distance.

With the plane gone, the airstrip was deserted but for Curlew Sandpipers, Grey Plovers and a little group of Sanderlings wandering about, heads down, bent on pecking amongst the grass. After the insistent engine noise of the flight the quiet was intense and reassuring. It was like arriving on an alien planet where nature was prodigal and unafraid – a paradise garden, an island of birds. Our first sea swim was a prolonged bird encounter: as we lolled in a sea the colour of school chemistry copper sulphate, Noddy Terns flew close by, oblivious of us, eyes down, heads dipping briefly to scoop floating weed to add to their nests. Even now, outside the breeding season when the population is residents only, this was indeed a bird island – later, from May to September during the south-east monsoon, half a million pairs of Sooty Terns would arrive to breed.

By night, living in parallel with the birds took on a new reality. Tired out by the journey we sank into bed in our simple bungalow, eager for sleep submerged in the quiet world we had encountered on arrival. By contrast, our avian neighbours seemed stimulated by the relative cool of the tropical night. Fairy Terns were arguing and socialising in the trees outside our windows and Noddies bill-slapped, chortled and cackled on the roof all night. By 3 a.m. whining mosquitoes had successfully reconnoitred the holes in our mosquito net and I was relentlessly gathering the offending areas into closed bunches with hair pins. Then came a sudden cool breeze which heralded a torrential downpour. The raindrops fell hard on the roof and ricocheted off the ground in spurts of dust. The sounds were unmuffled as the windows were without glass, the space closed merely by a wooden louvre, and the high pitched ceiling had airy ventilation gaps under the eaves.

The birds sang and it was dawn. For the next week sleep would be a reward of exhaustion. Such considerations were, however, irrelevant in the face of more precious rewards. Nights of ravishing bright indigo skies crowded with stars created nightscapes shining clear. At full moon, late flying birds cast dark blue ground shadows made from moonlight. In a monochrome world white cloud towers dwarfed silver trees and leaves. The unique rewards of day were the island's wildlife, above and below water. We felt very positively alive.

Bird Island is a vulnerable coral island, 1 ½ km (1 mile) long by ½ km (1/4 mile) wide, perched near the underwater edge of the ancient continent of Gondwana. At that time there was a very different distribution of land on the globe: Gondwana (or Gondwanaland) was one of two supercontinents, a big southern landmass which started fragmenting 170 million years ago. The giant pieces began slowly moving apart and continue to do so. As a young teenager I had read of the idea of 'continental drift' and was naively fascinated by the idea of actually living on the Australian piece – one of the oldest and earliest continents to break away and still retaining some of the ancient wildlife. The possible jigsaw of Antarctica, Australia, New Zealand, Africa, Madagascar, South America and India fitting so neatly together to make one landmass and the distribution of ancient versus modern plant and animal types were compelling. Not a widely accepted idea at the time, it is now mainstream. The tiny speck of Bird Island seemed to slot into place in a moving mosaic of overwhelming magnitude and timescale. The island emerges only a matter of metres above the sea, a green oasis of palms, Pisonia and Casuarina trees surrounded by a ring of shifting sand and reefs, far out of sight of any other Seychelles Islands, which themselves are a thousand miles from India in the north, Africa to the west, Sri Lanka to the east, and Madagascar to the south.

There was in the Seychelles a great sense of the continuity of history through different races and peoples meeting at a crossroads of trade and colonisation, and slavery. The facial features, stories of family ancestors and living relatives still link and reflect French, British and Malagasy influences. In Mahé we had found ourselves sitting on a high balcony overlooking granitic mountains and the sea, listening to the stories of two families. Husband and wife linked with history: the French Revolution and the Jacobins deported by Napoleon, the Belle Epoque, tropical timber trading, wealth from Hong Kong, wandering seafaring and living native and tropical. The historical contexts of both family recollections conjured the stuff of movies – riches, politics, murder, betrayal, intrigue, passing romances, love and adventure... Real historic events are often more exciting than fantasy.

By contrast, the living history of Bird Island reflected the basic challenge of making a living and surviving in a small place isolated in a big sea. The owner of the island came from an old French colonial Seychellois family; his great grandparents were with the French equivalent of the East India Company. He described how his work as a coconut plantation assessor had taken him to Mauritius and all over the Seychelles Islands. Bird Island had been abandoned as a coconut plantation and had become severely degraded as a tern breeding habitat. He bought it at the age of 25 in 1967 and over the years has returned it to the prime tern colony of previous centuries as well as initiating a turtle conservation project in 1995.

Long before the days of the coconut plantation, visiting ships of the eighteenth and nineteenth centuries, and subsequent islanders, would have relished fresh meat and eggs of the Hawksbill and Green Turtles that come to breed here. When the island was first sighted and named by the British in 1771, 'innumerable' birds were noted, and Dugongs, or sea cows (now rare), were lying on the beaches. In following years, ships landed in search of timber (poor) and fresh water (old and bad tasting from a pond). The long-established tern colony had created large deposits of phosphorous-rich guano which was mined for fertiliser in 1895. The human population peaked at 100 until the resource was exhausted ten years later. By 1931 only a dozen people remained, surviving on growing cotton and a small coconut plantation. In traditional practice large numbers of terns were killed as their nests damaged the coconut flowers. Later in the thirties papaya was planted; Seychellois tradition has it that the coconut and the papaya trees provide all the necessities of life – food, lodging and medicine – and both still grow plentifully on the island today alongside stray cotton plants. In the face of these human activities the natural ecology dwindled; the Sooty Tern population dropped from over a million pairs to 65,000, which had further reduced to 18,000 by 1955. The northern tip of sand was all that was left as a useful habitat.

In the 1970s, tourism became the most significant contributor to the Seychellois economy and chalets were constructed using what was available on site for buildings – the larger Casuarina trees, palm thatch, – and the old tree trunks were used as tables. The south-east side of the island is fickle and moving, subject to seasonal strong waves and beach erosion. Extreme weather between 1988 and 1992 partly washed away the tiny hotel which was rebuilt well back in the island's centre. The continual redistribution of sand and erosion affecting beaches and runway are part and parcel of all small coralline islands.

Introduced rabbits became a pest and were exterminated by marksmen in 1995, and rats, a constant threat to birds' eggs, were eradicated in 1996. Today, chickens peck amongst the grasses of the central utilities clearing and a few domestic pigs roam the forested path; home grown chokos (chayote), mangoes, papaya and fish also feature prominently on the menu. Solar power and very careful usage of fresh water make for an environmentally sensitive place which has received coveted awards. Appropriately, for once, humans are an insignificant minority in the natural scheme of things. It is indeed an island for the birds… and the turtles.

Fairy (or White) Tern. '... so light and delicate a body must be tenanted by some wandering fairy spirit': Charles Darwin fell under their spell. Their large dark blue eyes possibly enable fishing at night and the long blue beak carries small fish held sideways.

DIGGING FOR HATCHLINGS AND CRABS

It was 31st January, 2002. On the south side of the island the beach was completely submerged with a seasonal invasion of mounds of dead Turtle Grass and leathery brown seaweed. In pouring rain, six of us, led by Stephen, an enthusiastic island volunteer, squelched and waded through heavy, slimy, sliding fronds. As the slithering strands parted pale spiky sea urchins were exposed – rather too numerous a population for peace of mind for those wearing toeless sandals. With sea surging up to our knees, superfluous umbrellas were more use as impromptu walking sticks to assist climbing over arching roots and drooping heavy stems which effectively made barriers like trip wires encroaching through and over the deep seaweed. How had a female turtle, less than knee high, battled her way through this maze to dig her nest?

At the nest site, carefully noted in the turtle records book, the sand was soft and wet and sheets of tropical rain poured and dripped off overhanging undergrowth and trees. Stephen dug with his hands. Here and there were little eruptions of dark sand as darker shapes moved beneath. Discarded eggshells felt like very thin, pliable leather. Carefully he cupped each turtle hatchling (weighing 13.5–19.5g, approximately 0.5oz) in his hand and put it in the waiting washing-up bowl. Holding one energetic wriggling creature in the palm of my hand, it seemed ridiculously tiny for the present digging task, let alone tackling the immense challenge ahead. Encrusted with sand, tiny turtle eyes glinted, their flippers working back and forth, sliding about in the red plastic bowl. More and more of them – the bowl was a striving heap of reptilian life. The intricate perfection of hatchlings takes one's breath away. As with all young animals their proportions are very different to the adults; they have 'the Disney factor'- a larger head and face in comparison to the body size, and longer gangly limbs. The peaks and troughs of the tiny facetted shell are exaggerated: from a double central line of peaked plates the shell curves down to a pale fluted edge.

Halfway down the hole Stephen dug faster, his face hardening into fury and mouthing curses. We crouched closer over the hole, now nearly as deep as my arm. There was a foul smell of rot as handful after handful of half-eaten eggs and turtle remains were scooped out. Stephen gently filtered the dark stinking slime through his fingers, but in vain. Score: turtles – 151: crabs – 70.

Sodden and frustrated at the efficiency of crab predators we took the bowl of survivors to the beach further round on the west side of the island. To cope with the distance, I borrowed an antique 1940s 'sit-up-and-beg' bicycle (with cross bar) and pedalled at speed across the bumpy grass runway in the still driving rain. At the top of the beach the others – and the crabs – were waiting.

The six of us made a protective anti-crab shield, three either side of a smooth downhill slope to the sea. The battalions of ghost crabs multiplied, eyes vigilant and mobile on stilts. When these crabs are fully focused on a target they run staggeringly fast, fully sideways on, deftly teetering on the pointed stiletto tips of their legs. Ghost Crabs have been recorded speed running, covering 2.1 m (6' 10") per second in the equivalent of 'top gear', using only two pairs of legs instead of the usual four. They scuttled up and down and sideways between our feet as we rushed up and down the slope herding them off the turtle trail. We capered and stamped the ground like Khathakali dancers with footwork aimed to avoid squashing them, while Stephen released hatchlings in groups from the top of the beach. In their haste and being shorter than one's thumb, the hatchlings toppled helplessly into footprints in the soft sand, clambering over sand humps and hollows sometimes to fall back in again. At last tiny flippers worked a steady rhythmic track down the last wet stretch of sand. By the time they reached the smooth, firm slope downwards some of them were almost rearing up on their short hind flippers, front flippers clear of the sand, scuttling on two legs in order to rush on, frantically obeying that primeval instinct driving them to the sea.

There were rough pounding waves. Each time a wave surged up the sand, overturning a turtle onto its back or simply sweeping them back up the beach where they had started, we rushed to be in all places at once in the face of the relentless advance of crabs. When knocked on to their backs they reared their heads high above the scaly bellies, flapping their flippers wildly. That any of these little creatures could even reach the water in between these turbulent waves seemed impossible, let alone survive the ever larger pounding waves beyond. Once into that churning bubbling turbulence they seemed to be at the mercy of the great wave machine. They were being swept up as part of a transformation as each great water wedge unrolled to speed fast and forwards towards the shore. Bouncing and sliding on the water they were like surfers in a net of surging froth being pushed from below. Old memories stirred – of being dumped in surf, caught in a wall of water reaching high overhead, being tumbled, toppled, twisted and turned over, a wet sandstorm swirling into mouth, nose and eyes, and trying to distinguish between vertical and horizontal.

In spite of it all, according to film made by an expert snorkelling camera team, the hatchlings just keep on paddling at full strength and ride out the turmoil, in fact swimming so fast the cameraman could barely keep up. The film footage makes amazing viewing, and it is reassuring for those who have kept watch – anxious, horrified, relieved, but always shaded with apprehension of the next wave, the next predator. Crossing the fringing reef and coming face to face with its many waiting fish predators they show no evasive behaviour; they simply head on for the open sea. Scientific studies have shown they seem to rely totally on swimming speed – the fastest swimmers have the highest survival rate.

Secreted in dense vegetation with difficult access from the sea, a turtle's nest had been heavily predated by crabs. Stephen dug deep for surviving hatchlings; digging as a group, hatchlings can take two days to dig their way out.

Science aside, it was akin to watching one's children leave home. As a snorkeler one also had a particular shared feeling of the conditions: a dark rain cloud approaching, grey sky matching grey choppy sea, low visibility, an unexpected larger wave slopping and swamping one under, a loss of sense of direction below and above. We recalled the four small Black Tip Reef Sharks we had seen quietly swimming in a mere hand depth of water, and further out, six larger juveniles. A few hours later we returned to the beach, the sky pitch black, rain, fierce surf. Somewhere in the swell beyond, our turtles were paddling, bouncing and tipping against or with the force of the water, doing their non-stop 24-hour swim until the sea's currents carried them to the open ocean – not termed the 'juvenile frenzy' for nothing.

THE ISLAND HUMAN MINORITY

What of the human 'frenzy'? A little later that evening, a German lady politely enquired as to why we had been doing 'little Indian dances' on the beach in the rain. Tired, soaked to the skin, staggering about through heaving seaweed and sea urchins, slipping and crawling under low, slimy undergrowth, then racing across the island, rushing up and down a sand slope trying to outwit athletic crabs in an attempt to ease the passage of hatchling turtles – who were these eccentrics?

Chris, from England, was a conservationist and what could only be described as a manic aquarium fanatic. Chris, his wife, shared his enthusiasms as well as the name. We first met him crawling over grass peppered with dried tortoise droppings in an effort to get eyeball to eyeball with the heaviest tortoise in the world. Mistakenly named Esmeralda, this splendid male creature was mundanely munching, flanked by five Noddy Terns on the ground and a pair of Fairy Terns in the background shrubbery – quite a photo opportunity even if one compromised by taking a less earth-oriented view. An older English couple was similarly stalwart in the face of the torrential rain and hazards, although Geoffrey, like me, was slightly limited in mobility and also hanging on grimly to any strong bits of dripping undergrowth. He had been an actor and his wife, we presumed, was similarly inclined as she had a beautiful voice, diction and intonation. They were quiet and if one had met them in the street one might have thought them too orthodox and sophisticated to be thigh wading for turtles.

Michel and Ughette were from France, collected Morgan cars, and were energetically keen on retrieving hatchlings. Such an activity was almost commonplace when compared to some of their previous exploits: taking a year out to drive across the Sahara in an old car; and Michel had walked the Pilgrim's Way from Auvergne to Santiago de Compostela with a donkey. Their house was of extraordinary modern design surrounded by a hectare of garden containing 300 sculptures of wood, iron and metal.

Not all of the visitors chose to be so 'up close and personal' with wildlife in the raw. Many returned year after year simply to escape some or all of the relentless modern treadmill: artful advertising, conspired commercialism, contrived retail, manipulated media, hyped entertainment, machine whine, cars, crowds, fashion fads, food fads, city noise, building noise, telephones, television, junk mail, email, sham, scam, spam... Bird Island is the antithesis of all this: the lack of conventional tropical resort construction and air conditioning allow the feeling of a simple breeze passing through, a reality of being in touch with the natural world, an inkling of being close to the primitive life without actually having to battle personally with the intense elements in order to eat, wash and survive comfortably.

Visitors come from many cultures and many walks of life. Such a place is for many, in effect, a pilgrimage. A half-Russian, half-Swiss man has returned annually for 35 years, almost the entire life of the lodge. Whenever he appeared he was always carrying a huge tome under one arm and accompanied by a particularly pretty woman with the Scandinavian sculpted features frequent in St Petersburg. Enviably he lived in that city, just around the corner from the Mariinsky Theatre enabling him to walk to the opera every night, even in temperatures 40°C below zero (-40°F). Peter was eventually unable to contain his curiosity as to the title of the book: it had to be something other than 'War and Peace' – it was all the known facts on the Aztecs. Other regulars were Expat American divers from Europe who came with wetsuits and fish identification books; thankfully discreet closet-nudists, great and small from Germany, who came with nothing; demure ageing couples from well-to-do, well-behaved suburbs of southern England; keen German fishermen; photographers – feverishly focused, professional and amateur, sensitive and insensitive, from Holland, Germany and France; seasoned travellers totting up their list of unusual places; Seychellois families on holiday; many ageless young at heart just loving being part of life; and from all over the world a few disbelieving/horrified/bored trip tasters in transit on three island packages. Old timers swapped quintessential bird experiences, turtle incidents, fish sightings and meetings with sharks, and recalled with nostalgia a past bar lady, of generous proportions and a wonderful smile, who when mixing cocktails made theatre – shaking her entire being to the extent the vibrations continued some time after the drinks had been set down before the mesmerised clientele.

With so few guests spread over extended areas of sands, shallows, reefs, lagoon, runway, and wild jungled areas, one could indulge in place or activities without seeing another soul except at mealtimes. In such a place there must have been quite a few people of like minds who fortuitously coincided at particular sightings of turtles, tortoises or birds and maybe shared thoughts and experiences – and many who did not. They had passed by each other without realising – like ships in the night – as we had done with a fascinating scientist, but fortunately met her before it was too late.

We had noticed a lady walking with difficulty using crutches. Staff helped her along the path from her chalet to the dining room and obviously had known her for a while. She wore bright sarongs in optimistic colours and was obviously a positive person with perseverance – sometimes we saw her aiming towards the sea, wielding snorkel and fins. We marvelled at this, her courage to have travelled here alone, which I had gathered when chatting. It was when we left on the same plane that we discovered that we were both zoologists and both specialised in animal behaviour and fascinated by animals of the sea. She was a professor and her particular interest, and reason for regularly visiting Bird Island, was to research change of sex, known to be common in many fish species. When out snorkelling, she collected (with special licence) baby fish in plastic bags and had an aquarium set up by the wash house (no wonder the staff knew her so well, and what a shame aquarium crazy Chris had missed her, another silently passing ship.) At the end of each stay she transported them alive back to Europe in breathable plastic bags in an outer polystyrene box – which was there with our luggage on the old 'Fergie' trailer. She was obviously a leading authority on marine aquaria and the rearing of exotic species, which after a year might reach four inches long, after two years, nine inches or more. She had discovered a new species of parrotfish living on algae and named it after the owner's wife. She commented parrotfish were pale coloured when relaxed, which was interesting, recalling some colour flushes we had seen previously. She was obviously an expert snorkeler and diver, having carried out detailed studies on the erosion of living and dead coral by parrotfish versus sea urchins involving sustained swimming following individual fish. Her current limited mobility was due to a fall back at home which had broken her pelvis in six places – 'inconveniently' for her current fish-collecting trip. We silently marvelled even more. She regularly snorkelled along the outer reef amongst the sharks and, while there, had witnessed the Frigate Birds homing in on the turtle hatchling's frenzy swim as they headed out towards the open sea. I felt extremely humble on all counts.

CRAB CITY CULTURE

Following the 'turtling' night of torrential rain another nest of hatchlings emerged in more clement conditions. These behaved very differently and were very spread out as they ran down the shore into the sea. It was an evening to just sit, face into the wind and marvel... Score: turtles 120: crabs 0. Lives had been gathered and sown into the sea. The hatchlings were off safely and swimming for their lives so we could stand and watch the most extensive and dramatic bright sunset we have ever seen. A lone giant pink cloud suddenly transformed sky, sand and sea into an alien spectrum. The sea turned a metallic mauve with dark pink undulations; the wet sand reflected the same vivid pink as the sky, whilst the dry sand and the rest of everything seemed as if there had been one sweep of the pink-tinted brush.

As we formed our human barricades to keep the crabs off the turtle track, one couldn't help noticing that they were not simpletons: they had various mechanical and behavioural options which they employed appropriately.

Everyone knows crabs walk sideways on eight legs, but they have other possibilities. The Ghost Crab has an apt scientific name, *Ocypode,* from Greek, meaning fast foot. It changes its leg array according to the speed it requires. At general walking pace it ambles along on four pairs of walking legs, but when speed is needed it lifts the fourth pair off the ground. While at full throttle it becomes as airborne as a crab can – the third pair lift off enabling it to run at a speed – difficult to intercept, as in hatchling chasing. Crab locomotion looks strangely mechanical and awkward to our eyes – abrupt stiff actions with a touch of the robotic or cinema alien. Their fascinating movement works on a very different system to ours and the turtles'. Instead of an internal hard skeleton of levers worked by muscles arranged around them, crabs and other arthropods – insects, spiders, centipedes, etc. – have their skeleton outside. Their legs are more or less

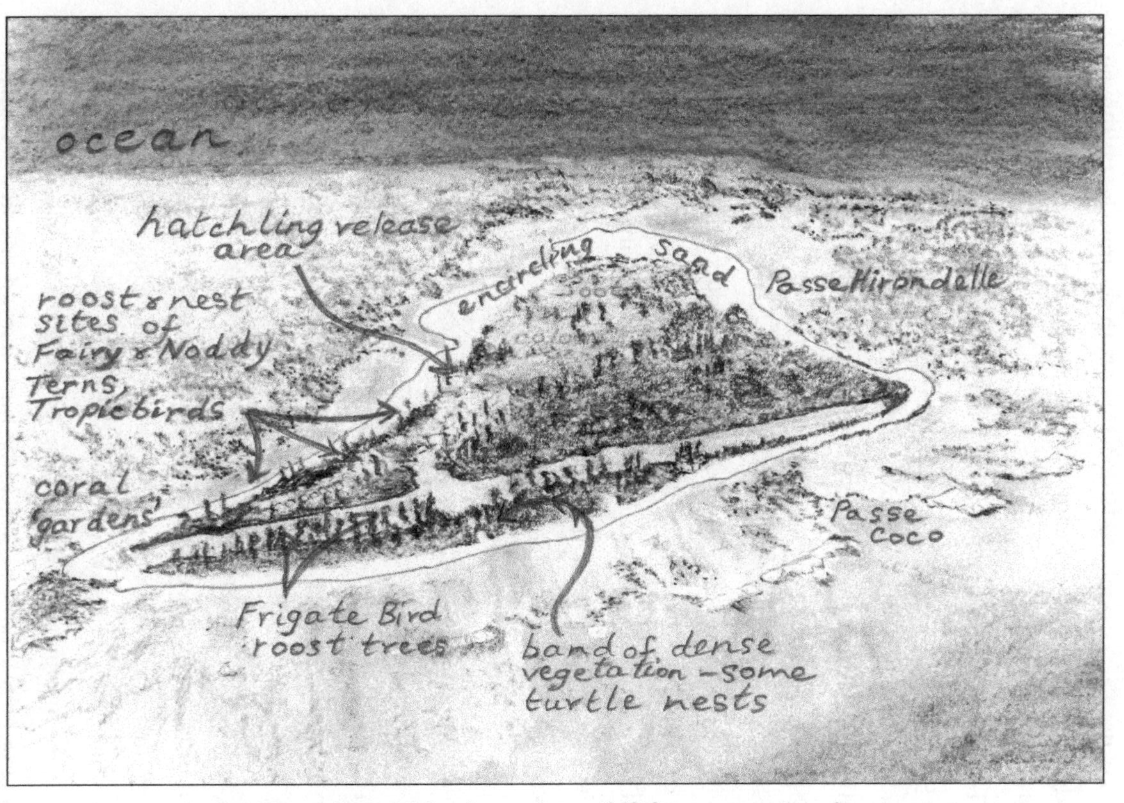

Aerial View of Bird Island – a tiny wildlife sanctuary in a big ocean.

like a sequence of articulated hollow tubes with the muscles pulling on the inside (and packed in very compactly as one can demonstrate by trying to dine on a crab claw).

This alien body design gets more bizarre when the crabs start grappling and dining. Having caught a hatchling, more legs – eating legs – appear which had been neatly stowed around the mouth when not in use. These are smaller, specialised, and such extreme tools for specific jobs of dissecting, shredding, manoeuvring, and accurate placing that their leggy origins are barely recognisable. Gruesome in their usage, the speed and expertise in synchronising these mouthparts at such speed puts knives, forks, spoons and chopsticks into a lesser context.

The Ghost Crabs are so named for their pale colours and dusk-to-dawn habits – we heard and felt them running about and over our feet when we walked in the dark. They are difficult to see even with a torch. From place to place their colour varies. Over a long period of time they have the ability to change hue to match their surroundings; they change the concentration and dispersal of pigment within specialised cells.

They feed on much more than baby turtles, which are only available from December to May. They are quick to grab any carrion, debris, ants' eggs and small creatures from the water's edge – burrowing mole crabs and small, clam-like snails – and, we observed, steal others' prey using the learning potential of their very small 'brains'. We watched at sunset as five Turnstones worked their way along the edge of the waves, using their shut beaks for sideways turning and then open-beaked for prodding the prize. At this point the waiting group of eight crabs rushed in like a gang of bovver boys, at which the birds hopped and flew a little, tried again, hopped further, tried again... The sequence was repeated over and over again until the birds eventually left. We also observed crabs bullying other bird species over food. With raised, elongated eyes like stick radio aerials (compared to the round eyes of the land crabs), they were alert to everything.

Their other preoccupation is mound and burrow building – which seems pretty basic until one takes a closer look and it transforms into an enigma. The best time to watch is at sunrise at a low tide. This time of day in such a place is like walking into the Garden of Eden. Horizontal stripes of bright, moving light – turquoises, pale and intense, smeared with purple indigo – entice one through the dark Casuarina tree trunks. The crisp purity of the light and bold verticals against horizontals recall a Hockney painting. The wind wafts the dry drapes of Casuarina needles, the Noddy Terns chatter in the tree forks and on the shore beyond is 'crab city'.

The slightly dishevelled beach of the night before has been scoured by the waves and is now as smooth and pristine as a new canvas ready for artwork. Bird tracks criss-cross at random. Most prominent are larger areas, unmarked other than by wonderful diagonal curving lines of patterned tracery – controlled, ordered, symmetrical, with a beginning and an end. They could have been the work of a person carefully dragging a pointed stick through the damp sand. These are the tracks of a Ghost Crab, leading to the edifice of its endeavours. The animal emerges from its burrow clasping a ball of sand with its pale blue front claws (one claw much larger than the other) and two front pairs of walking legs. These are a colour contrast of green and copper, joints and tips highlighted in orange. The crab runs along the beach for some distance before depositing it, slowly creating a conical heap. On each visit it runs in the same direction, sideways up the growing pile which thus takes on a spiral pattern with lines of crab tip print. In the final stages the crab pats, moulds and taps loose sand into a peak. The final mound, volcano-shaped, is higher than the width of the crab including its extended legs – an image of heavy earthmovers on stilettos comes to mind. It is a crab citadel. The excavated burrow shaft is long with a chamber at the end, occasionally it is Y-shaped with a second entrance. The male repetitively rams down the area round entrances with his big front claw. Inside he is sheltered from the heat of the day and winter cold.

Meanwhile, female crabs inspect the mountain constructions and, predictably, their choice is based on size. She moves in with the male in his burrow, but here is the riddle, the evidence that doesn't logically fit with the plot. The female has already been fertilised, she is carrying eggs bearing the genes of another male. Therefore, there seems to be no advantage to the male who has proved his strength spending all his time and energy on the construction of his exceptional mound and burrow. His genes do not enter into this strange transaction. This information was divulged to us by the professor with whom we had had our all-too-brief, but fascinating, encounter cut short by flight departures. She is gathering more information on this baffling behaviour, uncovering yet more levels of subtlety and interaction. There was also exciting work ahead in unravelling the mystery of the males underground making noise patterns to attract the females – which one can hear if one puts one's ear to the sand. Unfortunately, when we gleaned this extraordinary information we no longer had sand beneath our feet, only the sophisticated world of airport concrete floors.

Crab citadel construction. Clockwise from the top: a crab emerges from its burrow; climbs the mound, clasping a ball of sand; manipulates the sand into position. Left: crossed by bird footprints, an arduous trail of crab-trodden tracks leads to the completed construction, one of several close to the tideline.

HATCHLINGS VS CRABS

Later in the day, as the sun was sinking, the far end of the great empty arc of beach was our goal, specifically a numbered marker high up near shrubby undergrowth. As Stephen pushed the sand aside, scrabbling flippers and faces surfaced and gradually a bigger and bigger smile crept across his face. This nest was obviously a record – 213, the biggest number of live exits so far this year. (The average clutch size for this area is 100-200.) They were ushered down a crab-free track to the waiting sea along with some from a previous night which Stephen had held back as they had not completely absorbed the necessary nutritious stores of their egg sacs. These were very lethargic, some barely moving. We stood and watched, tense, – willing them down into the waves which unfortunately were becoming crashing masses of water.

Again it was sheer agony seeing them being swept back further up the beach than they had started. Stephen began to chain-smoke. Finally, that glorious moment came when their tracks began to well up with water and white froth encircled the wriggling little dark mound, almost trying to race the outgoing wave in order to keep up with it. Sometimes they were left stranded high and dry, but ultimately being swept away, leaving the hazards of the land and the crabs for the 'safety' of the sea and open water. Straining our eyes through the binoculars we could make them out for a few more metres occasionally rearing their heads up – tiny little black dots tossed about like dead leaves pitched into the ebb and flow of tides and probabilities before disappearing into the shining blue shimmer under beige-pink clouds of the sunset.

The next evening's hatchlings were a complete contrast to the lethargic Hawksbills. These were Green Turtles, comparative giants of 25 g (nearly an ounce) with darker carapace, more sprightly and with immense front flippers like oars rotating so fast they went down the beach like trains. The contrast between the two species was exactly like the long-life battery commercial of demented clockwork toys. Their tracks looked like plant stems incised into the sand, the dragging tail etched the stem-like path and the sprightly 'sprouting leaf' imprints were made by the windmill action of the front flippers. Under the dark flipper skin one could see intimations of the classic vertebrate bone structure beneath.

Their passage was easy – conditions were calm and clear, an infinite indigo of sea and sky, dusted with multitudes of dazzling silver stars and tinted bright planets. So far from anywhere, the clarity of the night sky was a timeless constant, independent of modern introductions of artificial light and polluted air. When the moon was full, walking at night was like being in a stage set, everything veiled in an unearthly cool blue tinted with shadows of violet, even the ubiquitous crabs on sand and paths. Nights were never silent, nothing seemed to sleep: fairy terns socialised, argued and threatened, and chattering Noddy Terns always added to the cacophony.

Overnight the calm weather gave way to grey clouds above the northern horizon, transforming into a heavy pink cumulus cloud as the sun rose. Then a complete rainbow arc crossed the sky above the western horizon and the whole became suffused with pink – even the rainbow colours had a wash of pink like an ephemeral veil. By the time one's eye had travelled the rainbow's length to the far end, the other end had disappeared completely.

By mid-afternoon the heavy cumulus clouds of dawn had contorted into a sky of wind and cyclonic turmoil – a spin off from the cyclone over Madagascar further to the south. Wonderful artistically dramatic skies and natural forces turned to apprehension when waiting at the grassy airfield for our diminutive aircraft with its 'bus seats' which was to take us back to Mahé. The 'strong Aussi pilot' (as described by one of the new arrivals, obviously thankful to be so) leapt out and ran into the office to phone Mahé to check we could still land there. Stephen looked at me with a wry grin and offered me the 1940s bicycle as an alternative option. Looking forward through the cockpit as we approached Mahé there was a view of thick cloud and rain, peering for the runway, with main tanks at zero, tiptanks not switched on and a notice saying 'On no account land without tiptanks if main tank less than three gallons'. I mused over what a tiptank might be. The strong Aussi landed the antique aircraft expertly and smoothly; obviously some outback training.

The first lap of the frenzy – Green Turtle hatchlings with focus in their glittering eyes stride out, rearing up clear of the sand, some running almost like birds taking off, some stirring up sand with flexible flippers making near swimming actions on land. Lucky females may return several decades later to breed.

IN THE SHADOW OF EL NINO – A DIVERSION

Previously the storms had been much worse. Before returning to the northern winter we snorkelled Isle Ronde near Praslin and saw a reef recently pulverised by the comparatively distant effects of El Nino. The effects of the full force of wind and sea at its most ferocious could be seen everywhere; the sea floor was a carpet of pale, battered and broken coral… but the tenacity of life was evident.

It happened to be a day of grey choppy sea, turbid visibility. Fish life was occasional and sparse: two sweetlips, black and white striped with their vivid yellow lips and eyes, and a few turquoise and blue parrotfish, sporadic Yellow Tang and Blue Tang … a small pipefish, as thin as its name, and deep blue flickers of Chromis. Two small pink and magenta squid came close and looked at us in their typical inquisitive, focused way, swivelling their eyes for every detail. Then the prospect of the devastated reef changed totally… there, a long way down through the murky grey there was a turtle, relaxed, almost flying with the easy motion of its flippers as it gently swam out of sight.

Nearby in the Marine Park San Pierre, close to a tiny island edged with great rocky outcrops, the coral was similarly smashed, but small shoals of fish were fairly abundant. They were obviously benefiting from the food-laden water being flushed through gaps in the rocks and waves breaking in a very heavy swell. We could just about hover still enough to focus on the pure metallic blue and silver sides of Blue Fusiliers, dark surgeonfish, Large Trumpetfish, and neat little striped Sergeant Majors. Long-armed yellow starfish sprawled and crisply striped black and white Pennantfish swam sedately with their unlikely twirling trails of dorsal fins and pert pouting mouths.

Then in the rough current full of noise and bubbles and cloudy bits and pieces of plankton streaming in between the rocks, there was a turtle – a Hawksbill. It was eating a sponge, hanging vertically, only an arm's length away. It had a distinctly dark-edged beak, big bright eyes, and a patterned shell smoother than one could begin to imagine. Images of Edwardian 'tortoiseshell' hair combs flashed to mind: the horny layer of a

Hawksbill Turtle's shell, pale mottled honey colours through tan to dark mahogany to almost black, cut and shaped, highly smoothed and polished. Memories of trinkets and jewellery my parents had bought in Fiji and Hawaii gave a particular focus to this living reality: the gleaming surface was never connected with any thought of grappling and stabbing a live turtle. At that time animal souvenirs and trinkets were part of travel. For animal lovers there was a comfortable assumption that maybe the animal was washed up dead on the beach. The other possibility was that it was a by-product from a hotel kitchen; turtle soup appeared regularly on hotel menus, not necessarily with particular gourmet pretensions – I remember it as somewhat akin to consommé, salty and not much else. Soup (usually made from the Green Turtle) and 'tortoiseshell' were desirable luxury acquisitions which had no association with the extinction of species. Today both species are listed as endangered but they are still eaten in some cultures and remain as coveted luxury items where old traditions die hard, or where burgeoning extreme consumerism still feeds off extreme poverty.

The feeding turtle hovered and tilted: the hydrodynamic shape of the shell was tuned to such conditions while we finned hard to avoid being swept against bruising rocks. The swell pushed the animal upside down and its bright yellow belly was gloriously exposed for one fleeting unforgettable moment of beautiful living turtle shell. We must return to these waters.

A Green Turtle swims on a reef unconcerned about quiet floating human observers nearby. Now endangered and admired, it was previously a soup ingredient across the world.

HAWKSBILLS ASHORE AND IN THE LAGOON

The same plane was still functioning six years later, bus seats that bit more threadbare, roughly repaired here and there with fraying edges. Apparently the runway had shortened a little more as the persistent power of the sea shifted sand slowly from one end of the island to the other.

The place had the lovely relaxed atmosphere of coming home – peace and beauty still staggering and not exaggerated by memory. But time had blurred the discomfort of unrelenting heat through a tired night punctuated by calls of birds on the roof and geckos on the rafters. At 2 a.m. we resorted to the beach, armed with insect repellent, water, torch and binoculars. Earlier the moon had been rich gold, close to the horizon.

By the time we emerged through the Casuarina trees on to the sand it had disappeared behind cloud but the myriads of stars seemed even brighter. There was a tactile strong breeze coming in cool from the sea – this was the place to be. It was a busy place: some Noddies and Fairy Terns were flying, there were crabs running everywhere – white ghost crabs, living up to their name – and purplish crabs with blue pincers. We were glad of the torch.

It was 2008. The turtle yearly cycle had moved on – it was now November in the peak of the nesting season. Time and people had moved on too. The owner's son was taking over the management of the island. The turtles were now in the care of Robbie, ex-warden of Cousin Island. By one of those strange coincidences in life, we had, unknowingly, known of him for some years via a conservation work colleague who had talked of living, Robinson Crusoe style, on a nearby island doing conservation work under his direction.

For ten years Robbie had been a warden on various islands and for twenty-five years had been in charge of Cousin Nature Reserve Island – one of great importance as a sea bird island, with a core of Pisonia trees full of Lesser Noddies, and rare land birds such as the Seychelles Magpie Robin and Seychelles Warblers, and, like Bird Island, a haven for Giant Tortoises from the remote island of Aldabra. While on Bird he had had the privilege of long discussions – and arguments, he said – with Sir David Attenborough. We had visited Cousin on an organised trip in 2002, so our paths could have already crossed. Conservation staff accompanied all visitors as it is a carefully managed habitat where people give way to animal priority and are not allowed to wander from designated paths nor clamber for a better photograph. Wayward humans may well have presented more of a challenge than the wildlife to Robbie and his helpers. On our visit the usual over-enthusiastic photographers needed discouragement, and, more engagingly, there was a plethora of European city ladies, bejewelled, immaculately manicured, clad in elegant *décolleté* glamour beach wear, wearing decorative, backless high-heeled sandals and totally unprepared to discover the virulence of hungry mosquitoes swarming on to sun-oiled naked skin following a beach landing in vigorous surf. Fortunately, we had plenty of spare insect repellent.

With a lifetime of practical conservation behind him, Robbie was now walking Bird Island's shore at first light, in fact six times round the 6 km island perimeter through the course of each day. At dawn there were no human footprints other than Robbie's, just multiple networks of bird feet and crabs, as if someone had decided on creating an immense carpet of repetitive claw patterns, variations on a theme, tightly packed against a fine white background.

The first rays of the sun cast long beach shadows and shafts of light through dark tree trunks and streaming curtains of windswept Casuarina needles – will o' the wisp leaves in drifts. On the sand beyond dry needles, white crabs still scuttled. Standing on this deserted long line of beach curving a way round out of sight, the air was fresh and bright, the horizon was crisp blue – a vista of freedom. An open wide sky was smeared with big brush clouds, shifting and reflecting, moving the light across the expanse of turquoise sea to mix with shadows from below. Near inshore it paled to limpid pale green streaked dark purple with Turtle Grass and floating pieces. Here was a glimpse of ancient space – spaciousness untainted and untouched… empty space, but intensely full. Total quiet was intense sound: near waves breaking, distant reef waves rumbling, ocean wind.

First out of the branches came pairs of Fairy Terns, darting over sand and sea – they flew like performing aircraft, sky diving in synchrony, swooping and swerving. They circled high and low, sometimes one bird above the other, sometimes tilted tight angles in strict unison, wings almost touching – two linked W's, sun glint illusion of almost pale golden wings against dark sea streaks. They hovered, accelerated vertically down like falcons stooping on their target; light shone through their wings making whiter than white primaries seem translucent. They braked and twisted, splayed tail feathers spreading light. They in turn were being tailed and overtaken by more pairs zooming, all at lightning speed until there were fifty individuals out on a flying spree in a brisk wind, speeding through one small airspace. Pairs split up, single ones intervened. They chased and competed in their antics – high speed aerial acrobats. They turn their heads as they fly, long beaks facing, and watch each other intently with big deep blue eyes. Large metallic blue 'eyes' seem to either fascinate, muddle or threaten them – on two occasions when I was wearing metallic blue sun glasses, pairs came and hovered less than an arm's length away, peering intently straight at my 'eyes'. Face to face at such close range, their large beaks brought a smile at their resemblance to Pinocchio's unwieldy, overgrown nose.

As the sun rose higher the acrobatic displays veered away from the beach and beyond the shallows. The Lesser and Greater Noddy Terns and a few Bridled Terns flew out of the trees and took over the sea centre stage. Taking off from the beach, their numbers seemed to double – svelte, dark birds tracked by their crisper black shadows flying across eye-burning sand to the sea. Noddies swooped low over the water, dipping and scooping up pieces of floating seaweed and floating Turtle Grass – materials for presentation, status and 'home improvements'. They were so focused on their activities they often flew as close as a few feet from us as we swam – as oblivious to humans at sea as on land. On one occasion a bird flew down and checked the material potential of my hair. Flying close to the water surface the relative angle of the sun and waves could create moments of magic . As the dark body tilted, wings outstretched, the underside of the wing would turn bright turquoise with the sea's reflection. Blink, and the wing turned darkest brown once more. As they skimmed the sea surface the water droplets sprayed out as they rose. With a quick shoulder quiver they shrugged off any remaining droplets and a shiver ran down the length of the body as the bird flew up and away.

There is little room for error in a Noddy Tern's life. Swooping down to the sea surface they pick up small fish near the surface. The angle of approach is critical: I saw one literally 'splat' into the water and it never reappeared, presumably drowned, or eaten, in a matter of seconds. Food skimmed from the sea included squid. This was practically demonstrated when a bird flew into our open-roofed bungalow, panicked during its careful removal and going into 'Frigate Bird alert mode' vomited a two-inch squid, perfect and entire, with large bright eyes and two long tentacles onto our settee.

We rose one morning to swim with the birds but in our path there were two silhouettes standing out between the striped shadows of tall tree trunks against a dazzling sea. Robbie was standing writing in his notebook and in front of him was a dark hump of turtle flicking puffs of sand. Her perfect carapace was dark brown, glittering and wet, just out of the sea. She was a beautiful animal. The dome of her shell did not look at all heavy and made a completely smooth sweeping curve which moulded round snug to her skin. Its edge was contoured and gradually tapered, as if by wear which had polished it glossy so that it almost glowed amber with the early morning sun. The beauty of her long coveted 'tortoiseshell' was very apparent. Every part of her body was touched with shades of yellow to orange: the plates of her carapace, fitting as tight as a new jigsaw, were delineated by a thin tracery of rusty red, and almost tufted (maybe some algal growth?). Yellow-cream skin intensified to dark yellow towards her tail on her under side. Her head marking was reminiscent of facetted skull bones; her dark eyes were accentuated by the yellow eyelid area extending to the sides of her head, paling to a cream neck with giraffe-style patterns of dark brown – like living crazy paving. The leading edges of her smooth flippers were flushed golden and caught the light as she worked, swinging them in a steady rhythm. It was hard to imagine that within this sleek, spade-like limb she had the same array of bones as the slow weight-bearing legs of her giant cousins nearby in the grass – the tortoises. Robbie pointed out there is a sharp hooked protrusion further up the flipper which helps with the digging. Having had an all too fleeting glimpse of Hawksbill gold previously, it was satisfying to see the detail of her colours at close range. Standing with Robbie behind her while she was digging, and beside when she left, the three of us were out of her vision range and not causing her any concern.

She was digging a deep, narrow diameter hole; her agile rear flippers working alternately in a rigorous rhythm: bending, scooping sand, twisting, lifting and throwing it aside. Her tail dipped down as the hole deepened. It was between two trees, so close that she soon came up against a large root. She abandoned that site and clambered over a thick tangle of stems nearby, forging in like a bulldozer into the thick undergrowth. Realising that was not going to be a success she retreated, managing to climb backwards – with flipper paddling – over high stems. It was an extraordinary performance. Having made two fruitless attempts, she gave up her mission and lumbered slowly back to the beach and accelerated down the easy wet sand slope with slow swim flipper movements and melted back into the sea. Early swimmers might have noticed just a few tracks remaining to tell the tale.

Later in the day we saw a turtle in the sea just off the beach, and two days later the same animal, now tagged and measured, laid successfully (probably about 120 eggs) bringing the season's laying turtles total so far to nineteen Hawksbills and fifteen Greens. The following day a second unknown female emerged from the sea and was tagged, photographed and measured for the record book – she was smaller than the norm, her carapace measuring 76 cm (30 ins) versus 86 cm (33–34 ins).

Top: a Hawksbill Turtle with prominent hawk beak paddles her way across the beach. Centre: Her sleek, low-domed shell is still wet and leaving a trail of tracks she starts digging her nest, head down, 'swimming' her foreflippers backwards and forwards, spraying sand. Below: Her tail dips down as her streamlined hind flippers dig deep to create a hole, paddling and twisting upwards as they flick away the sand (detail).

TURTLE PARADISE – LAGOON TO SHORE

Three days later, just off the south shore, three heads reared up, somewhat cylindrical and blunt, unmistakably turtle. A little later a fourth head surfaced and the animals swam about viewing each other and catching breath. Now and then a humped carapace broke through a lazy wave. Here the sea surface was softly undulating. Beneath, the sandy shallows were green with strappy leaves of Turtle Grass and strewn with myriads of tiny sculptured fragments of coral skeletons. For a turtle this is an idyllic spot to hang around and browse, ideal for meeting and breeding. Male turtles gather, loiter and wait. Females, mature and young, return to this beach of their origin. The young ones have spent twenty-five years away in the oceans since they left as hatchlings. Adult Greens can travel thousands of miles in a year. Hawksbills, on the other hand, do not swim far away from their breeding beaches, staying in shallow waters.

The lagoon oasis is cosseted by the wall of the outer reef where the continuous distant roar of crashing waves is a reminder that the hostile open sea is not far away. Only 500m from the north point of the island the ocean bed drops vertically 2,000m from the edge of the Seychelles Plateau, a piece of ancient Gondwana. Under a lid of stormy clouds this deep tropical sea can be a dark forbidding northern grey and there is a big ocean swell. Here in the open ocean there were Spinner Dolphins, small, sleek, very compact compared to other species we had seen – half the size of Bottlenose Dolphins – very slender nosed, pale grey with a wavy darker line down the side of their bodies. A pair leaping vertically out of the water had given us a clear sighting of their missile shape narrowing to an extreme at the tail base, and very pointed tips to the tail flukes. A double twisting somersault summarised their boisterous porpoising energy and muscle power, young and mature alike. Their speed denied a glimpse of their faces as they dived into memory.

Under a brighter sky, shoals of flying fish broke through the surface, free falling and skimming, shimmering, green-finned and blue, easy prey for the Frigate Birds. Below, swam Dolphin Fish, with skin a bright sleek intense sulphurous yellow, and myriads of others, which formed the mainstay of our diet. Fluttering above the surface, there were small flocks of Lesser Noddies hunting. Here our four Hawksbills had been swimming amongst their prey: comb jellies, near invisible but for their pulsating iridescent bands flashing like high- tech novelty lanterns; jellyfish floating and squeezing their rhythmic progress through the water; and ravishingly beautiful but dangerous Portuguese Man o' War (when eating these the turtles close their vulnerable eyes). These four had then safely traversed the surf and protecting reef, patrolled by heavy-bodied sharks. Their teeth can easily crunch through a turtle shell – a surprisingly fragile protection. To a human these huge fish can be almost invisibly hazy grey, and suddenly materialise into a looming presence, a great muscle wall of potential destructive power, quickening the heart beat to panic and scattering shoals of fish in an instant.

In the quieter water within, awash with renewed oxygen and nutrients brought in by the surf, L'Hirondelle and Passe Coco abound with more prey. Equipped with sharp, bird-like beak jaws, Hawksbills reach daintily for small sponges, anemones, tubeworms and shrimp from awkward coral crevices and scrape Turtle Grass: they are fussy feeders. Seeking out tiny creatures in a similar way, pairs of keen-eyed Threadfin Butterflyfish flitted and probed extended snouts amongst corals. Symmetrically striped black and white, chic and slim-bodied, their foraging was meticulous. We heard the sound of coral pieces being pulverised in the crushing jaw beaks of parrotfish as they hovered over coral heads. Here it was bright: flickering small fish, pale sand, rocks and corals reflected sunlight as the water became shallow turquoise – a habitat not dissimilar from the Maldives further north and sharing many reef species. In the protected water of the lagoon there were welcoming 'cleaning stations' above large brain corals where small striped Cleaner Wrasse could squirm in and out of gaping mouths and flipper skin folds and scrape the turtle's shell, delving for morsels. Turtle clients, as well as fish, relax into relief, freed from irritant growths and parasites.

Apparently our four visitors were males, eager to mate, hanging about waiting to catch a female returning to the water after laying her eggs. As many as six males at a time had been seen here, ferociously fighting each other over a mating opportunity. Far from Bird Island, on the uninhabited protected island of Aldabra, forty fighting male turtles at a time had been seen by our waitress, Annette Marie, who had been a warden there a few years earlier. In the heat of the day we had seen a female Hawksbill trying, unsuccessfully, to dig a nest high on the beach above this place, and then return to the sea. Her attempted nest high up the beach would have been less likely to be inundated by water, but set amongst tall trees emerging hatchlings would have been directly beneath one of their predators, Frigate Birds, roosting high on their favourite dead tree. Having returned to the lagoon, she may have been the target of one of the waiting males.

Snorkelling to retrace her route ashore to nest, we swam skimming low over shallow coral. Areas cluttered with lumps of dead coral rubble created a maze of tunnels and holes, welcome nurseries for juvenile fish and encroaching wafts of algae and sponges within easy reach of hungry turtles. Amongst moving seaweed tufts, a sinuous movement of white betrayed a thin, young pipefish – a seahorse relative which has not fully curled its tail. Pale, young Picasso Triggerfish, perfect miniatures of the striking adults, followed all that passed above them with high placed upturned eyes, swivelling and peering from carnival masks striped with bands of shades of brown and yellow, touched with pure blue. A Bird Wrasse appeared and watched us, then flashed by on fast beating fins, wing-like and perfect triangles edged pale. It was a tapered arc of richest blue reaching from tail to long turquoise tapir nose – almost a push-me-pull-you joke fish.

Interspersed with these sandy turquoise zones were the patches of dark indigo – meadows of Turtle Grass, lush undulating pasture where turtles feed, fish and breed. This is paradise for adult Green Turtles. Their beaks differ from those of Hawksbills in having a finely serrated edge, tuned to their eating habits of grazing grass and scraping algae. Undersea meadows would have also fed the plentiful Dugongs sighted in 1771; it is thought that the competition between Dugongs and turtles for food could have led to the decline of the Dugongs here. Turtle Grass is a terrestrial flowering plant gone to sea; but only a small percentage produce pale white flowers. It covers the sand, leaf blades rhythmically lilting in waves – a green monotony relieved by shreds of algae and ageing leaves streaking and darkening to dense dark brown, shot purple like silk, almost magenta-black. A dangling silver thread caught the light. Gliding sideways, it propelled itself by tiny fins vibrating fast, head held high. It was a seahorse, one of the huge numbers of small creatures seeking protection – worms, snails, shrimps, and darting juveniles. The sameness seen from above is deceptive. It masks an efficient, heavily populated habitat where sea urchins, sea cucumbers and starfish extract every morsel of organic matter from the sandy floor, and camouflage is vital. Olive green and brown flashes of sheltering fish appeared and disappeared as waving strands wafted apart. Background colours reappeared in a passing parrotfish – a sap green head, rust-brown, yellow and grey-brown, muting typical parrotfish turquoise.

The undulating grass could be ambiguous; straps of green suddenly seemed to ripple grey... a sudden large presence materialised as if from nowhere. Dark wing-like fins slowly flapped before becoming engulfed in shadowy obscurity, trailing the menacing spike of a stingray foraging for the small hidden creatures.

A first sighting of these bat-like fish is not one to forget. The first impression is alien – a creature seemingly faceless, apparently without a mouth (small and hidden on the underside) and small piercing eyes on the hump of its upper side, unable to see its food. The steady flap of their great triangular fins has something of a mechanical action, akin to an early film rendering of a pterodactyl. Thoughts of ancient ancestors were not wholly fanciful; rays are an ancient group, related to sharks and sharing their skeleton of gristly cartilage and visible external gill slits (on the underside in rays). Rays and sharks are very different from the more familiar design of fish frequent on a dinner plate which have bony skeletons and fewer gills hidden behind protective flaps behind the eyes. Like sharks, rays seek out their prey by smell and a sense alarmingly foreign to our human experience – electric receptors. These pick up electrical activity of muscle movement in the body of their prey. Clams, snails, shrimps and small fish sheltering amongst strands of Turtle Grass and beneath have little hope as a stingray churns up the sand. The image of the stingray has never been benign: animals to be feared and treated accordingly – challenged, dominated or killed – but the menacing barb on a thin tail held high is used purely in self-defence when the animal feels threatened. On my first sighting, a group of rays had been bombarded with projectiles, shouts and a youth splash-jumping on top of them, fully clothed, whilst clasping his can of beer aloft, aiming his heavy leather boots. Several decades later, attitudes of fear still linger, further fuelled by the film footage of Steve Irwin swimming very close over a stingray which then killed him.

When swimming over dark weed and Turtle Grass my Australian childhood had taught me vigilance – misunderstandings between different species is all too easy. We watched the stingray pass and drifted on, allowing little intermittent waves to carry us in surges towards the steep sand shelf of shore. The water was as clear as the air; in places it was tinted yellow-gold, similar to some Scottish waters coloured by peat. Possibly there was pigment leaching out of dead Turtle Grass. Pieces of swirling black leaf blades had collected in the shallows – a narrow corridor of white sand, coral fragments and shells – reflecting white and hot. Line after line of Small Spotted Darts, translucent and white, dashed along these deep narrow furrows, almost invisible, tightly packed against sand below and sea surface above. These small shoals were more of a passing flash than a sighting, an impression of a sharp scimitar tail, dark grey eyes and eyespots on the flanks. As the shallows ran out we were deposited in a wavy skein of bubbles and found ourselves face to face with a group of terns resting at the shoreline. They continued unperturbed by the two log-like shapes that had drifted up out of the water beside them. Young were begging for food. The adults ignored them, standing with beaks agape. Maybe they were hot like us. From here the female turtle had dragged her bulk out of the buoyancy of the sea water across the narrow beach and arduously paddling she had worked her flippers hard to haul her heavy weight up the steep sand slope to dig her nest in the protecting undergrowth. She had left those unmistakable tracks behind her, but two sets, as she had so soon returned to the lagoon and maybe the hopeful males, task unaccomplished.

In an isolated natural paradise, such as Bird Island, careful human assistance could help tip the balance for the critically endangered Hawksbill. The carefully kept records of turtle size and identity, nest sites, egg laying dates and expected date of hatching form the basis of increasing the number of baby turtles hatching and making it to the sea successfully. On the other hand, humans can also be intruders – through thoughtlessness or ignorance.

The Seychelles is the only place in the world where the Hawksbills lay their eggs during the day, which can bring them into rather too close an encounter with humans in the present era when the photograph can become the fanatical focus rather than its wildlife subject. We witnessed an unfortunate occasion when island guests stumbled across another female who had just finished covering her nest, high up the beach almost hidden in dense undergrowth. Robbie was not present at the critical moment. People stood between her and the sea. There were murmurs in several languages that people should stand back as unavoidably she was aware of their presence. Her path was made clear and she was already beginning to sidle out of the bushes and down the slope. Two amateur photographers immediately took advantage of her clear view of the sea and leapt in front of her to get head-on portraits at close range. Two more people, not to be outdone, dashed to the scene and walked backwards in front of her, bending low to her level, flashing cameras and mobile phones continuously in her face – only the prospect of getting immersed dampened their ardour.

Top: Spotted Dart – near transparent against sand; below left: Picasso Triggerfish – striped patterns become ambiguous amongst coral rubble; right: Bird Wrasse – a projecting long face (relative sizes comparable).

TORTOISES AND TURTLES

The phrase 'living with the animals' took on a new meaning when we emerged from our early swim with the terns one morning and heard a loud rhythmic booming resounding through the trees. There was a gasping, hoarse rasp to it and it seemed to be everywhere. It grew louder as we approached our bungalow which we soon realised was the source. A pair of Giant Tortoises were mating by our veranda. The dwarfed female somehow managed to stagger about six tortoise lengths carrying an extra 350 kg straddling her carapace. He had managed his compass bearing appropriately on this occasion, as opposed to a previous one when, 180 degrees out of orientation, the prospect of success had been improbable. Esmeralda, the misnamed male, was able to balance on the curved dome of the female's shell as his under-belly shell – plastron – is concave. It was a very noisy unambiguous performance, which entered the world of farce when an ostentatiously prim and proper couple walked briskly into view en route to breakfast. With looks of horror and indignation they immediately averted their eyes... such basic instincts were not on display in their demure home town. We were never quite sure if their disapproval stemmed from the tortoises' efforts to procreate or the sight of Peter in Attenborough mode filming it – with the noticeable difference of being clad in slim-fit bathing trunks rather than a fading blue shirt.

The architecture of their shells is a sculptural wonder, a transformation from the basic design of a scaly skin and some fairly standard bits of skeleton such as ribs and backbone like ours. These unpromising starting materials combined for a new purpose – an economical design for overall protection for an animal's back and belly – the distinctive protective shell of bone covered with horn. After that major step forward their body plan has changed little, beyond developing the facility to withdraw the head back into the protective shell. The timescale of the turtle and its distinctive shell belonged to the Age of Reptiles, about 190 million years ago, when dinosaurs, conifers and cycads lived on a very different distribution of land than exists today. The tortoises became purely terrestrial; the turtles reverted to an exclusively aquatic life with paddle-shaped limbs instead of feet, returning briefly to lay their eggs on land. Turtles date from 110 million years ago. Our reptilian neighbours and visitors were of a very ancient lineage.

Turtles and Giant Tortoises have shared aspects of their recent as well as past histories. Both have suffered severe depletions in numbers of adults, eggs and hatchlings at the hand of man and his inadvertent animal introductions. Giant Tortoises were once common on many islands of the Pacific and Indian Oceans; in the Pacific they remain only on the Galapagos Islands. There were originally eighteen species in the Indian Ocean, but all are now extinct except for the Aldabra species. This relatively recent decline is partly the unfortunate result of an otherwise advantageous evolutionary adaptation to living in dry places. Esmeralda and his kind are able to drink through their nostrils from tiny puddles of water trapped in crevices by virtue of the specialised structure of their nasal chambers and flat-ended nose, and they can survive long periods without drinking at all. Over the centuries they were seen as the low maintenance living meat supply on board ships bound for the long voyages of trade, exploration and piracy. By 1840 the only survivors were a few living free on the Aldabra Atoll or in captivity. Towards the end of the century Charles Darwin and other naturalists sought to protect the survival of the species on Aldabra, and 'a good number' of Giant Tortoises were transferred to other Seychelles Islands. The first two of the present population were brought to Bird Island in 1969 – captive animals donated from owners on larger islands in order that they could roam free.

A unique feature of these Aldabra tortoises is that the carapace ends well behind the head, enabling a tall neck stretch and an unusually large expanse of exposed skin to benefit from any cooling breeze. Their vulnerably extended positions when relaxing in the shade would not allow their survival in any habitat with potential predators, but is advantageous in these isolated islands. From ancient tales of hares and tortoises and given that this is a creature dependent on the sun's energy to raise its body temperature, one might imagine Esmeralda as a slow dozy reptile. However, he responded avidly to food gifts, observed human antics going on round him, and stretched out his long neck to facilitate and enjoy having it stroked. When washed and polished (with furniture polish) for a professional photography session for a postcard, he positively asked for attention by his majestic gesturing and postures – stretching his neck and standing tall, consuming fresh cut Frangipani flowers.

A young Aldabra Giant Tortoise sprawls gangly land limbs and flat feet as it sleeps in the shade of overhanging leaves. In contrast to turtles, its long neck stretches out of a high domed shell.

INCOMERS VS RESIDENTS

The introduced tortoises have entered the intricate web of plants and animals of the island's community. It is observed that seeds which have passed through their gut germinate far better than those which have not –

a frequent scenario in various habitats. Some of these seeds are foreigners too. Appropriately, the Cordia seeds germinate to produce trees festooned with the orange-red flowers which in turn develop into the moisture-rich white fruits, much loved by the tortoises, on which they feast, continuing the cycle. It is unclear if the Madagascan Fody (also known as the Red or Red Cardinal Fody) is an introduction or not – their habit of perching amongst the matching Cordia flowers is a visual delight.

Other introductions by man, accidental ones, do not fit into such a neat cycle of mutual benefit. The comical gait of the Common Mynas, gawky and reminiscent of Shakespeare's 'mechanicals', belies their true potential as alarmingly effective invaders, now increasingly widespread across the globe.

Giant African Land Snails were introduced accidentally to the island, possibly in cargo. We saw them in 2002, clustered in groups under palm leaves hanging overhead. They are not visually unattractive; in fact, they are advertised worldwide as ideal pets, but they are large – growing up to 20 cm (8 ins) – and are voracious grazers. Apparently they happily consume at least 500 plant species, and, furthermore, pose a health risk to humans. Their control was by the simple and effective act of collecting these very obvious targets by hand, adding an inspired incentive of a fun competitive element to the essentially tedious task. The prize was associated with much kudos and in 2010 the only obvious snails on the island were blowing in the breeze as an attractive mobile. Unfortunately, other new arrivals are a much more difficult proposition.

Ants arrived on Bird Island in about 1999. Isolated islands are incredibly vulnerable to invasion by foreign species; the residents are unfamiliar with and have no defences against newcomers, particularly those that are voracious and efficient breeders. Usually there are no predators in place to keep the invaders in check. The classic scenario is that some or many of the resident populations are decimated or become extinct – endemic New Zealand birds and Australian small marsupials are sad, ongoing examples. The ants suddenly appeared, accidentally introduced with some imported food or cargo. They have become a problem for the island's massive colony of nesting birds as well as turtle eggs; Sooty Terns begin to arrive in March/ April, and by the end of May they are nesting on the ground as opposed to roosting in trees, egg laying through June. Ants at the nest irritate the females who leave the nest, resulting in cold, lost eggs.

These new arrivals present a dilemma. Rapid responses are often seen as an immediate definitive remedy to a new pest – each threat to a treasured or endangered species often dealt with individually and in isolation as it comes along. Unexpected and often irreversible repercussions can result from what seem to be fast and effective control measures. Insecticide could, in the course of time, find its way into the surrounding lagoon and into the food chain affecting reef fish and sea beyond. For long-term success and the health of any island ecosystem, the ideal is a total view of links between species and their interdependency, particularly at the interface of land and sea, in order to forestall any unexpected outcome. It could be that the very visible 'baddie' crabs of the turtle hatchling scenario might bring some unexpected benefit; crabs eat ant larvae so there is potentially some degree of natural control available. See-sawing numbers and populations take time to stabilise into some sort of dynamic equilibrium and even more time to assess – the road to understanding natural relationships and systems never runs simple and rapid. And meanwhile the ants breed.

Inevitable sympathy and concern for the turtle hatchling's escape to the sea brings anti-crab feelings amongst human onlookers, even crab bashing, particularly amongst children. Occasional and very small-scale (and unlikely to have a very serious impact on crab populations) the resulting rotting crab remains actually make an extra food source for the invading ants to increase their colonies. More significantly, fixing attention on one species begins to close the door on any idea of understanding what is really going on in a small island ecosystem: the inter-relationships between species and between land and sea are diverse and subtle. As scavengers of carrion and detritus as well as predators of live animals, resident Ghost Crabs have been an integral part of the island's history and they may yet assist with the ant problem. The crabs are widely distributed around the tropics and subtropics and their populations are easily monitored which makes them useful beach health indicators. They are used to assess the degree of human disturbance such as trampling, constructions affecting sediment and chemical pollution on beach habitats worldwide.

An incomer in transit sits by the runway ready with alert eye and hooked beak for insects or geckos – a European Roller, possibly en route to Ethiopia.

CLOSE NEIGHBOURS – LIVING WITH THE BIRDS

OCEAN PATHWAYS

The horizon is a long way away, an empty place until apparently out of nowhere a speck of life materialises, having navigated an expanse of sea. Insects are most wondrous and baffling. Butterflies and hawkmoths are often seen from boats. Standing on another Seychelle shore we had watched as an Oleander Hawkmoth slowly came from the sea, into close view and over the sand with faltering exhausted flight. It settled: its green, olive and pink wings worn and only thinly scaled. It slowly lifted its wings high to open them. A bird plummeted down from a tree and the moth disappeared in one lightning gulp. Migration is risk and chance, the epitome of natural selection in practice.

Bird Island is a first landfall for migratory Eurasian species: an ideal stopover for birds crossing the ocean, on the move between the northern and southern hemispheres. The risks they are taking during such migrations are enormous: predation by falcons and other predators which gather in readiness along the migration routes, being blown off course by sudden storm or cyclone and dying from starvation. A long-distance migrant suddenly appeared on the runway. It was a European Roller, a species wintering in two regions of southern Africa. A beautiful individual, possibly following a route via India, took up residence for four days. Perched in the papaya trees it added a sea concoction of colours to the scene – bright blue, turquoise, purple and shiny black. It flitted and floated out over the sea in a buoyant flight. Back in the palms it flew on short sorties catching insects. We had seen one in exactly the same place eight years earlier. It was an exciting sight as the species has been in steady decline since the1970s; it was now 2010.

White-tailed Tropicbirds also frequented this airspace, soaring, slim winged and long tailed, a distinct white cross in the sky, looking almost like distant high flying jets. They were nesting, in prime positions, well protected between wide buttress roots of the trees or in deep trunk clefts. They sat, often in cramped niches, with their fabulous long tail streamers erect and somehow uncrumpled, even when the pair were mutual grooming – tails sometimes semi-projecting between buttresses and split trunks, like flags announcing their presence. They can sit thus for ten days without eating according to Robbie. He reached in to a nest and drew out a discarded broken egg shell, spotted a beautiful burgundy red.

White-tailed Tropicbird adult and young – long strong beak to grab flying fish above and swimming fish below, and to fend off nest intruders.

The newly hatched young peer from the nest: two enormous black eyes and wide-gape, grey beak emerging from a sprawling, shawl-like halo of ephemeral white fluff. Almost comically at the other end, two discernible tail feathers emerge, and in between, recognisable short wings have the makings of chic black chevrons. As they grow, the filmy white blur gives way to a crown of tiny brush flecks of grey and black, a shiny white breast framed by black-edged feathers making it seem the baby bird is wearing scalloped, frilly ruffs. They sit, impervious to people passing by within a few paces of them. Adults at the nest fiercely defend it against other birds, pecking hard with their very pointed beaks. The chicks were used to Robbie doing his rounds, checking, but this accessible behaviour makes them sitting targets for introduced predators on other islands. They have long been a goal of traditional food gathering on Pacific Islands. Andrew, our son, living with islanders on an extremely remote atoll, existed on and recorded the menu of hunter-gathering – fish, fish and more fish for three months – but occasionally tropicbird chicks with 'delicious' livers. Admiring their beauty, it is a terrible thought, but this is the reality of survival in a tropical island 'paradise'.

When the fluffy immature feathers give way to adult plumage the bird becomes clothed in a shiny gloss, gleaming white, with a radiant sheen, like the best silk – a perfect contrast to a strong, curved bright yellow beak, a dazzling black 'comma' accentuating round the eye, wing bars, and jet-black webbed feet. The flowing tail streamers, as long as the body, trail, float and curve as the bird flies, mirroring every movement like the flared swirling skirt of a dancer. Like some other sea birds, they are unable to perch on a branch – they move straight from air to ground or air to tree hole. Watching one parent flying in low between the trees, it approached its nest and slowed to the point of faltering in order to alight. The tail streamers stalled in a graceful S-wave, as curved and flowing as a single smooth sweep of a paintbrush, a time-lapse echo of the movement. As a bird 'brakes' or turns in flight the tail feathers spread in a perfect fan, its structure and symmetry etched against the brightness of a blue sky, while the two long tail feathers stream out in a floating wisp of white.

Even the mundane housewifery of the bird's intense food fetching and feeding the young was a balletic poetry in motion. Throughout the day the adults flaunted – as pairs and individually. Making white cross shapes in the sky as they climbed, then, as they turned and veered away over the sea, the tail streamers twisted and rotated, the birds receding into faint, streamlined streaks. They fly out to sea for 100 km (60 miles) to forage. They take flying fish in flight and plunge dive to five metres to catch small fish and squid, continuing to feed their young for up to twelve or fourteen weeks. The young stand, stretch their wings at the nest, but beyond that there is no preparation or training for their breathtaking flight. They simply get up and fly.

The freedom of flight: White-tailed Tropicbird with long slender wings, tail trailing. During the breeding season both sexes flaunt their tail streamers, fly in parallel, dipping tails and performing synchronised figures.

NODDIES AND 'BIRD-EATING TREES'

Tropicbirds frequently shared their Casuarina tree buttresses with noisy Noddy neighbours – we shared them as neighbours too. Our distance was less intrusive, at about 3.5 m (12 ft), but all over the island they seemed as oblivious of us as they were to the arrival of a nesting turtle or resident tortoise near their nests. We and the birds lived near and around an ancient Casuarina tree. A White-tailed Tropicbird chick nestled in a hollow bole, its world encircled by wood. The Noddy Terns got on with the everyday business of life: grooming, displaying over territorial disputes, mating, child rearing, loudly chattering and arguing continuously, day and night. When they greet, one of the pair opens its bill wide, the other 'replies' and then they indulge in an orgy of bill tapping and nodding. They break off intermittently to scoop and drag bunches of Casuarina or old, limp Pisonia leaves for their nests – a dual focus of ritual and housewifery.

Pisonia trees as a home base or a source of construction material are a mixed blessing for them. It is a tree with a definite relationship with sea birds, sharing their habitats of small tropical islands in the Indo-Pacific Ocean. On our visit to the Island of Cousin in extreme heat, we had thankfully walked through a lush forest of Pisonia, for its bright green shade and nesting birds, with the inevitable, slightly rancid smell of guano and heavily populated with mosquitoes. The tree is unable to regenerate without a phosphorous-rich soil, best achieved with droppings from such a seabird colony; it is one of the few species which positively thrives on acidic guano. If the birds abandon their island site, the tree also disappears. There have been unexpected and sinister reasons put forward for this close association; the tree is also known as the 'Bird-Eating Tree'- an image recalling the nightmare floating island in 'The Life of Pi'. From the bird's point of view, it makes an ideal nest site, with lots of large spreading branches bearing large leaves – good for flamboyant presentation and nest building material. But there the bird's gain ends.

Several times a year the tree produces clusters of 250–500 seeds, coated in a sticky resin which attaches to anything it touches, particularly to bird feathers. The birds fly off and the seeds are transported, fresh and fast, to another venue, even another island. This is the ideal scenario, but in reality a number of birds never fly again. The resin is incredibly sticky, sometimes causing wing and tail feathers to become so entangled they are unable to fly, forage or feed, and slowly die of starvation. A sinister conclusion was that there was a direct link between Pisonias needing fertiliser and its seeds killing birds. The number of dead birds is large and is having a serious impact on the seabird colonies of Cousin, particularly White-tailed Tropicbirds and Fairy Terns – a matter of concern as worldwide, seabird populations are at present in decline. Investigations on Cousin have clarified some of the possible explanations of such an aggressive botanical assault.

The idea that even a large number of birds killed by seeds is significantly fertilising a Pisonia forest overlooks the fact that the amount is still trivial compared to that accumulating from dropped eggs, dead chicks and the guano in a seabird colony. The expansion of a forest is mostly vegetative – new individuals sprouting from fallen branches rather than growing from seed. Seeds would seem to be the means for 'long haul' spread of the species to distant islands. The intense stickiness of the seeds is essential to keep them securely attached during immersions in sea water, such as when the bird dips into the sea to feed – the resin retains its stickiness through four weeks of periodic wettings. The seed cannot survive prolonged soaking, as when attached to a floating corpse, so a live arrival is better for the tree than a dead one. It was an alluringly macabre proposition that a seed arriving on a new site with a ready supply of fertiliser in the form of a dead bird has an advantage over a lone seed, but it has been shown not to be the case. It has been demonstrated that crabs and other scavengers scrabbling bits off a body disturb such apparently advantaged seedlings so much as to actually lower their chances of successful germination.

Thus it appears that natural selection favours a particularly sticky glue so that seeds can be successfully transported by sea birds, diving or skimming the sea's surface for food during their flight to another island. The fact that the bird mortality rate is high seems to be an unfortunate by-product which has no advantage (or disadvantage) for the Pisonia. On Cousin there are ongoing experiments into the possibility of providing areas of alternative native trees for nest sites instead of the inadvertent 'Bird-Eater'.

Noddy Terns on Bird Island have provided a perfect illustration of the ideal scenario: it was noticed that Pisonias were establishing under palm trees habitually used for roosting and preening during the moulting season. Sitting in the trees, the birds were successfully removing the seeds, or feathers with them still attached, and the dropped seeds were germinating on the guano-fertilised soil beneath. Robbie told us of sticky seeds killing some Noddies, but we were extremely glad not to witness them floundering with caught up wings or literally glued to the ground – even noisy neighbours had their charm.

Mid-afternoon there was always a lull, the shortest possible respite for them and us. It was around this time that single birds came to sit on our veranda and one could study the crisp delineation of their white eyelid with its scalloped edge. They could almost be frowning, with their pale cap seeming to overhang their brow and white line under the eye. The smooth texture of their plumage had the appearance of perfect velvet, essential for life relying on flight. Like all birds, they spent much time ruffling, cleaning, combing and prodding their own feathers, and each other's, with what seemed to be perilous vigour for such a long pointed beak – or so it seemed through the eyes of a clumsy hand-oriented human. Having groomed, they stretched energetically, reaching up to an astonishing height as they stretch their long wings vertically in a straight line, just like a human raising both arms straight up touching the ears. Dealing with insect parasites was a quieter social occasion. Roasting these irritant passengers off their skin and out of their feathers, they stand in a group, motionless in a hot sun reflecting off the bare earth, wings half-extended sideways, juxtaposed in an abstract striated jigsaw of wing patterns. Their dark feathers can heat up to 67°C (152°F).

The fluffy feathers of baby terns are white and dark grey: balls of whitish down peppered with dark dots, dark face, pert black beaks, eyes and feet. They are agile at an early age and back up to the edge of the nest in order to defecate. For those between tree roots the risk is slight, but for those high up in the tree forks, falling to the ground is probable. Noddy habit is for both parents to tend young, but a major problem occurs if there is only one parent, either due to natural causes or indiscriminate culling by humans to reduce numbers. While the parent is absent foraging up to 50 km away, lone lost chicks who have survived the fall are treated as intruders by other Noddy parents – harassed, pecked, tossed and mutilated. Their continual misguided efforts to return to the nearest, wrong nest at ground level and its aggressive adult are heart rending to witness. Each renewed, rebuffed effort leaves them more exhausted and injured but they still persevere, chided too by passing Common Mynas and Moorhens – a pathetic downy heap which might lie for an hour, its feet quivering occasionally, then up again, standing and trying, but weaker each time until they finally succumb. Their fate is to be ignominiously carried off by skinks or a waiting crab to be buried and dismembered, dead or barely alive. A tuft of unwanted down feathers at the mouth of a crab burrow is the only evidence left for the single parent returning with a bounty of food at the end of the day. In our little one tree community during two weeks, it was a minority of hatchlings which survived. Chance was a big part of natural selection.

Fairy Tern families were aloft in the trees. The single young simply clung on to a bare branch with big clawed feet – no nest, no shelter, just gravity. The female had chosen a branch, one with a v-junction, laid her egg there and then just sat... which stopped it falling. Robbie was trying to encourage them to nest on strategically placed upturned coconut spathes which offered a shallow bowl shape and a more secure future. The young resembled owlets – large eyes, forward directed and very observant, peering from a ball of dense furry feathers, pale fawn and white. The parents feed them small fish carried across the beak, sometimes three held at once. Although chiefly seen as inshore birds, they have been observed 600 miles from their islands at night, apparently foraging; their big eyes may well allow them to fish at night. Certainly they are flying about the island at night; we frequently saw them – one flew in and perched high up on our four-poster bed in the dark.

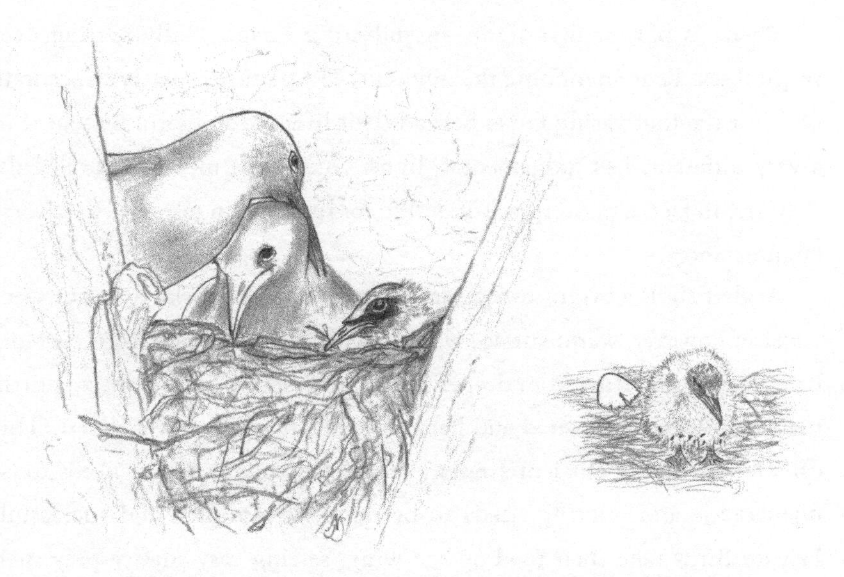

Left: A Noddy Tern grooms its mate and their young sits on an untidy nest safe up a tree. Right: Unprotected on the ground below, a lone chick - later pecked to death.

FRIGATE BIRDS – PIRATES OF DESERT SEAS

Birds of a very different character were the Frigates – Lesser and Greater Frigate Birds, mostly black, with angled arc wings and long forked tails, a forceful presence accentuated by a long beak tipped with a sharp, powerful hook – visible as they twist and move their heads, decisively scanning life below. Mostly young males, these birds were passing their immature days just hanging out, being *frigatti* – pirates: like their namesake, seemingly always there, even at an invisible distance, a menacing presence waiting for unsuspecting prey. Their image was accentuated by an austere design, sparsely stripped down to essentials and with a superficial resemblance to pterodactyls from a primeval world.

Theirs is not, at first sight, an endearing image – idly soaring over tropical seas bent on robbing the innocent. The picture is partly an accurate one, but the motivating forces behind their lifestyle and form present it in a very different, less judgemental, light. One of the most aerial of birds, they are, in fact, a masterpiece of design for function in response to adverse circumstances.

At first sight a bright turquoise blue sea under a hot sky does not seem adverse; however, warm surface water restricts circulation of cold currents bringing up nutrients from deeper down. With few nutrients there is little plankton: prey is scattered and hard to find – it is like a wet desert. This calls for an energy efficient strategy of strict economy. Flight needs to be unenergetic and hunting needs to be rapid, streamlined and successful. Frigate Birds take their food on the wing, seizing easy surface prey such as flying fish in flight, baby turtles and small fish; they cleverly make use of hunting dolphins and tuna which push prey fish up to the surface. Tern chicks from land colonies make relatively easy prey, interestingly, for females exclusively.

Options for low energy expenditure in the natural world are either parasitism or piracy. Piracy supplements their diet. At their most spectacular, Frigate Birds have been seen to seize Tropicbirds by their long tail streamers. More typically, they swoop down on Masked Boobys which have emerged from a deep dive with food in their beaks. Faced with imminent attack by a great black bird, the victim hastily disgorges its catch as an avoidance tactic, hence the Seychellois name – Benign Booby. The attacker then twists and U-turns with acrobatic accuracy and grace and dexterously catches the ejected flying food. The victor's feet never touch the sea surface – they can't. Their feathers are not waterproof, their feet are tiny, only partly webbed and completely lacking in propulsive power. Not able to paddle, or run over the surface to get airborne, they are essentially a superb 'flight only' machine.

Their agile manoeuvrability is the product of anatomical alignment and fusing of bones to make a narrow body. Their bones are amazingly light and flexible, only 5% of their total body weight – a far lower proportion than other birds. The shape and length of the wing (2.3 m, 6 ft) is purpose built, for soaring with minimal wing beat and effort, similar to the albatross but not as extreme. Their proportions are tempered by the need to switch to active fast-flapping flight when pursuing their targets. Their weight is about the same as a duck, which gives them the largest wingspan to body weight ratio of any bird. Such a masterpiece of design allows them to hang and ride warm up currents from a still ocean where there may be little or no wind for long periods – they can be airborne for a week.

Food scattered thinly over a large area of ocean requires very long-distance foraging flights as well as energy efficient ones. In the Seychelles their distances are large: Aldabra to Aride is nearly 1,200 km (750 miles) for birds on the home range. 'Foreign' tagged birds have been casually observed here from distant lands (in this location, very distant). In the Pacific, extremely long flights have been monitored where tagged birds have travelled 8,000km (5,000 miles) between nest site and roost, and they have been seen riding high on thermals up to 3,000 m (10,000 ft). It is not surprising that these impressive masters of flight are seen as an iconic species in the Seychelles. The 10,000 breeding pairs on the closely conserved island of Aldabra form the biggest colony in the Indian Ocean and the second largest in the world. On the islands of Bird, Cousin and Aride smaller numbers habitually gather in roosts, but they numbered in hundreds.

As dawn broke and we started our early swim with the birds, the

Frigate Birds were beginning to leave the spacious branches of their most favoured roosts in stark skeletal trees, and were lazily winding upwards with the warm air. By day they drifted and many disappeared – up to 250 km (155 miles) away in search of food. Later in the day a few Frigate Birds floating motionless in the sky would imperceptibly multiply to hundreds – stationary, hanging at different levels on the island thermals. As the afternoon matured into blazing sunset, the slowly idling flock dropped down, closer. At an even lower level, close to the sea, 300 or so Noddy Terns would fly in from beyond the horizon, some circuiting for a quick extra feed. At 10 p.m. Noddies were still making sea sorties in and out of the trees.

The Frigates just hung about, somewhat reminiscent of Alfred Hitchcock's birds. It is at dusk and nightfall that turtle hatchlings naturally emerge. At the outer reef, from the sea surface, the sinister black shapes of Frigate Birds loom large. Far out there, snorkelling amongst the larger denizens of the outer reef and sharks, our research acquaintance regularly saw large gatherings of Frigate Birds hanging, waiting for the next batch of turtle hatchlings and timing their dives to the hatchlings' needs to surface to take a breath. At this moment the birds picked them off – lots of them. Once underway to the open sea, there are further numbers of predatory fish of all sizes awaiting the hatchlings. Big predation has always been a natural part of the equation – both in the sea, and en route to it.

Frigate Birds spread their wings - a wide span ideal for long-distance flight using warm thermal updrafts; angular wings and forked tail give manoeuvrability to take food in flight with a beak hooked at the tip. Their small feet are unable to run or paddle over the water.

THE CRYSTAL BALL

In a study on the predation of turtle hatchlings in another venue it was found that during the exposed vulnerable half-hour transit from the nest down a 45 m beach to the sea, 12% of them were eaten by predators, which are various. Our Ghost Crabs are the most abundant species on sandy shores of the tropics and subtropics, (replacing sandhoppers of cooler zones). Ubiquitous predators are the sea birds, and, depending on beach location, ants, mongoose, raccoons, dingoes, monitor lizards, rats, and also dogs, cats and foxes introduced by man.

By 2010, the Turtle Conservation Project on Bird Island was routinely digging out and retaining hatchlings for a short time in ideal conditions. It is unclear if the turtles slowly digging their own way out of the nest is as important to their memory of place as scuttling down the beach to the sea. Robbie's period of artificial protection gave them time to absorb all of the yolk sac and attain maximum strength; then several large groups were released simultaneously en masse at a pre-appointed hour. An organised tourist spectacle was thus created as well as raising the possibility of muddling the efficiency of waiting predators by sheer numbers of prey, but there must be a minimum number of prey, and a density of predators needed to make the conversion of predator's feast into baffling frustration. Objective scientific assessment of the degree of success of mass releases is complex as there are many variables at work: a complex convergence of many behaviours, species and random events.

Turtles cast their young into the vagaries of a planktonic existence, as do many other sea creatures which will grow into turtle hatchling predators, such as crabs and fish, but they all compensate by producing large numbers of eggs to better the chances of survival of a few to mature, return and breed. Overall it is estimated that land, sea and aerial predators take 90% of turtle hatchlings in their early years, and that one in 1,000 to 10,000 survive to become breeding adults.

This has been the slender lifeline of survival for the various species of turtles so far. However, since the beginning of my personal odyssey, the world and the marine environment have changed dramatically. Floating plastics take a toll on adults, and present alarming nursery conditions for juveniles in the Atlantic and the Pacific. Whether their survival rates can keep up with such insidious modern hazards or not remains to be seen. Their vulnerability on land is being well cared for on Bird Island, which although fairly remote and protected from many modern influences, is inevitably a microcosm of the wider world. It shares problems of accidentally introduced species, and the knife edge of sensitively managed ecotourism, and one of the biggest challenges of the age: climate change and rising sea level. Like many others, it is a tiny island with limited freshwater aquifers vulnerable to intrusion by the sea, and not very far above the waves.

A Noddy Tern rises on long wings, having scooped floating seaweed from the surface to carry back to its nest.

Chapter 2

WILD DOLPHINS SEEK HUMANS FOR PLAY... IN OPEN SEA

Bahama Bank

As far as the eye can see there is nothing beyond the tiny boat. Nothing but sea and sky, in any direction. Out there, beneath us, the shadows move, flickering pieces of mosaic images. The sun reflects off wavy peaks of blue, masking fractured long shapes... gone... there... not there... maybe moving closer.

I fumble with fins, pull on the heels, grapple with my twisting mask strap. With a quivering hand I push back wind-blown hair, trying to breathe steady while my heart rate is racing. Walking backwards without tumbling over fins, there is a sudden rocking movement of the boat. I'm scrambling, grabbing hold to balance, standing in line, pushing wet mask on tight... 'Go!'

On command I step forwards to the edge. It's a long way down to a big sea. I'm high above where I thought I was and way beneath is a rippling surface. Beneath that is lost in moving reflected light. There's no time to pull out now. I push my mask close and point fins down then jump out and away from the reassuring solidity of metal deck. Anticipation gives way to terror.

Crashing through the barrier the impact sounded deafening. The splash rushed upwards – all known tones of blue, silver and white. Exploding droplets subsided into a rising curtain of bouncing bubbles, dancing as they disintegrated into the air of our world up there above the shimmering roof of water. Peering through a haze of turquoise there were shadow shapes, then in a moment of stillness, there was clarity. It was a serene blue world apart, a beautiful but alien place. Two dolphins, a mother with a calf, materialised out of diffuse light. They looked across at my sudden, clumsy arrival. For a finite time it seemed there was only them and me – the only beings in the universe, from two different worlds, aware but separated by species and limits of perception and communication. The moment was intensified by its context – the realisation of a dream held through years of work and saving, at the end of a traumatic time tunnel of family illnesses and deaths. This long awaited fantasy had come abruptly, but had been there all the time.

The baby dolphin was in constant touch with its mother – its dorsal fin touching her belly – a touching infant bond. Colours were drained by the sea and they were both tinted aquamarine – a harmonious scene of delicate watercolour wash spread over them; two distant swimmers, water and pale sand below. The mother was darker than her calf, spotted all over except for a pale belly, indistinguishable from the sky above when seen from below, dark when seen from above – counter-shaded – like many sea creatures. Her sleek young was almost white on the belly and a plain light grey above – the spots come with age. The mother was longer than I was tall. She kept her distance, moving imperceptibly, as slow-cruising dolphins do, without so much as a glimmer of muscle movement visible near tail or back. Both seemed to move by magic and as one. Dolphin mothers and calves sometimes swim inseparably in this way for up to five years. The very close association is retained through the first four years of a calf's life, while it still suckles milk. At about two years old the calf starts eating fish, lessening dependence on milk. With such affinity, this calf would be observing its mother's every move – foraging for food, social relations with other dolphins of the group, noticing us, boats and other aliens in their area, and watching out for and avoiding dolphin predators – sharks, occasionally some larger cetaceans, and, sadly, man in some parts of the sea, though not this area.

A small group of swimmers kept within sight of mother and baby for a short time, and a larger animal approached. It squeaked at us, head-on – maybe it was warning us off, although it need not have worried about our underwater potential. Two more dolphins joined the group and as the five of them swam away it was with speed and was effortless. The two latecomers rolled and exchanged sexual overtures as they went. Sexual play happened frequently and incidentally, very much *en passant*, as part of tactile communication. Young juveniles spend a lot of time with contemporaries of the same age, learning the ways of courtship and culture of their society by trial and error and play – from each other as well as from adults, like other very social mammals.

This day had been unique, and continued so as we headed into deeper water for the night and the yacht began rolling intensely during dinner on deck. The generator ran continuously; it was hard to sleep, and I was sea sick.

DOLPHIN WAYS

We awoke in shallow water again. It was vivid turquoise as far as the eye could see in any direction – too bright for more than a glance with the naked eye. As the boat pushed on, two dolphins appeared from nowhere and swam high-speed swerves backwards and forwards across the bow wave.

There they could coast along at the speed of the boat, expending little of their own energy. Presumably we and they share a similar experience of forces in the exhilarating activity of bodysurfing – feeling that extra surge from a wave pushing from behind, and the thrill of acceleration and staying within its driving force.

We leapt overboard in sequence as before, but the animals were not interested in us – our swimming did not measure up to the excitement of the bow wave. One hesitated, dived deeper, stopped and swayed, nearly vertical, dabbling his beak into the sandy bottom, listening for echoes from 'one-eyed flounders', lizardfish, blennies or other snacks hidden in the sand. The dolphins make specific sounds – buzzes, trills and whistles – when searching for buried prey, scanning and pinpointing it by echolocation, which also seems to disorient the small creatures, making them easy pickings. Our particular dolphin did not appear to have been successful in his snack seeking, and quickly re-joined his companion. This community mostly lives on the great shallow sandbank beneath us, where the depth is around 9–12 m (30–40 ft). Every few days they consolidate their snacks by visiting the surrounding deep water, about 60 m (200 ft), where there are squid in plenty.

No sooner were we back on deck and dry, than another six arrived. There was hurried grabbing of fins and masks and we were over the side again. One of them made a direct approach to Andrew, and boy and dolphin communed quietly beyond: it rolled on its back with eyes shut, and another swam near and peered down on them.

Rapport beneath the surface – a dolphin rolls on its back close by Andrew's side, eyes closed – a position of trust, whilst another dolphin watches from a distance.

Below them, the main stream of five dolphins were fanning their tails up and down nonchalantly. They were being frantically pursued by five humans who were swimming wildly, flailing arms and legs in multi-directions or floundering, or treading water trying to see the dolphin whereabouts from the surface. I had entered the water last and was lucky to submerge and accidentally meet up with the dolphin group as they arced round, away from the main group of swimmers. Just hanging there, quiet and stationary, I had a perfect close-up view of sleek, silky dolphin skin, wide 'grinning' mouths, active bright eyes, and, one might be tempted to say, their vigorous enjoyment of the fun of the race.

There were two on my right which were larger than the others; one of them appeared to be a male. They rolled round to show their very pale bellies as they glided past me. Unsure of dolphin etiquette, I meekly followed suit. Body posture between animals is part of their subtle communication and copying them seemed a means of bridging the communication gap between our species. If Andrew stood vertical, or rolled over, he was mimicked, so it seemed an appropriate response to their initiative. Two on my left belly-rolled around each other and one mouthed the other's thin tail base as they slid by. This behaviour might have been connected with their well-developed sense of taste – which, it is thought, could be a means of communicating more information on age, mood, sex, sexual state and prowess.

The main phalanx of swimmers caught up with them and we all followed for a very short distance until they increased angle and push of tail arc, accelerating up several gears beyond the most optimistic human pace. Several of us retired, vanquished by speed, and the others soon lost sight of them. As if to tease, the animals returned a short time later, and we were over the side yet again, but they immediately worked their tails at high power and sped away into the turquoise haze. Their vitality conveyed a force larger than life, almost joy in athletic prowess. We imagined they were probably indulging in the cetacean equivalent of a good laugh. This extraordinarily efficient swimming propulsion is achieved by long muscles lying along the spine powering vertical tail movements that drive the horizontal flukes up and down against the water. The spine is the key to this action by virtue of variation in flexibility and form along its length. The body acts like a spring which propels the dolphin using minimal energy. The beautiful economy of the spring design is comparable to that in the steady bounding action of a kangaroo's hind legs. This unique cetacean design and mechanics enable it to store elastic energy, damp down excess movement and help control changes and reconfigurations within its structure during its powerful movements.

BY DOLPHIN INVITATION ONLY

After a morning of expending maximum human energy, and achieving very little propulsion, we anticipated a quieter afternoon with a little gentle snorkelling. Our schooner moved on to a place where an old sugar boat had been wrecked in the 1920s, creating an artificial reef. As we sat about the deck eating a leisurely lunch, someone spotted five dolphins approaching our official jumping-off spot. Their heads kept popping up and looking at us, like comic strip 'kids next door': 'Where are you? When are you coming out to play?' Plates, lettuce and bread hit the deck and in silent film mode eight people flung off clothes and rushed to find fins and masks. With a mounting score of false starts, and with a couple of people not yet having seen the animals close up, the captain was cautious about overpowering our visitors with an excess of human interest. Two people jumped in. The dolphins distanced themselves. Then they started leaping – three at once cleared the water in unison, with energetic arching backs and splayed tails. One could almost feel the striving power, an earnest intensity of concentration. Others appeared and started 'porpoising' towards us, rhythmically bouncing up and down through an undulating sea, almost bounding like deer. The captain directed another two swimmers into the water: more people needed to be in there quickly before they lost interest in slow humans. But we were too slow and the dolphins had disappeared before we had surfaced. Wet people and wetter lunch were reacquainted, after which we decided to follow the pattern of the dolphin's usual routine – a siesta during the heat of the afternoon. Atypically, the dolphins reappeared at the usual jump point, but, as was becoming a norm, they had gone once we were in the water. It was quite clear who was in control and making the choices.

It seemed to be a very thin line between entertaining them enough that they would choose to engage with us, and possibly, at the other end of the scale, overwhelming them. They seemed to be almost like children with a short attention span. Their timescale of living is very different from ours, but then, each animal has its own very different baseline of speed, interest and relevance, and our human one, even setting aside our inadequacies as land creatures in a world of water, is completely different. Looking up from below at the underside of the surface 'roof' the disconnected bits of slow-moving human anatomy must have appeared ungainly to dolphins: they were more in tune with a twisting body-roll and eye contact.

Dolphin's-eye view of humans – a surface swimmer becomes disconnected bits of anatomy which dip through the sea surface 'roof'. Below the surface, Peter rolls on his side for a better look and a dolphin imitates.

There were also the dolphins' alternatives to be considered. They could choose to be sleeping – one side of the brain at a time, the other checking the surroundings and controlling breathing. Or, they could get on with dolphin life – foraging for snacks, hunting in deep water for a substantial feed, nursing or babysitting the young, teaching juveniles pod protocol and social behaviours, socialising, playing, experimenting and learning, courting, copulating, fighting amongst themselves, interacting with the Bottlenose neighbours, watching for predatory sharks, checking distant boat sounds and other human intrusions... or there was us. It seemed rather arrogant and humanly self-centred to imagine that our meagre swimming and gaming efforts should take preference.

The captain had said at our first briefing that experience had taught him that dolphins could be choosy and avoid people whom they disliked or who behaved badly, and the crew often shared the dolphins' judgement. Was this true, or was it a ploy to encourage people to be civil? The one strict rule we had been given was 'No Touching' (and certainly no nonsensical attempts at intrusive kissing, hugging or riding). Such selfish and human-oriented behaviour would spook the animals and could damage their very sensitive skin, which is an integral part of their friction-free, fast passage through the water.

There were mutterings and queries. Animal reactions to human body language can be full of surprises. Experiments on animal choice and perception are conducted such that no unconscious human gestures, facial expressions or eye movements can be seen by them and used as a cue. The reality of dogs and horses sensing human mood and fear has been significant since their domestication began. Particular people have a relaxed natural rapport with them and can rapidly bond, creating communication and some degree of control with an unknown, even 'delinquent', dog or horse by eye contact or body language. Such people seem to enter into the vocabulary of their animal's body postures and do not push the boundaries too far outside that framework. On the other side of the coin, animals can be choosy about their human associates. It has been observed that animals as apparently 'silly' as sheep notice if their handler is frowning or smiling and move out of range as appropriate. Dolphins have complex interactions within and between groups, other cetacean species and have a culture of learning and teamwork. Their brain is big; their perception must be very different from ours, using echolocation as well as vision. Had someone been reaching out to touch? Had they mistaken an underwater camera on an outstretched arm? Did they notice interaction between us humans? Had they misinterpreted spluttering from first time snorkellers with ill-fitting masks? Could they have misinterpreted swimmers' detours and bursts of speed when they tried to avoid splashing plastic fins and walls of bubbles? Could our own diverse repertoire of body language be an obstacle? It was anyone's guess.

There seemed no doubt that they had interacted most with the relaxed and confident swimmers – Peter, Andrew and others – who could cruise along with them, easily duck dive, twist, roll or interact rapidly mimicking their own movements, conjure up new antics – and stay submerged apparently forever. Dolphins approached them, standing upright in mimicry, pointing their white-tipped noses as if investigating.

Underwater mimicry – dolphins 'stand' upright, one rearing up straight with nose pointing upwards, like Andrew.

The order of entering the water came under careful scrutiny and management. It had become apparent that the dolphins were definitely attracted to Andrew, which, according to the captain, fitted with his own past experience and the pod's unique history. Not only did they seek out human company, but they apparently recognised and particularly sought out the young – Andrew was just sixteen. This pod's interest in humans was initiated by children in the 1970s as a by-product of a find of gold on a wrecked Spanish galleon. Hopeful divers flocked to the area, and with parents preoccupied with diving, children swam and romped in the sea around the boats. The dolphins joined in the fun – they play their own version of Chase, throwing and fetch games and indulge in competitive racing (as if someone shouts 'Go'). Dolphin mothers teach their calves to play games with Sargassum seaweed or anything which comes to hand. They have also been seen at 'play' harassing sea birds and turtles. Thus, it was not extraordinary that mothers and minders regularly exposed their young to this new human playground. The habit entered into the culture of the pod, and was handed down from parent to young through the generations – they can live to 50.

Thus it was that from then on, Andrew was usually overboard first – as bait. To watch dolphin and young human cavorting was a delight, with a particular hint of humour when punctuated by a stream of white particles and dust passing out of the dolphin and pluming towards his mask. As I pointed out at the time, many dolphin admirers would give anything to be in such a privileged position of close intimacy.

DOLPHIN GAMES

The first sighting next morning was two Frigate Birds, a yellow-beaked tern calling overhead and a distant dolphin fin... or was it a shark? Whenever we swam one of the crew of three was on watch, keeping alert for that sudden surprise.

Two dolphins approached the boat, the bait was dropped, followed by a further six swimmers. A mother dolphin awaited us with her baby in constant touch. When they disappeared two others circled about each of us to the point of close scrutiny. I twirled round in a tight circle and was eyeball to eyeball with one of them while we completed several circuits. Finning hard with hands linked behind my back I made myself as hydrodynamically shaped as possible, trying to mimic, and trying desperately not to bump or touch my fellow dolphin by accident at this unaccustomed speed. I need not have been concerned; the animal was so expert and so accurate a swimmer that it constantly corrected for my clumsy manoeuvres and we kept in tight parallel, about six inches apart, without the slightest brush of skins. The aquiline shapes swirling around me were mesmerising. We swam in the tightest circles possible for my curved length, round and round, looking into each other's eyes. The face next to mine was quite slender, the eye dark, peering and alert – a deep penetrating gaze – watching me as I panted into my snorkel with exhaustion and spouted the odd jet of water.

The eyes can move independently; the other eye could have been watching Peter, who was deeper, playing a similar circling game.

'Suddenly four raced up from behind, passing inches under me as they sped out in front, turned and dived deeper as they came back towards me. Head down, I finned deeper as one of the dolphins circled around me. I circled too and tried to swim as fast, but couldn't. For four or five complete revolutions we played this game. I was as sure as I could be that the dolphins enjoyed the game just as a young dog would relish this kind of sport. Then my lungs began to ache to bursting. I had to give in to my human need for air, while the dolphins, engineered for long dives, played on with each other. Down again and this time we swam alongside each other and looked each other in the eye, measuring each others' enjoyment of our contact... '

Deeper still, at six or seven metres, Andrew was twisting and twirling with them as if he, like them, had been born to it, and the dolphin who chose his company rolled round and round by his side. As Andrew pirouetted, slowly kicking, he wondered how long he could keep holding his breath. Three other dolphins were copying his every move. He noticed the pupils of their eyes were coppery, maybe an artefact of reflected sunlight.

'It was a strange place down there – undulating white sand and blue as far as

the eye could see. The emptiness focused all attention on the dolphins.'

As the dolphins left, two swam by in tandem, one with its flipper in the other's genital slit. They seemed at ease with our company now and I could hear them squeaking to each other for extended periods.

The close-up underwater view of their skin had been closer to a tactile experience than one might consider possible for a visual stimulus. It was patterned with elongated charcoal-coloured spots. But most prominently, it had an extraordinary, almost 3D texture, like silver shot silk, with multi-layered depth. While beside the dolphin I had battled to think of words to capture the memory of this uniquely beautiful skin. The closest description I could conjure was a recollection of deep lustrous layers of patina of polished wood from an ancient buried Kauri tree, 45,000 years old. In fact, dolphin skin is not multi-layered, but has an unusually ordered structure, simplified by having no hairs, fewer glands and different layers than other mammalian types. The outer layer, the epidermis, is about ten to twenty times thicker than that of terrestrial mammals. Its unique appearance reflects 50 million years of dolphin skin evolving for reducing friction drag. The skin structure varies according to the position on the body and is compliant with flow conditions, reducing instability and turbulence in a manner in which the details are still not totally clear. Synthetic coatings for reducing the drag of ships and boats have been made and are in use, in a crude imitation of their skin – limited by our present level of understanding.

Our encounter with these masters of hydrodynamic efficiency had lasted for twenty-two minutes. We were all totally drained physically, and somehow dragged ourselves back onto the boat. Once aboard, a hushed quiet descended on everyone, as with our very first dolphin meeting. Possibly we were all thinking our own version of Peter's thoughts:

'There is no thing in this world like meaningful contact with another intelligent and sensitive species for ennobling the spirit and putting our life on earth into its proper perspective. These are experiences you do not forget.'

Our next visitors appeared soon after; a larger group of ten dolphins came up ahead. As we focused for the usual scramble, the captain said no – these were the Bottlenose neighbours, uninterested in relating to humans, twice the size of our dainty Atlantic Spotted companions, and could be fairly rough. Instead we admired their 'porpoising' in the slight bow wave of the slowly moving boat. Their movements were precisely choreographed, heads out, bodies gently arching out, gliding down again – moving together exactly as one. The group included a baby and its mother; the infant began a sequence of zooming off and speeding in a circle around all of them, but was soon hauled in by the parent. Dolphin discipline of juveniles is always impressive. We could hear squeaks, but lower pitched than the smaller Spotted species. A second baby appeared accompanied by several more large adults, all bouncing gracefully and effortlessly in and out of the moving wave. As the tiny animal leapt clear out of the water it turned its face towards us. In the grand finale this little individual returned with the mother and swerved feverishly back and forth in the bow wave, eager to pick up every morsel of thrill, as the boat began to accelerate away and leave them to continue with dolphin activities. They zigzagged faster and faster, then dived, in perfect synchrony. After a short time they returned, rushing in all directions, squealing. Then, as suddenly as they had appeared, they sped past and were out of sight, still whistling.

It continued to be a morning of superlatives as five of our Spotted Dolphins arrived. We were quickly to the side of the boat, where the dorsal fins were cutting lines into the smooth sea's surface. Feet first into the water, we used fins to slow the descent. Sudden silence, bubbles, diffused light and down into the seemingly empty world of turquoise and white that had become so familiar, but still took one's breath away. Then, through the quietness, there were whistles – but no dolphins in sight.

Suddenly I was with a duo of dolphins, swimming very close together as a group. As we swerved sideways, a third accelerated up from underneath me. I had no idea it was there until a taffeta textured head appeared in front of mine. I shrieked with shock and delight. Dolphins and human swam on fast, at crazy speed (as judged by the human), as a parallel group. With piercing eyes they peered and steered – and took me in a circle, faster and faster, round and round in a decreasing spiral. Dolphins darted in and out of our spinning vortex, and way below beyond my reach. Gasping for breath back at the surface I watched their deep nonchalance enviously.

In a calm moment, a gentle, observant little female swam close in front of me. Females have one genital slit and two mammary slits on either side of it. She had strange zigzag marks on her shoulder. It was difficult to decipher if these might be mechanical scratching from a sharp metal edge, or sharp scraping tooth marks. Such scars are common amongst adults and are a record of their lives. Dominant dolphins nip less dominant individuals in the group, as in many social mammals. Shark's teeth, Remora suckers, fishing tackle and boat propellers leave a record on the skin besides nicked and split dorsal fins, tail flukes and pectoral flippers. Such permanent signs of wear and tear are vital in photographic identification of individuals, which was realised in the 1970s and revolutionised research studies.

Their skin is not the only record of these past tactile experiences. This group of dolphins shared an indelible memory. We carried a Gemini on board which was never used. A while previously, our boat had been chartered by a professional photographer who had insisted on continually driving the Gemini at its highest speed to maximise his photo opportunities of these wild creatures. Whether the propeller grazed one or not was not known, but the dolphins became terrified of the craft and their shared experience rendered it unusable in the area.

There was an older, spottier big dolphin with wire or fishing line caught in his back encircling the base of his tail fluke. There was a cluster of large lumpy calluses – it had been there a while. Dolphin healing is impressive and something of an enigma as they can cope with and recover from severe injuries such as shark bites. They do not bleed to death even from very deep wounds, and infection seems to be rare (as in crocodiles). Their skin integrity is important: dolphin skin qualities make a vital contribution to their efficient movement through the water. To keep their skin surface in the best possible condition, it flakes and peels like ours, but faster – nine times faster in the Bottlenose Dolphin where the outer layer of skin may be replaced every two hours. Thin nylon line, nets and drift nets are invisible to various sea mammals, as we have witnessed with an injured Scottish Harbour Seal resting for days on the sand (chapter 7). Slow death by drowning caused by fishing tackle holding animals submerged and unable to reach air is well documented and makes harrowing viewing and reading. This animal had been lucky to avoid that fate. The vital muscles operating his main propulsion system – the tail fluke – were tightly constricted, bound by several windings, cutting in deep. The fresh injury must have created difficulties and constraints to swimming at any speed, and there would have been the aggravation of the wound and impaired muscle action during healing and callus formation.

Some people deny that animals, even mammals with sophisticated nervous systems, feel pain comparable to ours, and that such considerations are teleological and projecting human feelings of inappropriate sentimentality. It might be that the question needs turning around. Is it a possibility that in extreme pain or fear (what one might term 'gut' reaction) it is we who revert to a deep-seated animal level? Mammals share many physiological and orienting responses of pupil dilation, raised heart rate, changes in brain rhythms and more. In extreme circumstances one is only aware of these sensations, without adornments of human reasoning and words. Could it be that we, in those moments, switch back to animal consciousness? This permanent dolphin injury was news to the captain who entered it into his dolphin records, along with the human cause.

There were two further dolphin alerts during the afternoon, two Bottlenose, then five. As they swam by slowly in calm, clear water their heavier submarine-like shape was very visible, also their subtle gradation of dark to pale to palest grey. On deck, in the quietness of the night, there was an audible whooshing wave as a Barracuda grabbed a fish at the surface, almost against the metal hull. A Golden Spotted Snake Eel wove its way near to the boat, and a scattering of fish finned by in the torchlight. The boat was rolling too much to sleep, so we went on deck to remind ourselves of the intensity of the starlight, and saw Orion, clear and bright. No one could sleep much, there were low voices on deck on and off through the night.

Day dawned with a Bottlenose in the distance. The boat was moving fast, cutting frothy edges through the water. Two dolphin fins appeared, racing towards us. They seemed so exhilarated they leapt clear out of the water for what seemed enormous distances; their action and speed emanated a feeling of earnest intensity and intense striving power. Another appeared, trailing far behind, 'porpoising' rapidly in and out of the water in low leaps, keeping its head clear of the water for breathing. It squealed like an excited child trying to keep up with the big boys. They darted in and out of the bow wave ... and were gone.

Eventually, two last playmates joined us. These were definitely testing our skills to the limit. They swooped under the deep hull as soon as we were all in the water. Our first challenge was a swim around the boat through an impenetrable haze of plastic flapping fins and walls of bubbles that seemed wide enough to stretch to infinity, obscuring direction, dolphins and sun-glinting surface. The dolphins initiated their chosen game of eyeball circuit swim, which took their fancy only briefly. They accelerated out of our sight, leaving an empty sea full of whistles. I was fighting to recall every detail of that last privileged wild contact before it blurred into a vague happy memory – a fragmented mosaic of impressions of smooth shining silkiness of skin, a nebula of bubbles and speed, spectral shapes disappearing, whistles fading into an aquamarine haze.

As we sailed back towards the real world we stopped over the sugar boat wreck. There was hard coral: some ochre and white Fire Coral and various fawn brain corals with attendant Neon Gobies. Mauve soft coral fingers waved amongst purple based sea fans fading up to edges of blue. Half submerged in the sand, lines of old boat ribs like railway tracks, were buzzing with yellow fish. A Black Durgon looked strangely out of season in this tropical sun, with wintry northern colours of olive green, dark purple and terracotta brown. A Cleaner Wrasse patrolled his area; grey striped Sergeant Majors, Blue Tangs, grunts and a turquoise parrotfish passed a fleet of silver Barracudas – long, lean and mean – on the hunt. Below old bits of structure, a Green Moray Eel lurked and red squirrelfish watched, wide-eyed, from safe overhangs.

It was a fitting end to the day, but there was still a surprise out there. With everyone out of the water, wrapped in towels and exchanging fish sightings, there was a cry from the sea watcher, 'Bullshark!' A long, dark shadow below the surface, with tell-tale dorsal fin exposed above, was moving steadily across the old wreck we had just left. Old memories die hard. The presence of shark towers where Australian lifesavers kept watch and tales of lone swimmers disappearing had been part of my youth, and I had been a witness. On a vast long arc of wild Queensland beach early on a cool winter morning, I saw a lithe young woman sprinting into the small waves, bouncing with energy as she leapt into the bigger surf. The sea was pale in the early haze. She was a lone swimmer in a big sea. Later that morning we returned for a day's fun, but in the centre of the beach there was a small crowd. The lifesavers had improvised a low enclosure of screens and looked grim. She was a sister of one of their number and had not returned from her accustomed early swim. The dead shark was behind the screens and we were invited to take a look and put a donation into the club collecting box. The firm muscular rounded body of the pale grey shark, its cold, grey small eyes and sharp, slim pointed teeth curving inwards remains indelibly in my mind. I vaguely recall a story that they found her arm in the shark's belly. Times change – feeding and photographing sharks is big business and killing them for human safety or revenge is a matter of increasing concern as populations of these top predators in the food chain decline. And the deserted beach on an unpopulated shore was Surfer's Paradise.

There was a brief information exchange: Bullsharks are amongst the most aggressive sharks, more likely than most to attack humans as well as dolphins, ranking with Great White, Tiger, and Oceanic White Tip. They frequent warm, shallow water – hence its proximity now – and, like many of their kind, being tolerant of fresh water are found in estuaries and rivers. It is now thought they are and have been a presence in Sydney Harbour and responsible for some attacks there. We were glad to be high up on deck, and not preparing to engage in dolphin encounters at this moment.

Dolphins in control underwater – three dolphins eye the observer as they speed away leaving struggling humans behind at the surface.

DOLPHIN COMMUNICATIONS

Dolphin whistles and whines have become the most evocative of memories. The range of 'notes', frequencies, intonation, and contexts of these squeals, trills and high speed clicks conjure our image of the essence of all dolphins – communication. Communication is at the core of everything: group organisation and cooperation, socialising, and responding to the outside world, including humans. Within close visibility there is the possibility of body posturing and copying – they constantly touched (sketch), postured to each other, and eventually postured with us. When out of sight and far apart there is sound – travelling four times faster in water than in air and keeping group members in close touch. When vocal high notes and clicks merge into sea distance, tail slaps on the surface and body leaps create long-distance messages.

Communication enables long-term group learning and a shared culture. The evidence was that our group was passing on their habit of playing with humans. Particular groups, often quite small ones within a bigger population have learnt, copied and communicated, creating coordinated hunting strategies which are unusual and innovative. Some create their own bow wave as they surge dangerously close towards the shore in order to beach prey fish. Another group cooperates with local fishermen netting from the shore in Brazil, another on the Irrawaddy River in Burma. In Shark Bay, Western Australia, the nose-down behaviour foraging in the sand, which we had seen here on the Bahama Bank, has been refined to a very high degree amongst some Bottlenose Dolphins. Young learn from their mothers where particular sponges grow, select a convenient basket sponge to fit their nose, prise it off the substrate intact, and put it on their noses before scouring the rocky bottom for buried and sheltering fish, presumably as protection against abrasion. This ingenious procedure allows them to hunt for hidden Sandperch which are out of reach of the dolphin's normal hunting method. This fish has no gas-filled swim bladder – which is what reflects the dolphin's sound search (echolocation) allowing it to home in on its target. With no sound signature this fish is safe. It is a labour intensive, though reliable, way for clever dolphins to find Sandperch protected by silence deep in the sand. The behaviour has become a source of bonding and seems to be the driving force of who associates with whom in this Australian population. Females who have learnt to 'sponge' group together, forming a clique with the mutual interest of 'sponging'.

Atlantic Spotted Dolphins use ten distinct vocalisations which have been identified and analysed. Individuals identify themselves by their own particular whistle and sometimes accompany this 'name' signature with a trail of bubbles expelled from their blowhole. Their sounds emanate not from the mouth, but the nasal sacs which connect with the blowhole, and are projected forwards through their melon hump forehead. They call each other selectively. Babysitters, male as well as female, give their own signature whistle before retrieving young dolphins. Mothers and calves whistle when reunited. Young males also form strong associations with their contemporaries and some form 'amigo' relationships, lasting for fifteen years or even a lifetime. In a study of Bottlenose Dolphins copying each other's signature whistles, one of a pair of allied males was still copying the other's whistle, in intricate detail, twelve years later.

In distress and excitement, the signature whistle is overlapped by different sounds. Aggressive and sexual behaviours are accompanied by specific ones. Animals attempting courtship and mating identify themselves to each other and there is a specific sound used in this context, the 'genital buzz' which has a high repetition rate of clicks. Squawking is part of fighting and resolving conflicts, accompanied by head to head postures with stiffly arched bodies and open mouths. Further along the scale there is synchronised squawk, scream and bark.

This wide repertoire of sound, tactile and postural communication weaves each individual into the social web. Gregarious living starts early; calves tended by babysitters as well as their mothers, grow up to spend most of their time with age contemporaries, learning from each other and adults. Juveniles progress to become young babysitters. Young females may join an itinerant group of young males for a time, but return to their mother's pod in order to raise their own offspring. Like elephants, the grandmothers are the repositories of learning and expertise. Females with their first calves share assistance as well as needs with other females at the same stage in life. Males can form groups and cooperate in coalitions – threatening other males, influencing who is involved in mating and who is thwarted, overseeing and defending the dolphin community, a topic which becomes more complex and unique as more behaviour is observed. The Atlantic Spotted Dolphins of the Bahama Bank spend time travelling, playing and socialising with their Bottlenose neighbours. The two even associate sexually.

Socially acceptable behaviour within a group, as in any society, is an essential for peaceful coexistence without conflict and chaos. Dolphins can be disciplinarians; researchers have filmed mothers making the genital buzz sound, aimed at the genital area or centre of the body of her errant young. At a gentler level of coercion, we had seen the bow riding Bottlenose calf being obediently brought back into the group. Other disciplinary action can involve physical contact on the flank with the mother's beak, and, in the extreme, holding the calf down on the sand. These measures are also used by the group on older miscreants.

In touch: a tail fluke and a right flipper intertwine – two dolphins swim as a pair as they accompany Andrew to the surface to breathe.

AFFILIATIONS

During our very tiny glimpses of dolphin social life in progress, we had seen the close bond of mother and young in everyday circumstances. In extreme circumstances this strong relationship can be intense to the point of suffering, involving mothers lifting injured calves to the surface for days or weeks on end. There have been recent extraordinary sightings – Sanniang Bay, China, July 2012 – a newborn dead baby dolphin had a long cut across its belly, probably hit by a boat propeller. The mother worked for three days and nights to keep its blowhole above water in rough seas. Singapore, July 2013, the third such incident in a month – four or five Pink Dolphins took turns assisting a mother trying to support her dead infant, probably poisoned by polluted harbour waters ingested and passed on in mother's milk. Mothers have been observed supporting their calves for two weeks, going without food, exhausting themselves, with other dolphins rallying to help. California, March 2013 – an infant Bottlenose Dolphin had been dead for days or maybe weeks, with flesh visibly decaying: the mother bore it up, draped across her dorsal fin, steadily swimming towards deeper water, flanked by other dolphins. It has been observed that Bottlenose Dolphins react differently depending on whether death is gradual or sudden. Mourning is not unique to dolphins; it has been recorded for whales, elephants, chimpanzees and others, including birds.

There are well-known incidents of dolphins gathering round and lifting a fellow injured adult animal to the surface for every breath for days on end, followed up by intermittent support. A recent observation recorded a team effort involving twelve Long-beaked Common Dolphins forming a raft support. Amongst the forty or so species of dolphin there is some degree of joint activity and coexistence: herds of Pilot Whales are accompanied by small numbers of Bottlenose Dolphins; Spotted and

Spinner Dolphins associate; and Northern Right Whale Dolphins are seen with Pacific Dolphins; our Atlantic Spotted Dolphins associate with Bottlenose Dolphins. Assistance in threatening circumstances extends to the different species as well as their own. New Zealand has been the site of some extraordinary incidents: two tiring and distressed Pigmy Sperm Whales, repeatedly beaching in spite of one and a half hours of rescue attempts by persevering humans, were suddenly and easily led out to sea by a well-known, local Bottlenose Dolphin. In an incident in 1983, dolphins took over from humans guiding seventy-six stranded Pilot Whales away from the beach to safe deeper water. In a previous similar whale stranding and rescue by dolphins, a helicopter followed them as they guided the whales several miles out to sea.

Their interspecies assistance extends to humans and is one of the most fascinating and endearing aspects to dolphin enthusiasts. Incidents of injured and exhausted humans under threat in the sea, as well as boats, are almost commonplace. From 'alerting' and leading a dive boat out of range of the 2004 tsunami, to herding swimmers for forty minutes to thwart the Great White Shark below them, or a single dolphin assisting a surfer already badly mauled and bitten by that species, the survivors' accounts make thought-provoking reading. There could be long speculation and rethinking ahead: given the discovery in four cetacean species of the specialised brain cells – spindle cells – specially linked with speech, social organisation, 'gut' reactions, empathy and intuition about other's feelings.

FOR THE LOVE OF DOLPHINS

In this context of socially organised, cognisant beings, the idea of permanently splitting up family groups, isolating individuals or putting them into alien groups becomes unthinkable. In the context of creatures ranging freely over large areas of sea, the idea of confinement within a comparatively small blocked off area or smaller artificial pool becomes abhorrent. Turning their play, games, curiosity and intuitive toy and tool use into circus tricks becomes grotesque. Converting the animals themselves into cute animated cartoon-style performers for a highly lucrative entertainment industry seems barely credible. The light dusting of factual information which renders this 'family friendly' activity 'educational' speaks less eloquently than the records of captive dolphins and killer whales known to have resorted to self-mutilation and stereotyped behaviours equivalent to big cats repetitively pacing their cages. The fluffy toy dolphins with big eyes in the gift shop by the exit complete the fantasy.

As our boat turned stern to the bright turquoise expanse of the shallow Bahama Bank and the wild free dolphins, I was glad I had long resisted the temptation to admire them in captivity. If I could not see them on their own terms in the wild I had vowed not to see live ones at all – television films conveyed their wonder and excitement. Having seen them in their own environment I knew I would have felt a nagging guilt if I had succumbed and subsidised dolphin captivity in order to see them. To have had these highly sentient wild beings seeking a few minutes of our company had been a privilege beyond comparison.

The turquoise sea disappeared into deep blue, and the 65 km (40 mile) crossing back to West End, Grand Bahama brought the rediscovery of fresh water showers and shore supply electricity. Next morning, we cast off, leaving the mosquitoes behind, and sailed into the dark at 05:40. It was a thin hammock of a new moon, languishing on its back, dwarfed by the dazzle of Venus in an enveloping sea and sky of rich indigo. Slowly the colour drained and drifted to a mauve hedge of cloud, and behind, a yellow and blue horizon intensified. Even as the sky turned blue, the moon and stars still shone a path of glory across inky purple sea. The sun rose and switched the water to a crisp dark blue. A solitary yellow-beaked tern was flying with us again, swooping and diving in the wind. It caught a small morsel, dropped and dipped and caught it in mid-air. Three white sails billowed to steady the boat as we sailed 130 km (82 miles) to Fort Lauderdale… and reality… or was it?

'Dolphin adventures available locally… with kiss, feed, dance and rub the dolphins… the kids may get to ride a dolphin across the pool'... The higher prices of summer '…do not include pictures of you with dolphins or videos of you swimming with the dolphins… Natural dolphin encounters… swimmers go snorkelling with the dolphins in their seawater home. Visitors should not touch the dolphins during this type of swim because it is considered non-work time for the dolphins…'

Reality? Not for the dolphins.

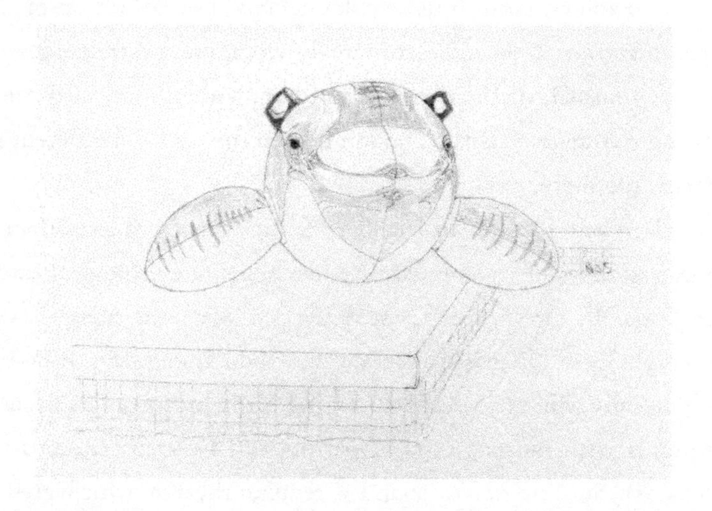

A dolphin fit for hugging, kissing, riding and rubbing.

Chapter 3

GIANTS AND BABIES – CARING IN THE CARIBBEAN
Tobago

NESTING GIANTS AND HUMAN GUARDIANS
GIANT LEATHERBACK TURTLES ON AN ISLAND SHORE

One of life's greatest thrills is to arrive in a tropical place after dark, travel-worn and tired, to be escorted through unaccustomed sounds, sights, smells and temperature. To snatch a few hours' sleep and then to wake abnormally early to a dazzling bright dawn is to see the world afresh: with crisp shadows, clean intense colours, and clear definition of shapes, textures and forms. Trees and plants are different, more extreme; leaves and flowers are unusual, distinctive – from unknown families; bird song is a tantalisingly strange melange, and loud. Even the sea has a different sound as it meets the shore.

The place was Tobago; an island with more exotic species than other Caribbean islands due to its proximity to and being a geological extension of Venezuela. In forest trees Crested Oropendola nests hang down like fruits, vivid Green Iguanas stretch and flex their silken skin. Blue-backed Manakins court while iridescent humming birds and jacamars fly, and the air resounds with raucous calls of parrots and Cocricos (Rufous-vented Chachalacas). Surging waves sound a regular rhythm which crescendos cyclically into loud crashes making beaches vibrate underfoot, a reminder that nearby is the point at which several oceans meet. Off the north coast of South America, the Atlantic and the Caribbean Oceans clash with the Gulf Stream pushing up between them, catapulting nutrients into circulation. This meeting point of churning seas at the eastern end of Tobago is punctuated by rugged dark rocks and the wild uninhabited St Giles Island. In this place of plenty, fish flourish as do the sea birds that feast on them. Hundreds of Frigate Birds nest on the stunted shiny-leafed trees, babies white and fluffy, males disporting their puffed-up red throats. Chic Red-footed Boobies compete for the brightest red, along with ravishing Red-billed Tropicbirds, resplendent against the dark rock background. Their tail streamers of purest white and longer than their bodies trail in graceful curves as they fly side by side into the wind. They hover with arched backs in balletic courtship display, ephemeral and seemingly too fragile for this turbulent ocean crossroad.

This was a first morning – 5 a.m. and waking to a new world. Between spasmodic waves of loud power, the sea lay quiet and still, the air cool. A soft subtle clatter of the palm fronds floated on the breeze. A mockingbird called first before the sky was light. The first rays of sun picked out black rocks and touched the tips of distant palm fronds. Gradually the entire ring of palms edging the bay blazed into crisp bas-relief. The magic of small birds' twitterings followed, until their calls in turn were finally masked by monotonous *oo oo*'s of doves. By 6 a.m. the sea birds were flying in low, heads tilted, eyes alert, scanning the sea, their incessant calls dominating the skies.

Half an hour later a few hotel guests emerged, but briefly, threw hats onto sun beds and retreated back to bed. The mile-long beach was now empty but for a lone fisherman. The sun had risen above the skimming wings of the seagulls. Behind, palm fronds flickered between being moving straight lines and superimposed curves sharply etched against the pale pink sky. Thus it was when I saw my first wild turtle. Far in the distance a group of four people were crouching around a dark round shape in the sand. From a rim of low creeping spume there were wide tell-tale tracks leading up the steep slope – two large scooped 'tyre' marks either side of a sharply cut tail trail. Usually leatherbacks nest at night, around 3 a.m. This was an unusual and privileged sighting.

This largest of all the marine turtles, the Giant Leatherback Turtle, more than 1.8 m (6 ft) long, had laboriously dragged her 454 kg (1,000 lb) bulk up to the top of the beach to dig her nest. The mechanical effort of such a transition must have been immense: her norm is for her great weight to be supported by the sea. She rhythmically swung her immense flippers in arc shapes, monotonously and steadily, as if to swim through the sand, gradually deepening the circular body depression. Working incessantly, her head held tense, she made gasping noises, distracted almost as if in labour, distantly focused on a remote elsewhere. Her eyes looked glazed as if in a state of trance, running with tears besmirched with sand. Traditionally it was said that female turtles wept because making the nest was so difficult, so many eggs would be stolen, and she would never see her young. All of these fanciful tales are true facts; though her tears are in fact salty secretions, ridding her body of excessive salt from drinking the sea. One could well sympathise with any tears of effort, for a turtle works for about two hours non-stop to create her nest and our turtle was no exception.

Puffs of sand sprayed upwards and sprinkled her dark bluish-grey back, coming to rest in the shallow gullies running down her shell. The strewn sand accentuated rough-edged long ridges along its surface. The back looks almost like a hard pressed patchwork of long pieces of leather, crimped along the seams and stretched tightly over a frame. These deep grooves and ridges run from head to tail along the belly as well as the back and act like the grooves in the hull of a boat – a hydrodynamic shape. As the name 'leatherback' implies, this turtle's 'shell' is thick, tough textured skin rather than bone as in other turtles. In other species the bony top shell (carapace) is formed by the fusing of rib bones; the Giant Leatherback has dispensed with such heavy bone construction. Instead it has a fibrous rubbery skin with a layer like a mosaic embedded with thousands of tiny bony plates – strength without the disadvantage of excess weight, as well as flexibility. This leather-skinned innovation allows them to swim faster, further and deeper.

Her hind flippers swung deep, flicking sand in the air, scooping further for a deeper hole under her rear end. On and on she dug, monotonously turning, shifting, sweeping, scraping, gouging – one fancied these might almost be the repetitive actions of a being possessed, a body performing a predestined ritual controlled remotely. In a way it is – her rear digging is without visual directive as not only are turtles quite near-sighted in air but she can see nothing of her progress, with her relatively small head obscured by her humped carapace. From the point of view of the human observer this rear action blindness has its advantages as one can approach unseen and watch quite closely without causing her any disturbance. Though infinitely more talented than us at navigation and place recognition by particular wave frequency, water and sand characteristics, her brain power is not great. Her brain is small. She is still a creature from the Jurassic Period, akin to a living dinosaur.

Eventually, at about a metre (3 ft) deep when there was no more resistance to her outstretched hind flippers, our turtle ceased excavating. From under her tail we could see small round white eggs like wet billiard balls dropping down into the sand. There could have been 120 of them. They would remain protected beneath the warm sand for sixty days, the incubation temperature determining the sex of the developing baby turtles. A higher temperature produces a female; in some locations El Nino effects cause a female-biased sex ratio.

Her task completed, she laboriously carried out the long excavation process in reverse, moving her flippers backwards and forwards filling in the hole. With her enormous front flippers, used butterfly-stroke style, she then swept sand back across her body imprint. Finally, she wielded her great bulk round, twisting and turning about the entire area and far beyond, energetically sweeping and spraying sand in all directions creating a chaotic maze of marks as if there had been a mass manoeuvre of large vehicles. It was then impossible to see exactly where she had deposited her eggs.

She faced the frothing waves and lumbered slowly down the beach, lifting her pointed head as she touched the first swell. As the wave broke over her head she disappeared down the steep slope into deep water. Intermittently, a nose tip surfaced to breathe and we had an occasional glimpse of a dark ribbed mound between the waves diminishing beyond the surf to a shadow, probably imagined as it was lost in a wide jostling sea.

She was back in her natural element for a short while, with the males who never leave the water. All being well, she would mate, return in about ten to twelve days to nest again, revisiting her sandy nesting beach, or another in the vicinity. Having a leathery rather than a hard bone shell this species avoids traversing stony beaches and sometimes changes beaches – appropriate where erosion is frequent. Our turtle would return several more times, through June to maybe as late as August. Then with her tropical sojourn of breeding over for two or three years, she would be off to seek out enormous quantities of jellyfish, a few octopus, squid, sea squirts and floating kelp. Her search would take her immense distances into colder, open ocean – largely a desert where gatherings of her jellyfish food are few and localised, reflecting the sparse scattering of plankton blooms on which they feed. In 1990, twelve individuals followed large schools of their prey jellyfish north into British waters, becoming entangled in fishing nets or stranded on Cornish beaches. Leatherback turtles swim to the even colder seas north of Norway and south of New Zealand. They forage relentlessly and explore into waters so deep and cold that their only company is Sperm Whales and a few rarer whales, deeper than 1 km (0.6 miles) and at less than 5°C (41°F).

The pressure of such depths creates decompression problems which they have solved in ways similar to the special adaptations of other animal divers such as dolphins, whales, seals and diving birds. Leatherbacks have been recorded submerged for 85 minutes, but unlike many animal divers they descend with a lungful of air. It is thought that they avoid decompression sickness (the 'bends') by ascending slowly. Like other deep divers they have collapsible lungs and their heart rate slows in order to conserve oxygen and energy. It also seems that their body temperature lowers the risk of gas bubbles forming in the blood.

The Giant Leatherbacks are unique amongst turtles and amongst reptiles. They are warm-blooded and keep warm in cold seas. Other reptiles, such as crocodiles, lizards, snakes and tortoises need to soak up warmth from their surroundings before they can function efficiently, hence their prevalence in the Tropics and their need to hibernate in cool climates. This turtle regulates its body temperature such that the centre of its body is 18°C (32°F) higher than surrounding water. How they do so was long mysterious and misunderstood. It transpires that their body warmth is not solely due to anatomical design. Their behaviour is linked into a clever sequence of cause and effect. They rest very, very little, swimming incessantly after a prey which is not a high energy food. They need jellyfish in giant quantities even though some of their prey species can weigh 20 kg (44 lb). Like any athlete, the turtle's intense sustained swimming causes muscle temperatures to rise. This is their heat source. Their immense size is another part of the heat equation. A large volume with relatively small surface area loses least heat and this species is huge. In 1988 Giant Leatherbacks made newspaper headlines when the largest ever seen was washed up in North Wales, Britain, drowned in fishing gear. It was 3 m (10 ft) long, weighed 916 kg (2,019 lb) – as heavy as a small car – and had a 2.7 m (9 ft) flipper span. They have to grow to a minimum size before they can retain their heat efficiently. Heat is also retained by insulation. Even when a turtle's shell is cold their core heat is further held steady by fat.

The power house of this clever mechanism is the giant flattened forelimb. Circulating blood is kept warm by an ingenious design of a tightly packed network of blood vessels serving the flippers. Blood is cooled on the way out to the flippers and warmed on the way back so that returning blood is not lowering the body's core temperature. Thus blood flow combines with giant size and insulation to hold the heat of muscle activity.

Our Giant Leatherback was in her element once she submerged. Equipped with temperature control, diving adaptations, streamlined body shape and stability keels she became a superb long-distance cruiser flying through the ocean, travelling far and deep. Her brief sojourns on land had belied her true nature, although her powerful and sustained sweeping of sand gave an inkling of her muscle power.

This first sighting of a nesting turtle was the most outstanding of several more encounters. Its evocative setting was visible; subsequent viewings happened at about 2 or 3 a.m. and inevitably were mosaics of glimpses and shadows by torchlight. These nightly encounters took place under the eye of Roger, a hotel security guard, of African origin like most Tobagans and a giant at over 2 m (6'9") tall, ever watchful for the turtle's privacy and safety. He warned off any over-enthusiastic photographers from flashing a camera in her face eager for the perfect picture. He was a keen practical conservationist and eagerly shared his turtle knowledge. He carefully explained the necessity for newly hatched turtles to dig their way out of the sand and scuttle down the beach without assistance. Regardless of their vulnerability, this was their only opportunity to experience and remember the taste and smell of their birth beach and the sea of this bay. Without these vital clues the females could not make their astonishing return to nest on these beaches years hence when they were sexually mature. The protective impulse to pick up these tiny hatchlings and carry them to the sea is strong, but misguided.

In his twenties, Roger was a conservation soulmate. He had been on security duty all night and we struck up conversation – talking turtles and the dilemma of tourism and conservation, then the joys of exploring underwater. I mentioned our unsuccessful local attempts, somewhat frustrating after briefly seeing the corals and fish of the Nylon Pool for real and Buccoo Reef through the grubby glass of a viewing boat. Roger described his favourite snorkelling place near Castara, his home village set in a lush forested valley around a bay. As he talked it became obvious he was like a duck out of water here, standing stiffly in khaki uniform in the artificial contrivance of a modern hotel. His voice changed, his face relaxed and his eyes softened and looked into the middle distance of private memory. He promised to take us there.

Top: Seen from behind, a Giant Leatherback Turtle digs her nest, tail tucked down; sand sprays into the air and settles in the grooves of her leathery ridged shell.
Below: She wields her huge fore flippers backwards and forwards, scooping sand. Her head markings are distinctive – a means of identifying individual animals.

VILLAGE VOICES

Castara was a small fishing and farming village with a lackadaisical atmosphere. Iron-roofed houses teetered on stilts down slopes of lush vegetated hills. Bunched strappy leaves of bromeliad plants were growing on the electricity wires, their aerial roots twining the wire and hanging down catching the moisture from the air, some with red, white and purple sprays of their eccentric flowers. In the central heart of one there was a core of thin dried grassy strands, held snug by the encircling crown of leaves – it was the tiny nest of a humming bird, which flew in and out fast and direct as an arrow.

This was no gingerbread village with tiny timber houses, brightly painted and ornate. It was more a place of a few minimal concrete houses, some with overhanging verandas for extras and welcome shade, and makeshift lean-tos. Workaday furniture was sometimes basic: bits of wood roughly aligned and nailed together; babies were being bathed in plastic washing-up bowls al fresco, entertained by iridescent humming birds darting to and fro. In a warm climate and outdoor way of life furnishing assumes less importance, function sensibly far outweighs appearances – refreshingly real, an alternative to the carefully contrived 'look' of modern affluent aspirations. There was the homely clucking of comfortable chickens on the air, twittering bananaquits and the occasional squawk of parrots in overhanging trees.

Life had not always been so casual here in the past: on the way we had passed a 'Jumbies tree', carefully left growing by the roadside. Most had fallen in hurricane Flora in 1963 which destroyed 75% of Tobago's forest trees. According to Caribbean and some African traditional folklore, enormous Silk Cotton (Kapok) trees harboured 'old ghosts' and were objects of fear and superstition. Some local people were reticent when it was mentioned, but later we were told slave ancestors had been hanged from this tree – about fifteen on a branch so all could see.

Village people not living off the land and the sea were employed in 'government work', alias occasional road repairs. Cricket was played with passion at any time of day and in unorthodox venues – as is so often the case in countries far from its origin. On this occasion, the pitch was in the middle of the road, with improvised stumps which included a wire crate containing a python-like snake, folded to fit its prison conveniently, mouth agape as it was taunted mercilessly. I politely declined the player's offers for me to photograph it for $10. (Animal welfare was not the norm here. At Buccoo and Scarborough we had seen a pathetic monkey chained to a bare tree, complete turtle shells hanging up for sale, caged toucans, macaws and parrots, and starving mangy dogs were not an unusual sight – not that unexpected in a place where human life had been so cheap.)

The character of the village was in keeping with the island custom of painting biblical texts in black Gothic script as banners over public entrances. Roger's family owned the local bar, a large establishment with first floor veranda, everything very neat and freshly painted. Inside, its walls were austere cream, each one bearing an immaculately painted slogan in plain upper case lettering, enormous. By the toilet door there were gentle words of encouragement: 'Let us be tidy'. In the main room there were moral messages: 'NO BARE BACKS' (with the B artistically shared by both words), 'NO OBSCENE LANGUAGE' (with the foot of the L heavily underlining the remaining letters), 'NO SMOKING OF NARCOTICS'. The instructions presented something of a juxtaposition, positioned near a poster of a voluptuous bronze beauty kneeling and leaning provocatively forwards to emphasise the sizes of her nakedness, advertising a rum for 'Peak Performance'. Outside, Roger's unsmiling father sat under a spreading Breadfruit tree, apparently oblivious of our presence, reading the bible out loud to an intent gathering.

One of Roger's friends, Bertil, joined us. Seriously committed and knowledgeable, he was studying in the hope of becoming a conservation guide. We saw his father, a traditional fisherman, sitting making four-foot square fish traps from specially selected pliable sticks. These boys were passionate about their village way of life and the surrounding forest and sea – an enthusiasm for tradition and the reality of growing or catching daily food in a bountiful place.

Roger's Bay does not appear on any tourist maps. With no road, access is by sea. We went in Bertil's boat, *The Ark of Safety*, and it was. Having boarded in shallow water off the beach, the wind in our hair was exhilarating as the boat skimmed and bounced across the waves. There were glimpses of Red-footed Boobies, and a short distance from the boat a turtle's head rose briefly out of the waves to breathe.

Beyond several wooded headlands, very compact and small, the deserted bay was everything Roger had promised. Surrounded by sloping cliffs covered in forest, the sheltered cove was nearly circular with only one quarter open to the sea. Rocks were strewn across it, the large boulders at one end of the beach heaped up into a tall barnacle-clustered ridge. Beyond this a secret deep pool of turquoise water was protected by a stack and an unexpected blowhole. The sand was white and silky smooth leading down to the rocky edge of water and reef. A solitary palm tree bowed over and draped as if placed for artistic effect.

BENEATH THE SURFACE

The reef beyond was an equally perfect microcosm. Submerging beneath the surface was not a feeling of flying down through tree tops of coral branches; this was creeping into a fern-spangled grotto. The 'ferns' were delicate lavender and pink sprays of sea fans, related to corals. Some were edged with yellow shading down to a dark purple base; others emerged bright pink out of bright greens, yellows and browns. Their close trellises faced into the prevailing current to better catch their tiny prey; drifting animals and plants of the plankton. Mauve sea feather corals seemed to mimic willows dipping and waving with a flowing stream. A miniature rock plateau was scarred by deep channels which dropped away to steep canyons and overhangs down to the bottom of the reef. Wherever one looked there were micro habitats offering different life opportunities. On the reef floor big boulder corals, green or purplish-grey, grew amongst gentle coral bushes and yellow Smooth Flower Coral – true to its name. Sea anemones draped over the rocks like rugs and their finger-like tentacles were mimicked by neighbouring soft 'sausage' corals. Beneath them there could be all manner of creeping creatures eating and being eaten. Here and there, small round humps of yellow brain corals emerged, crowned with meandering lines of turquoise and lime-green weed growing in between the tight 'brain' folds. Some of them hosted what appeared to be opening splayed fans made of the most delicate feathers fit for an eighteenth-century lady. These were magnificent Christmas Tree Worms, extending their delicate striped tentacles in perfect symmetry. They were sieving the sea for passing food from the safety of their protective hard tubes anchored firmly in the coral. This underwater landscape was a complexity compounded with more colours and shades than one could differentiate or remember. No matter how hard I focused my senses were supersaturated. I now totally understood Claude Monet's frustration when he had described attempts to capture colours changing by the minute in shifting light – moments of detail lost in moments of change.

Here and there tiny little 'fish in waiting' were propped – heads held up high and eyes scanning upwards, mouths at the ready. A nearby rock was a perfect hunting ground for a larger Spotted Scorpionfish. It was resting through the daylight hours. Its flattened splayed body shape, irregular jagged outline and spreading fins were lost amongst the random shapes of compact sponges and encrusting growth. Its colour furthered the illusion with patchy blotches in browns and grey; its skin covered in ridges and spines added to its anonymity. The venom potential of the sharp spines of its fins and an upward facing wide mouth at the ready gave it an aspect of menace.

Inevitably it was the most dazzling fish that competed for attention. There were Slender Filefish with their giraffe like patchwork of brown and white; Jewelfish with dazzling turquoise spots on a rich purple-blue background. Foureye Butterflyfish appeared from behind sea fans, fluttered then disappeared, the brightest and biggest two of their four eye spots being strategically near the tail fooling predators to aim away from their head; and a Spotted Moray Eel snarled at us.

The parrotfish were a source of total delight and fascination. They glided about singly or in groups – a dazzling array of patterns and colours, living examples of the bright colour extremes of psychedelic 1960s art juxtaposed with subtle drifts of translucent watercolour. As they moved they became creations of shifting spectrum facets. Their scales, like feathers, reflected light at angles changing the boundaries between colours. When their movement slowed one could focus, but as we looked turquoise-green bodies transformed imperceptibly to blue then to mauve then shocking pink and as we tried to memorise the detail of each they vanished like phantoms. Their beauty is as transient as life, fading unrecognisably to a dull ordinary grey on the fishmonger's slab, possibly due to changes in the way light reflects back off drying skin which has been subjected to touching and abrasion. Living, their skin is coated in a mucous substance, thought to possibly have antioxidant properties and to give protection against ultraviolet light.

Head and body patterns of parrotfish species are varied and complex – spots, patches, streaks and wavering stripes, seemingly at random, or else repetitive, regular and geometric. They looked, watching us with dark piercing eyes like parrots; faces dominated by pouting prominent lips framing their parrot-like beaks – the origin of their name. Parted lips showed protruding teeth on the outside of the jaw bones: fearsome in appearance but efficient as scraping and crushing bars. Their teeth are tightly packed into a mosaic, growing continuously to cope with their tough diet of encrusting growth on coral and the coral itself, prickly sponges and small hard-shelled animals. Watching their swimming style was sheer delight; their small front pectoral fins beat fast, fluttering in a blur like the whirring flight of their namesakes. At first sight the fins did not appear powerful – delicate tapered bones splayed in a perfect tight fan supporting translucent thin skin. Their efficient, economic design allows them to beat up and down fast, pushing the fish forwards while the tail gives quick bursts of speed.

Stoplight Parrotfish: a 'lesser' female and a top male. The dull female on the left, buff brown with red fins, can swap dress and sex and change into the dominant fish on the right with flamboyant patterns of blue, green, pink and gold. Parrotfish features are visible: bar-like mosaic teeth and small fast beating fore (pectoral) fins. In the foreground, an enlarged sea fan.

Stoplight Parrotfish, rather mundanely named for the yellow flash near their pectoral (front) fins on green and red, were everywhere as if posing in the spotlight. I commented to Roger on the amazing ability of parrotfish to change sex. He was adamant I was talking complete fantasy. Such fantasies of parrotfish ambiguity have been the subject of careful research. In the Stoplight Parrotfish, as in many other types, the dominant male in a harem of females is the largest, most aggressive fish, extravagantly coloured and intricately patterned. He is a dazzling dandy, the 'terminal' supermale. His swivelling blue lids frame big watchful eyes: dark pupils in a pale surround are accentuated with a long pink stripe. The prominent mouth is outlined with pink and extended back as if an unsteady hand had exaggerated lipstick. The scales seem green but shift in the light between turquoise and blue. Arrayed like stretched hexagons around the body, each scale is delineated by crisp pink edges drifting ambiguously to bronze. The fluttering pectoral fins are blue, as are their crescent tails trailing long wafting tips, and sharply accented with a bright yellow moon, hence one common name, Moontail.

This dazzling male has a harem of females, subdued in comparison, although beautifully coloured – a rim of yellow above the eyes, pale brown, greyish or pale bodied with dark bordered scales giving the hexagon wrapping effect. This restraint is offset by vivid red fins, tails and bellies giving rise to one of their common names, Red Belly. If the big aggressive male dies, the largest, most dominant female takes on a completely different persona, changing colour and character with her social circumstances. She changes sex and colour during two or three weeks and then takes his place as the solitary male. This individual is then the head of the harem of about seven lesser females with whom he breeds. As well as this supermale, who was previously female, there are other males who started life as males and continue to be so. They have the same brownish and red colours of the harem females and breed with them, but they spawn in groups, rather than singly. Initially these variations were identified as two separate species: the green fish and the red. The many Parrotfish species vary; in some the situation is even less straightforward. There can be lesser adult males in different dress and sometimes one of these, rather than a female, may mature into the power-dressed top fish. One species does not change sex at all.

Even in the brilliant clarity of sunlit turquoise water this was a reef of extreme contrasts with depth, dark secret caves, crevices and shadows. In a shady corner a band of turquoise and blue dots materialised into a central band of papillae down the back of a wandering sea slug. It could have been a surreal contrived adornment for the 'toadstool corals' beside it. A fire worm scuttled like a centipede across the head of a boulder coral, boldly advertising itself with pale cream and bright red.

As my eyes grew accustomed to shadowy details I began to notice I was being watched. There were animals deeper in shadow looking, lurking or slowly grazing. A convoluted curved arm betrayed the presence of an octopus tightly curled up in its lair of a dark rock crevice. Far from being ugly and repulsive, as seen by many, this contorted derivative of a basic snail design is a masterpiece. The small slit opening into its lair was such that one could imagine the animal had almost oozed itself through the gap – they are renowned escape artists in sea aquaria. At that moment the animal was dark reddish-brown, merging into its background. If it took fright it could turn almost white, change shape, sprawl and crawl; or, extend long and slim, streaming its tentacles behind it to streak past like a torpedo powered by a jet of water. Now only one eye moved to follow us. This dark highly attentive eye was peering out through a gap between its folded arms. It was nice to see and be seen by such a sophisticate; the eye structure is complex, working on the same principle as a camera or telescope focusing by moving the lens, rather than changing the shape of its bulge as in the eyes of humans and other back-boned animals.

Here and there in dark recesses, long tapered wands waved about, unwieldy, ambiguously, questioning the surroundings. These were the segmented antennae of lobsters, their shells in shades of blues and purples. Bertil dived, pivoted and twisted through the rock labyrinths, familiar with every turn... *'Twenty lobsters, but not big enough to eat any yet...'* He pointed at a giant black and white shell swirl – something like a periwinkle as big as a hand, delicious apparently, but also too juvenile. Roger and Bertil both swam as if born to it. Bertil had had his first swimming lesson at the age of three: his father had put him overboard and told him to swim for the shore. The method was a visible success, if tough. It was in a different class of risk but shared a smattering of similarity to my blunt introduction to snorkelling at Buck Island. I had improved slightly in the meantime but, in total contrast to my underwater efforts, Bertil dived down further, leisurely and effortlessly, 20 feet, without fins, to the lowest rock shelves. He pointed out four foot of deceptively smooth-looking skin, in reality rough as sand paper, lying still on the sandy bottom under a wide overhang. The familiar cold grey eye triggered memory – it was a young shark sleeping. Slim barracudas were not asleep, and lurked in the background, maybe with lunch in mind.

Roger had successfully trailed a fishing line over the side of the boat and our lunch lay in a bucket. Before our eyes he had transformed into a different being. From a laid-back, somewhat lackadaisical dreamer he became a totally focused hunter. Even his face seemed to change shape as his features tensed and became almost pointed. The boys had selected a perfect pale curve of deserted sand, a turtle nesting beach, backed by aged trees with spreading low branches and even more spreading gnarled roots, lumpy enough to use as armchairs. Behind, in thickets, tall stems in shades of green were splashed with garish scarlet and yellow notches – sprays of heliconia flowers, so bright, so shiny and wax-like that they seemed to be plastic imitations. Pendulous sac-like nests hung from twigs – these were the intricate beak woven workmanship of Crested Oropendulas. Against a perpetual hum of cicadas there was a constant small bird twitter and gossiping croon of doves. A little creek wound through an arch of tall, thick bamboo stems on which a dark shape sat – with tell-tale tail streamers projecting down, perfect and spatula-tipped like two oars. It was a Blue-crowned Mot-mot, stolid and seemingly immovable, perched low on its short legs as its red eyes scanned for food below. It turned to the light and was instantly transformed into artifice – with bright blue crown, face and turquoise wing flashes painted with colours from the sea behind. Below it the creek was protected from the sea by a high sand ridge and as still and clear as a pond. Beneath the surface fish drifted slowly and two crabs were heavily engaged in dispute. Both held blue and white pincers aloft, disproportionately large. With fast moving rear flipper legs, the crabs were decidedly manoeuvrable and agile: they performed a stereotypic square dance round each other face to face, menacing and gesticulating with their claws, but now and then actually getting to grips with each other.

Roger hacked wood with his machete and made a fire on the foreshore, cleaved fish into pieces for the immense cooking pot and improvised a lid with large leaves. Bertil made dumplings, mixing flour and water, squeezing out sausage shapes and then mercilessly twisting and wringing them into submissive recalcitrants of compacted solid dough, which remained so throughout the cooking process; but he will make an inspired wildlife guide. Roger cut a length of bamboo and using his multipurpose machete, split it, and fashioned spoons to eat lunch. He and Bertil ate prodigious quantities, a whole casserole pot each: possibly they had not eaten for a while. The fish was fresh and delicious. A young woman came by and briefly joined us, and in a very proper traditional manner throughout she was respectfully addressed by the boys as 'Miss Judy'. As well as polite they were diplomatic. We had been wearing eccentric garb for snorkelling in order to avoid magnified sunburn reflected back from a virtual mirror of white sand underwater. Long sleeved T-shirts were part of the answer but we had pondered on some available leg covering suited to hours of lying on the surface face down. One of my school pupils had come up with the answer – navy blue woolly tights – uniform straight out of school, a little holey here and there, but a layer between our pale skins and the intense Caribbean sun. I explained the protective purpose of our outer layers to Roger and Bertil. They looked at each other wide-eyed… *'Oh, we thought you were feeling the cold as you came from England!'*

Fish and fresh utensils: leaf lid and bamboo spoons.

AN ALIEN ENCOUNTER, PARLATOUVIER BAY

We returned the following year. Further along the coast at Parlatouvier was another turtle nesting beach, a near circular arc of uninterrupted sand, sheltered by high hills. Rainforest fronds draped down the slopes like giant ladders; lianas and roots of epiphyte plants dangled from trees; single leaves were the size of our twelve-year-old son Andrew and Silk Cotton seeds fluttered in the air. These lush hills curved down to a bony finger of an encircling promontory which petered out to jagged rocks jutting out of the sea. Looking down on the protected water a dozen small boats were anchored like toys and the tell-tale areas of dark purple interspersed with shades of turquoise promising a coral landscape beneath – a sight to thrill any snorkeller's heart.

Village houses were neat, some roadside walls and balconies bordered with old cans carefully painted red as pots for spider lilies and gourd vines. The village shop stocked essential fare: canned orange drink, old-fashioned cotton shred dish mops, rum and flour. A lonely parrot sat in a cage and two squirrels were crammed tight into another.

Around the shallow quiet lagoon behind the beach, trees shading benches created almost a city park. One tree was as pink as a Matisse fantasy, full of fluffy flower – dotted with a protruding haze of long stamens and vibrating with humming birds feasting on nectar and insects. As is their way, their darting flight and acrobatics were so fast that their individual detail was lost in a whirr of flashing green and bronze iridescence punctuated with an occasional flash of dazzling blue. One individual was darting to feed on small insects at the end of a bare twig; another was accelerating down in figures of eight, looping the loop like a stunt plane, upside down, backwards, but better than any plane. Tanagers, dusky pastel blue shades almost to lavender, were sharing a mango tree with noisy gesticulating green parrots. Occasional outsize lizards crossed the grass and massive glossy black bumble bees flew between trees. The marshy edges of the lagoon held rich pickings for water birds. The Green-backed Heron was near invisible when its head was held down and its long black crest laid back sleek. By contrast, the Purple Heron was clothed flamboyantly in rich blue-purple with magenta-pink tinged neck and pale blue on its beak. A chic Tobago Ringed Kingfisher streaked past with a fish in its beak, leading our gaze to its nest secreted under the bridge.

An old man walked by and struck up conversation in the friendly way of so many Caribbean people. On country roads, cars often stopped level to converse through the window – to ask our origin in case they had a friend or relative nearby or had heard of our town. Our new acquaintance, Boris, was eager. We were English, he knew lots of English history... about Nelson. As he warmed to his subject it developed into an address, delivered in splendid rhetoric with a musical lilt, and in a delightfully archaic language not heard in Britain for more than two centuries. He waxed eloquently on how the British presence on the island had opened the eyes of the people to the potential of education. Not having been to high school himself, he was a civil servant. He looked the part – carefully dressed, with a pukkah grey beret and the perfectly furled black umbrella so typical of old London and city streets of India. He continued his walk to the shop and thence half a mile back up the steep hill home, but could not resist stopping again to continue – the story of ' Lewis' XII of France, Christianity, the Bahai faith and his belief, and finally, improving the world. It had been a charming but lengthy interlude, and we learnt that the government had financed the park and the village council had made the decisions.

By then the beach was deserted but for a fisherman returning home with bunches of red snapper and bonito draped from his shoulders. The sand was fine, peppered with shell pieces and threads and fragments of dark 'netting' – not fishing net – pieces of broken sea fans. These colonies of small animals, similar to corals but flattened, branching, and standing erect, grab food from passing currents with tiny extended tentacles. Out in the bay there were great stands of them like fantasy stage sets of lace screens. Aptly named Venus Fans, they lent a sense of mystery, obscuring and revealing occasional glimpses of life behind them. They surrounded us on all sides, far taller and more numerous than at Roger's Bay, and intermingled with the Elkhorn Coral and golden textured sponges.

The sponges were in curving elegant vase shapes, round bowls deep or shallow, all supported by embedded stiffening of protein mesh or tiny struts of chalk or glass-like silica – spicules. The shapes of these are various and beautiful: crosses, jagged spikes, smooth spears, three-dimensional stars, anchors, hooks. Some appear like snow crystals of the sea and their creations can be as fantastical: glassy constructions with evocative names such as Venus' Flower Basket. Spicule shapes are used in identification of the thousands of different sponge species perfected during 500 million years of existence.

The graceful forms and intricate textures of these sponges gave them the look of an artist's design, apparently inert and almost plant-like, belying their primitive animal simplicity and very significant place in the scheme of things surrounding us. They act as efficient filters of the reef, extracting and recycling minute matter, living and dead. This vital lifestyle is achieved by a conglomeration of single cells held together in a colony without nerves, senses, muscles or other systems – a strange animal. Strange is too weak a word. Uniquely, individual sponge cells can change their role, and amazingly they are capable of rebuilding their team after being passed through a sieve. Even different species reduced to their single cell components by mutilating, mixing and sieving can recognise their own kind and reorganise back into species aggregations and form new individual sponges. These surprising humble colonies hide even more significant mysteries; their immune defence is achieved by a wide variety of chemicals: antibacterial, antiviral, anti-inflammatory and antitumor.

This gathering of sea fans, corals and sponges was unlike anywhere we have seen before or since. Looking down into this reef it was neither a bird's view of a forest, nor descending into a giant rockery; it was more like floating down into a pastel herbaceous flower border, delicate and drifting with colour. Many residents of the reef were familiar from other Caribbean waters. Blue Tangs with plate-like slim bodies, yellow juveniles and adults of pure sky-blue swam by, mouths small, refined and delicately nibbling plant life. These fish defend themselves with sharp spines – a prominent pair of sharp blades sticking out horizontally at the base of the tail appropriate to their family name – surgeonfishes. Banded Butterflyfish with wide black vertical body stripes and eye masks prodded pert snouts amongst corals seeking out exposed small shrimps and worms. In stark contrast to such flattened thin body shapes, there were Smooth Trunkfish resembling children's clockwork bath toys. Their squat stiff bodies, wide-based to the extreme of being triangular, moved as if magically propelled from elsewhere. The invisible force came from two fast beating fans – transparent pectoral (fore) fins, steered by a brush of a tail on a narrow 'handle'. These belong to the appropriately named boxfish family – the 'box' being their hard covering of plate-like hexagonal scales. An alluring fish with character, their scales, large dark eyes and pouting lips give them an uncanny resemblance to a cute giraffe-patterned concoction from a cartoonist's imagination. The illusion is intensified by their hunting behaviour of blowing a water jet from their mouths in order to shift sand hiding small snails and worms. They also direct their attentions to sponges.

The sudden arrival of Gold-spotted Snake Eels took us by surprise as they contorted and gyrated through the water. At a quick first glimpse we mistook them for venomous sea snakes, animals to be approached with caution, particularly snorkelling with a child novice. At a metre long they are creatures of presence – pale with regularly spaced sequences of golden spots, each encircled with dark brown. The easily visible and reassuring fishy eel characteristic was the delicate ribbon of the dorsal fin running all the way down their backs, and being a fish as opposed to a reptile they have the familiar gills and gill cover. They are as impressive as any snake, with the strength to take on hard-shelled crabs as well as Mantis Shrimps which have spectacular reaction speed combined with a hard punching club claw or a sharp spear.

There were also some more staid old friends from our visit the previous year: the Christmas Tree Worms on the first rock out from the shore. Their crowns of spiralled 'branches' were splayed open, but it was a tangential sighting at speed and lost; they instantly withdrew and were stowed safe and secret in their tubes, closed off with their 'lid'.

Further out in the bay we had a most memorable encounter, now a part of treasured family memorabilia – our first meeting with 'The Aliens' who abruptly materialised from the invisible with no preliminary sighting or visible approach. We suddenly found ourselves face to face with a straight line of sixteen pairs of eyes just below the surface. Regularly spaced, side by side, as orderly as for a military inspection, there were sixteen little Caribbean Reef Squid, their large dark eyes looking directly into ours. They hovered, like a line of helicopters in perfect formation, smaller individuals at the outer edges. Motionless and wide-eyed they looked at us. Floating and equally wide-eyed we looked back. We all just looked, eyeball to eyeball, hanging in blue oblivion. After what seemed a long time, the line moved forwards as one towards us, still peering. Then, equally synchronised, they all moved backwards, viewing us from a little further away. They did this several times, as if the move had been choreographed and rehearsed. The glide was smooth, achieved by rapidly rippling the fin edging their bodies. How long we all spent marvelling at each other it was impossible to say – it was an experience outside of any normal timescale. There was ample opportunity to scrutinise their detail.

Their skin was a colour drift through purple and brown, with a pale stripe down the back and shining turquoise spots. Their colours and patterns change at will, and even their texture, in order to blend in with their immediate surroundings and to avoid a predator's gaze. Against cream and pale brown vertical growing coral they adopt a brown stripe on pale background; surrounded by a dark brown coral they assume the matching dark colouration with amazing accuracy. Their body is covered with complex tiny organs which include muscle and nerve cells which control the shape of an elastic sac of pigment granules. By distorting the elastic sac, the translucency and reflective qualities of the granules within can be manipulated to make dots or blotches separate or merge, thus changing the colour. The shimmering skin effect is controlled by altering grooves and folds of specialised cells which changes how light is reflected. Forty different patterns have been recorded – such as the belly striped or speckled, body bars, streaks, zebra striped, yellow flecked, and in slight alarm, shining golden eyebrows and white central arms. No doubt their sudden manifestation from the invisible to visible to us was the result of assuming reflective pale sea shades on approach, then turning on the bright colours on arrival. Immediate colour change is not only a defensive matter of not being seen. Taking the talent a step further, they are capable of mimicry – these squid have been recorded imitating parrotfish by holding tentacles close, swimming backwards. They assume disguises for hunting their prey of very small fish, other molluscs and shrimp.

They gather in socialising shoals for many of life's activities: to forage, rest, court and defend themselves, and as we had seen, for close inspection of incomers. Such communal activity demands very obvious communication between individuals and within the social group. They are not only capable of switching shades at will, but can flash brilliant colours in sequence and repeatedly. An individual can communicate one message to its right hand neighbour and send a different message to the animal on its left. Thus equipped these social creatures can alert each other to prey, attract a mate, threaten competitors and no doubt much else besides, but research so far has not recorded them hunting cooperatively as a pack. With such ambidextrous and detailed communication potential it is no surprise that there is some suggestion that Caribbean Reef Squid may have their own 'language' of visual signs, complete with vocabulary and syntax.

A high level of communication needs finely tuned senses. We had noted that their forward-facing tentacles were neatly folded away so that their faces seemed all eyes: bright, alert and encircled with such shining turquoise it was as if they had iridescent spectacles on a somewhat 'roman nose'. Their very seeing eye – bright, moving and checking everything – is a characteristic of all squid and octopus – the cephalopods. This group is very much more sophisticated than their distant cousins, the slugs and snails of sea and land, and clams. Superficially the squid eye, like that of the octopus, resembles ours, but it has a hard lens, which focuses like a camera. Their eye to body ratio is the largest in the animal kingdom: small wonder we felt a strong sense of being scrutinised and a form of communication through eye contact.

Many animals glance at swimmers as they pass, but squid and dolphins, and some fish such as Batfish, seem curious about humans entering their world and regularly seek out snorkellers and divers. There is something very special about animal encounters when it is on the initiative of the animal rather than the human. At different locations in Tobago we had two more squid encounters, one with even more individuals, and both following the same synchronised sequence.

To my delight, we had a haunting glimpse of a squid relative – a cream, brown and yellowish cuttlefish, striped zebra-style. Its tentacles were stowed and held tightly together out in front as it moved, looking like a strange smile with a purse-lipped look. The smooth glide of its body seemed disconnected from the source of its movement, which was a mesmerising ripple undulating along its encircling fin. It changed its striped skin pattern as it moved, so that it quickly disappeared amidst the vagaries of fine camouflage. This keen-eyed stealth hunter sneaks up on its prey before shooting a water jet to shift covering sand and grabbing it with two long feeding tentacles – another extraordinary brainy cephalopod.

Back in the human world in the heat of the late afternoon we sought refreshing drinks at a local shop. Behind the counter was the mother of Renwick, another of Roger's friends. She was an alarming and powerfully dour lady for such short stature. It was all in the eyes. I smiled in an attempt to break down barriers. Her eyes were very purposefully averted and instead of my eyes meeting hers, I faced a large notice written roughly on crumpled paper pinned to the wall behind her: 'The DEVIL comes with a friendly face'. Near the till was a thought which seemed to be in conflict with its location: 'We trust in God: others pay cash'. All smiles, Renwick was outside by his beloved car which he ran as a local taxi when not under it in his garage pit wielding spanners. There was a prominent placard with a bouncy 4-line Rap message urging people to look after his tools, admire, not walk off with them, and the fee for using his pit. Cages of rabbits were arrayed around the pit edge: he took time off from taxiing to fatten them for sale for feasts such as the Easter Monday dance at Buccoo in a few days' time. The feast was obviously a great success; we snorkelled with them two days later (Roger having been 'under the weather for a day') and I had never seen such heavy sleepers, faces down in the sand, in total relaxed abandon after swimming.

Four Reef Squid display distinct gleaming white patches above their enormous eyes. Swimming and manoeuvring with undulating fins and with their tentacles held tightly together, the three on the right scrutinise swimmers. The animal on the left is focused on a smaller squid below (out of sight) and has changed its skin colour from iridescent turquoise and mauve longitudinal stripes to wide dark-green bands running round body, head and wide-splayed tentacles.

THE HATCHLING'S REALM

FISHING AND THE HATCHLING'S DEBUT

It was the peak nesting season: female turtles arrived night after night. We felt unable to resist the timeless spectacle of these giants from a Jurassic world going about their nesting ritual. Our stay was in danger of deteriorating into an exhausting test of stamina. It was at this moment that the season's hatchlings made a sudden dramatic entrance – on two stages set for two human activities.

The beach was covered with traditional seine nets in readiness for the following day's fishing for Easter celebrations. On the attempt a week previously, twenty-six people had worked on and off through the whole day, rowing several boats out to place the long net in a great arc across the bay. Both ends had then been hauled in by those on the beach. The procedure was long and arduous. It had been a disappointing catch, with much disagreement followed by a sudden wild 'free for all' delivering only a handful of small fish for those with the toughest push and grab. Optimistic stray dogs got nothing. There were high hopes for a better catch for Easter. The sea had turned dark purple with a dense moving mass of juvenile fish. Brown Pelicans and Laughing Gulls were diving, scooping and emerging with fish still on their heads and backs. There were 'tiddler' fish as far as the eye could see. It was nightfall and the enormous nets had been carefully placed in position once more.

A few metres from the beach an evening of outdoor entertainment was in full swing behind a low retaining wall. Local girls clad in Creole costume danced their exit with easy rhythm; their facial features, eyes and hair a living testament to this island's trading and slaving history – Portuguese, French, English, Chinese, African, like a textbook illustration of ethnicity. A fire-eating limbo dancer took his place. The audience, lethargic with heat and heavy aroma of Planter's Punch, stirred and refocused their attention on whirling flames. As the dancer leant further and further back, passing his body under the descending bar while swinging the improvised blazing rags, the audience gasped.

Then a child's voice rang out from the dark beach behind and a silhouetted head and shoulders appeared over the low wall. Momentarily some heads turned. *'Look what I've found!'* A childish hand brandished a baby turtle frantically waving diminutive flippers.

The entire audience rose up, vaulted down over the wall onto the net-covered beach; the life threatening efforts of the limbo dancer were forgotten. In the dark without torches there seemed to be baby turtles everywhere. There were white crabs all over the beach, running with lightning speed eager for a turtle meal. The hatchlings were surprisingly strong and agile. Digging their way out of the sand, they were scrabbling over each other with clockwork energy, toppling into deep footprints, dispersing and disappearing. They were rushing in all directions into a chaos of shadows, hurrying human feet and layers of mesh which trapped and entangled them.

Roger was not yet on night guard duty; any coordinated attempt at rescue was out of the question. Amidst shrieks of delight and shouts of warning, people were trying to free them, picking them out and rushing to get each squirming creature into the sea as quickly as possible. Such acts of mercy were misguided. In a wild natural situation their guiding light to the sea would have been moonlight and its glittering reflecting path across the water. During this transit the hatchlings somehow sense and learn the identity of the beach and water for the future. It is also thought that during this first approach to the sea they may set an internal magnetic compass used in navigating away and out to sea. Their emergence from nests on populated shores is very different amidst the ambiguity of modern lighting. Here in the bay natural darkness was replaced by bright hotel lights behind and flickering village lights to the side which competed with the moonlit 'path of glory' forward and across the waves. Modern life and tourism, even ecotourism, have interfered with the natural course of events.

To combat this disorienting light pollution Roger's procedure was to gather them into a group and shine a powerful torch about 9 m (30 ft) ahead of the group mimicking moonlight, moving it ahead of them at their own pace, in the manner of an old time cinema usherette. One needed to continue the guiding beam on out onto the waves until they were safely away from shore illumination and following the moon's inviting path towards the distant horizon. Someone needed to lead them into safe water and in the absence of anyone familiar with 'emergency turtle evacuation' there was no alternative but for me to try to lead the way.

With a weak torch I was paddling tentatively at the water's edge, walking backwards to better illuminate a path. A large wave broke, took us by surprise and I and my very flared evening trousers were partly submerged. There was nothing for it but to shed swirling fabric and continue the operation half dressed. At least it was dark. We saw at least fourteen animals take to the waves into the dark. From there they swam continuously and rode the undertow to deeper water. These had so far avoided their ancient land-based opponents, the crabs, and preying birds, and their more recent predator introduced by man – the dogs. We moved the nets back into position as best we could and by early next morning the nets were already being set out in the bay for a big catch.

A few hours later the nets were slowly hauled in. We hoped the young turtles had made it out beyond the great loop of floats. The mesh out in the bay would have been dangerous enough for them, but above it Brown Pelicans swam and scooped, Frigate Birds hung in mid-air, dropped and scooped, and Laughing Gulls and Roseate Terns circled and dived to grab at trapped fish. As the catch was dragged into shallow water the cries and splashes of the hunting sea birds became a tumult; people shouted, dogs barked. Vigorously writhing tails and fins vibrated the whole net as flapping turned into thrashing. Shimmering scales scattered on to the sand below along with tiny sunfish like silver dollars. Together they created a wake of scales which drifted into deeper water like shining diamonds in the sea.

There were many more fish than previously. There were the staple hand-size food fish, small and silver, and also more spectacular species. Intense dark blue and verdigris green backs vied with pink and greenish lines and blue stripes. There were two Lesser Sting Rays – one very young with skin like a tanned leopard, a Red-fin Needlefish tinted delicate green with dorsal fin and tail tipped subtly with red, a bonito with vicious looking protruding spurs and a pink spotted squid. The local girls screamed with mock and genuine terror as the boys adeptly seized Flying Gurnards with their flashing sharp spines and threw them into the water, targeting legs. These fish sped across the shallows, just clear of the sand, their large pectoral fins fanned open like butterfly wings daubed with greenish and bright blue. Two wicker baskets were filled with the catch, but how many of these fish had fed on hatchlings?

Terns, gulls and pelicans scoop for the catch.

THE 'LOST YEARS'

Now, far out and beyond the net there were the threats of a pelagic existence. On the scale of the world's oceans our fourteen hatchlings were dots lost in a watery universe. As snack-sized morsels they were running the gauntlet of tuna, jacks, sharks, and more – all roaming these sparsely populated 'desert' zones of the oceans in search of a meal. Only a quarter of them survive their first few days in the ocean. One hatchling just might be the incredibly lucky one in thousands to survive and return as a mature animal 15–25 years hence. Meanwhile they had disappeared into a hazardous domain; for turtle researchers these have been the 'lost years'.

Sporadic fragments of turtle's lives during these years have come from casual mentions from fishermen, yacht logs, and divers. Latterly, focused research with tagging and tracking devices on juvenile turtles have uncovered some jigsaw details which trace a startlingly unlikely story, and in the way of research enquiry pose more questions than answers. Juvenile leatherbacks are very rarely sighted close to the shore. It seems that as babies they are not totally passive drifters, they actively swim and navigate using magnetic fields. They move far away to ocean zones where several currents converge, in particular the deep blue Sargasso Sea. This is an area of 1,100 km wide by 3,200 km long, between the West Indies and the Azores, mid-Atlantic, south of the Gulf Stream and north of the Tropic of Cancer. The converging currents sweep seaweed and flotsam into thick rafts, along with any small floating animals. The Sargasso Sea surface is covered by a floating living mass of seaweed (Sargassum) like an isolated floating jungle – a wondrous world of vegetation with bacterial and primitive life rich in diversity and food potential and crystal clear water. It is a mid-ocean nursery which nurtures all manner of sea life in their early, often unrecognisable, stages of existence. As a bonus this brown vegetation absorbs sunlight and heats the sea in its vicinity.

The drifting maze of interwoven live and dead seaweed, storm strewn trees and driftwood debris provides a network of cavities. Here itinerant small creatures have some protection from rough conditions and can hide from the wandering predatory fish of the open ocean. Permanent residents are few and strange: they disappear invisibly into their background by virtue of bizarre body flaps and appendages which perfectly mimic the weed.

Others are here temporarily. Seven species of hatchling sea turtles find sanctuary here amongst the weed. More famously, it is also the mysterious destination of the 5,000 km breeding migration of the European Eel which initially heads south to pick up a conveyer belt ocean current which gyrates towards the Sargasso Sea. Amongst the weed the young turtles slowly build up their size and strength, feeding on the habitat's diversity and anything else available which is sharing the protection of the Sargassum.

The various turtle species only diverge into their more specialised carnivorous and vegetarian diets when they leave this drifting opportunistic existence and return to their particular chosen habitat. The Giant Leatherbacks (and Loggerhead Turtles) are favoured during their Sargasso sojourn as the ocean currents sweeping into their seaweed home also bring in drifting jellyfish and the bright blue Portuguese Man o' War which are their foods of choice later. They are nurtured in a sea of food, or so it was for millennia, up until about the time I was introduced to turtles in a Queensland bathtub.

SEA OF CHANGE

As far as the turtles are concerned nothing seems to have changed: they continue to do what they have always done. Looking upwards against the blue ceiling of a light and shadowy rippling surface, ephemeral shapes, almost transparent, almost shadows, gracefully drift into focus. They see sunlight glittering on the pale pulsating circles as enticing tentacles trail like flowing ribbons in the swell. They grab the jellyfish with toothless scissor-like jaws, and have a good lunch. The modern version of the tale reads the same... until the jaws close on the catch. It is a very modern, virtual jellyfish: it is a plastic bag. And it is all to do with a good lunch. Picnic lunches used to be 'gift-wrapped' in carefully folded greaseproof paper secured with rubber band or string – days when everyday plastic experience was a few kitchen containers and implements. As the Swinging Sixties came and went, the synthesis of plastics also moved on: life al fresco and otherwise became wrapped, transported, plated and disposed of in plastic. Metal, fabric and wood could be replaced by bright alternatives as this exciting, and innovative, infinitely adaptable and convenient, hygienic product became the linchpin of modern life – cheap and disposable. Recycling advanced slower than plastic usage. Inconvenient disposables were, and in many places still are, simply dumped out of sight, the ultimate destination being the biggest ubiquitous dustbin of all – the turtle's domain and ultimately the source of much of our own food.

From a sea animal's viewpoint, the plastic is transformed to the promising and beautiful. Put a plastic food bag, or shiny party balloon, in a glass bowl of water, rock the bowl and watch it transform into facets of glinting moving light, billowing something like a jellyfish. A generation of children endorsed the turtle's judgement when I created the illusion while teaching during the 1990s. At that time, 44% of Giant Leatherback Turtle intestines contained trapped plastics. To prevent their jellyfish prey escaping their upper gut is lined with flexible, backward pointing spines, which unfortunately hold back the plastic and they ultimately starve or suffocate.

More recently it has been discovered that Sperm Whales, sharing the deep with the turtles, are similarly deceived. Hunting their squid prey by echolocation they, too, misinterpret the identity of sinking plastic bags. Large ones are masquerading as squid: both have roughly the same sound signature picked up by whale echolocation. Domestic and mundane plastic items have also caused death by blockage – rope, hosepipe, a flower pot, spray canister, bottle caps. As with the turtles, ingested plastic slowly deteriorates the whale's feeding and digestion and the animal may eventually starve. The potential effect of this extends far beyond the lives of individual whales. Importantly for the ocean ecosystem, the whales are feeding near the deep sea floor and surface every forty minutes to breathe while at the same time emptying their bowels. This activity brings recycled nutriment up from the ocean floor to the surface. Without their feeding and breathing activities this nourishing soup would remain out of reach in the depths without benefit to surface dwellers. Each whale with plastic blockage thus translates into nutriment lost to the surface ecosystem and its fish – which includes our fisheries.

A sampling study of floating objects of the Pacific was unknowingly carried out by albatrosses nesting on a large breeding beach in Hawaii. Old toothbrushes, printer ink jets, biros, and bits of toys were found in the digestive tracts of their dead offspring. Lined up in categories, these plastics completely covered the beach. They had inadvertently been scooped from the sea surface and fed to the chicks together with the volumes of tiny fish which their diligent parents had collected across great ocean distances.

During forty years of casual beachcombing by foot and bicycle along a remote 3 mile Scottish beach we have noticed obvious changes, both gradual and abrupt. It is a wide very shallow shelving stretch of golden sand on the north coast, facing the Atlantic. In 1969 the high strandline was strewn with driftwood, dried seaweed, seabird remains, occasional creels, wood planks and many wooden fish boxes, ideal for improvised holiday furniture. Gradually the back of the beach towards the dunes became a less enticing place. By the 1990s the norm had become grey and green plastic milk crates, bright blue plastic fish boxes, plastic drinks bottles entangled in the seaweed, very occasional driftwood and much plastic rope and fishing nets in vivid orange, green and blue. In 2013, returning after two years' absence, a strandline of dark brown seaweed was brightly dusted with what seemed to be wedding confetti. A closer look revealed these were myriads of tiny plastic fragments caught amongst the twisted stems and fronds. It extended on and on along the beach – an unexpected first sight of degraded, unrecognisable plastic pieces in large amounts.

Modern developments of biodegradable plastics reduce today's waste load, but the remnants of all our 'plastic years' still remain. Older and now very much smaller, these pieces are suspended in upper levels of sea water. The Sargasso Sea has gathered this new detritus into its protecting raft of drifting Sargassum, presumably ensnared as in the dried seaweed in Scotland. The plastic pieces have accumulated to the extent that an area measuring hundreds of kilometres across was officially named in 1972 – the Huge North Atlantic Garbage Patch. It is not apparent in aerial or satellite photographs, but can be caught in fine mesh nets – over 200,000 tiny pieces of debris per square kilometre. There is a larger Pacific equivalent: the Great Pacific Garbage Patch or Pacific Trash Vortex. These oceanic Patches are the 'heritage plastics' spanning just one human lifetime.

Long-term floating plastics unfortunately carry persistent extras: tiny particles act as nuclei, attracting and absorbing mercury, cadmium and chromium. There are old pollutants which continue to linger long even though usage has been outlawed to past history, such as the insecticide DDT and PCBs (from electrical equipment). Many new chemical compounds have now entered the arena, such as fire retardants. It has been estimated that this toxic plastic marine debris affects more than 250 species worldwide, many remote and not actually living within it. Amounts taken in initially may be small, but they accumulate and travel far through food chains. Small amounts are ingested by tiny creatures, which are consumed in great numbers by larger ones, and these in turn are eaten by fish, then ever larger fish, birds, seals, dolphins and sharks. At every step of the food ladder chemicals become further concentrated en route to sashimi, a tuna sandwich and fish supper destinations.

New plastic particles have been purposefully created minute and multipurpose. Industrial uses of these micro particles are extensive. At the everyday, every person level, 'microbeads' in facial scrubs, soaps and toothpastes, are washed down our domestic drains to waterways and the sea accompanied by accidental tiny fibres and dust from synthetic nylon and acrylic clothing. Their danger is in their micro scale – capable of ingestion by the very small in different sea habitats. They have already appeared in a range of creatures, familiar fisherman's bait – lugworms and shore crabs, animals of the ocean floor and tiny drifters of the plankton. Modern innovations can inadvertently create new problems. International organisations and some nations are investigating various aspects of the Atlantic and Pacific Trash Vortices and possible methods of reducing the accumulated plastic.

No effort can ever stop freak waves, storms or catastrophic typhoons and tsunamis delivering segments of modern existence into the sea, but the planet also sustains an enormous number of people each of whom contributes significantly. It is the everyday that counts and as with most worthwhile achievements, real success begins close to home – individuals reducing waste and being aware of the significance of disposal.

A HATCHLING'S RETURN TO TOBAGO

One of our saved hatchlings may have matured through these 'lost years' in the Sargasso Sea, survived toxic plastic pieces and gillnet fishing. What will this young turtle have found on its return?

It will have encountered fewer of its own kind during its journey. Those turtles that have returned to Tobago since our sightings are smaller than previously, but it is a return to a friendlier place. In the island's distant history Amerindian native tribes would have hunted for turtle meat, eggs and shell products, as would the various British, Dutch and Latvian settlers who followed Columbus' European discovery of the island in 1498. After them, the various European warring factions, their slaves, labourers, hopeful immigrants from Africa, India, and the Middle East, all tried to live off the bounty of the sea and one small island. Turtle meat and turtle eggs were nourishing and large and habitually eaten.

The second half of the twentieth century brought change, and latterly tourists like us. In the early 1990s turtle eggs and meat were still on local menus and there were still many stalls and shops in main tourist centres selling bits of various turtle species for the souvenir trade and quality markets: entire carapaces polished, gleaming and costly, for wall decoration or coffee tables. Hunting turtles is now banned between March 1st and September 30th. Over-exploitation is seen as their biggest local threat combined with inadequate legislation and resources to cope with poaching. Enforcement of Fisheries Legislation reflects such biological difficulties as the ambiguity of trying to differentiate between males and females when immature. As in most holiday destinations tourism brings deterioration of coral reefs, increased beachfront lighting, coastal development, beach erosion, sand mining and accidental boat strikes.

But here at a local level there is wildlife action in the 'here and now'.

Amongst the exuberant rappers at the beach there is now a group of volunteers who in 2000 formed an organisation, Save Our Sea Turtles (SOS) Tobago. Thanks to their continuing efforts, turtles returning to the beach are protected from being harassed or killed by humans. The spectacle of a female turtle carrying out her amazing primeval nesting ritual has become more than a privilege, it is now a valuable tourist potential and an economic asset to the people of the island. However, the hazard of significant light pollution remains and has been studied (2012) at Turtle Beach; disoriented hatchlings head inland rather than towards the sea. As the sun rises and the ground absorbs heat like a sponge they die of dehydration; in the bright daylight they fall prey to birds and dogs. So far the most successful solution has been rescue and redirecting the hatchlings to the sea by the SOS volunteers – ordinary people making future change.

I wonder if Roger and Bertil are amongst them. The breeding turtles of Tobago are mirror indicators of the sea's health and part of a much bigger picture which is still in the making.

Great flippers in swimming mode: a Giant Leatherback Turtle powers downwards hunting Moon Jellyfish.

Chapter 4

FISH FRIENDS AND FOES – A SWIM AROUND AN ISLAND

The Maldives – Baros

PATTERNS OF ISLANDS

From a satellite point of view there is an infinite dark blue stretching in every direction, but for strands of miniature dots strewn like a string of beads in trailing circles and elliptical patterns. The shapes are the ghosts of landscapes from a very different past – imprints of ancient sunken volcanoes visibly etched by the old coral reefs that had built up round the exposed rims of their craters. The beads are 1,000 tiny islands – the Maldives – coral and coral sand, only metres in diameter, linked and encircled by reefs and lagoons. It is an image spanning a vast distance in space and time.

From a human point of view looking down from an aircraft, there is the unnerving realisation of a planet of sea, not of Earth. Here is an uninviting blue emptiness relieved only by a very few isolated patches of pale turquoise and brown. Some have dots of green vegetation and white sand, fragile specks far too small to be reassuring, encircling inner deep blue lagoons of dark indigo blue like an alien unseeing eye – deep, unknown, large and with a hint of menace.

From a turtle's perception using senses which humans can barely imagine and only partly measure (such as magnetism) these bigger pictures from satellite and aerial maps combine. Here is a paradise

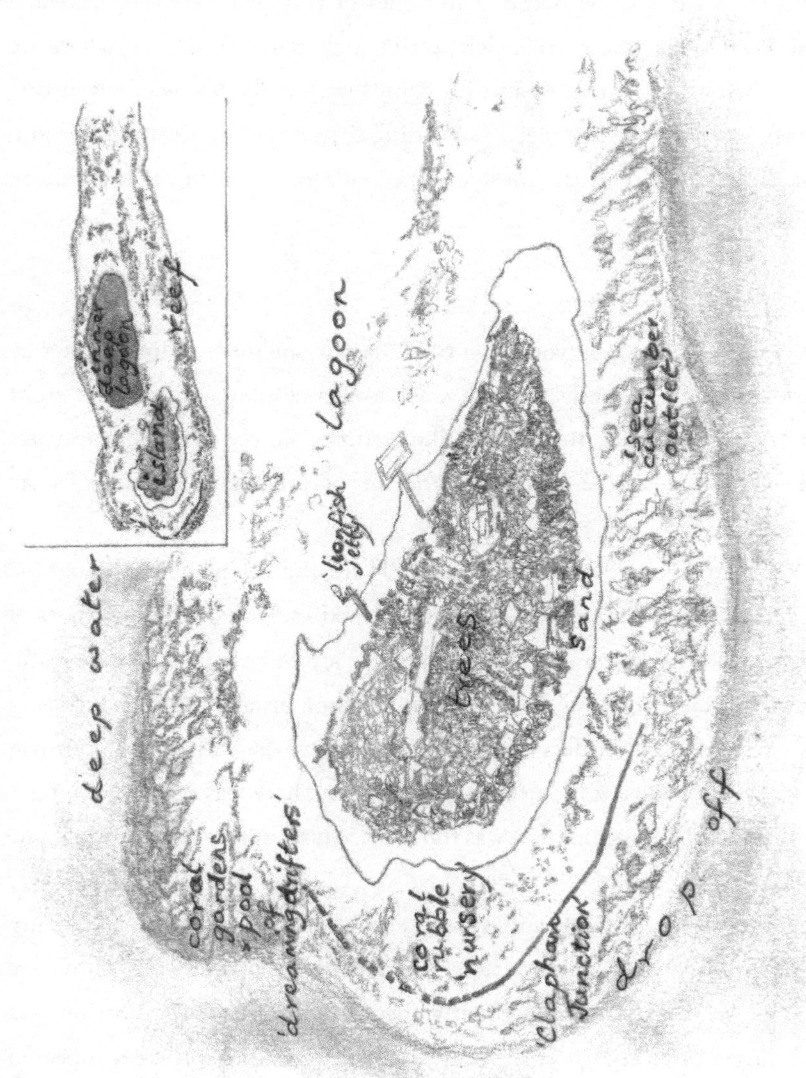

Aerial view of Baros Island in 1994. Inset: The island and part of its lagoon

of reef after reef, abundant with the necessities of life – an oasis in an immense ocean that is home. The riches of this place are only revealed when one adopts the turtle's perspective and swims this place where we do not belong. To become part of it brings with it the *frisson* of adventure, danger, awe, and the unexpected. Wildlife encounters are always uncertain, sporadic, and come at the most unexpected moments – a bit like falling in love.

A TURTLE'S EYE VIEW

To begin to see the reef world as a turtle sees it one must swim all the way round one of the islands. A brisk walk would circumnavigate it in eight minutes. To swim it, to swim it like a turtle, slowly, observing features and creatures along the way, is a journey beyond the bounds of an everyday time frame.

For us arriving at Baros in March 1994 the infinite hemispheres of blue sea and sky seen from above were transformed into small choppy waves of deep blue indigo water and spattering spray around a small boat. Beneath, life was going on deep and out of sight but for a brief spangle of fluttering fins emerging like bullets out of a distant wave as a shoal of flying fish energetically powered themselves into the air. There was no sign of land – our distant island destination was too low to show in this enveloping dome of blue.

Far away, high spray and splashes smacked the surface – a fleeting glimpse of dolphin tails in a leap. Another shower of spray and they were gone as we bounced on. Eventually the empty circle of the horizon was interrupted by a tiny irregular lump of green.. Recognisable trees appeared on this pathetically tiny dot of land. Around it, the round, tracery shapes seen from above materialised into brown and tan corals breaking the surface intermittently in the ocean swell.

Slowly on through a narrow clear passage there was calmer water. Looking down, layers of corals appeared through flickering fractured facets of clear green-tinted water. The sandy floor was dotted with coral mosaics of tans, browns, pinks and ochres. Dark and light fish shadows darted, dashed and cruised. Down there was a seething world of life, while above there was an enveloping quiet.

Inside the protecting reef was the quieter inner lagoon, edged with a shallow reef like a frilled collar overhanging pale turquoise water, darkening to the intense dark blue eye at its deep centre. At one end the reef widened and the powdered coral sand had accumulated forming the tiny island, lush with trees and shade, a few metres above sea level. By day the shallow beach of the lagoon shone blisteringly bright white to unprotected eyes, like crystalline white sugar, but in reality glossy fragments of white shells and powdered coral. The tideline was defined even whiter and shinier by myriads of big pieces and entire shells, some conical and liable to walk away: itinerant shelters for tiny hermit crabs. At the island end of the lagoon the beach sloped gently into pale turquoise water and there were coral 'gardens': miniature islands scattered along the sandy bottom like submerged fabulous rock sculptures, multi-coloured and multi-formed.

From above, these coral gardens had seemed brown blotched mosaics. Swimming and seeing them from below, Boulder Corals rose to massive mounds and large plateaux supporting miniature 'alpine rockeries'. Corals spread like miniature trees overshadowing smaller ones with textures of woodland undergrowth, prickly and spiky. Stark naked branches, erect or bowed over, were piled up like discarded antlers – the aptly named Staghorns. Flat-topped toadstool shapes grew erect like tables, some with convoluted edges fluffed into undulating frills while others jutted out horizontally, mimics of wafer thin bracket fungi. There were curved vase shapes and long fingers reaching up like flickering flames; amongst them, and largest of all, a curving twisted grouping of tall fluted columns grew vertical, one against another, tier upon tier like an isolated giant sand castle (we nick-named it 'Castle on Fire Mountain'). A competing castle of horizontal stacked storeys resembled a ceramic fantasy of tiered stalked bowls, layer overlapping layer, spreading outwards and upwards.

By day these hard corals appear inert as rocks, stony and spiky and are sometimes mistaken as such. They are a tearing sharp hazard for the careless snorkeller – but the more painful aspect is in the soft living occupants within the hard skeleton, armed with poison barbs. These hidden animals are like many joined sea anemones or jellyfish linked up as one colonial being. Using the sea's calcium, these simple creatures, polyps, constructed their hard outer limestone protection – the coral reef on which all resident and visiting animals, and the island's very existence, depend. Year by year the construction grows; each year's progress marked like rings in a tree trunk – good years and bad years – in minute details of growth. Corals are a timeline of the varying conditions and temperature of the tropical seas, an invaluable record in the study of climate change.

Swimming through them carefully, one stood out from the rest – large, floppy and looking as flexible as curling cabbage leaves, spreading bunches of beige-pink, and looking positively benign. It was a soft coral, appropriately named Toadstool Leather Coral. The colony was completely covered in what appeared to be soft moving dots – the delicate living animal polyps. Instead of a hard outer skeleton they create hard little shards, spicules, within their cells which make for some support and unpleasant eating. Even more distasteful to passing grazers are the chemicals they waft into the surrounding water. Secure in such defences they could survive exposure by day and were there to delight us with a close-up view of individual polyps and their minute movements.

By night the sharp-sculpted hard corals are moving too. They then show their true soft animal nature. Far from being hard and pitted these corals become covered with coloured gossamer layers of soft waving undulations. Looking closer at the animals emerging from every pit in the coral surface, each is a flexible delicate tube splaying out into a soft circlet of moving translucent tentacles, sometimes vibrating, surrounding a central mouth. The tentacles extend gracefully into the current with its wafting passengers of microscopic plants and creatures of the plankton – ranging from simple single-celled beings to complex crab larvae, tiny shrimps, krill, worms, even fish larvae and juveniles –but to our eyes a mere cloudiness, dustiness and floating 'bits'. These are their potential prey.

The exquisitely delicate appearance of the coral polyp tentacles belies an internal battery of lethally efficient poison barbs – nematocysts – neatly inverted specialised cells, stowed ready to eject for action at lightning speed. It is one of the fastest movements in the animal kingdom, shooting out at a speed faster than a bullet. Creatures that touch a tentacle are immobilised by the nematocyst's poison and trapped, embraced and enveloped by surrounding tentacles and then slowly consumed. Humans are inflicted with prolonged pain and slow healing wounds.

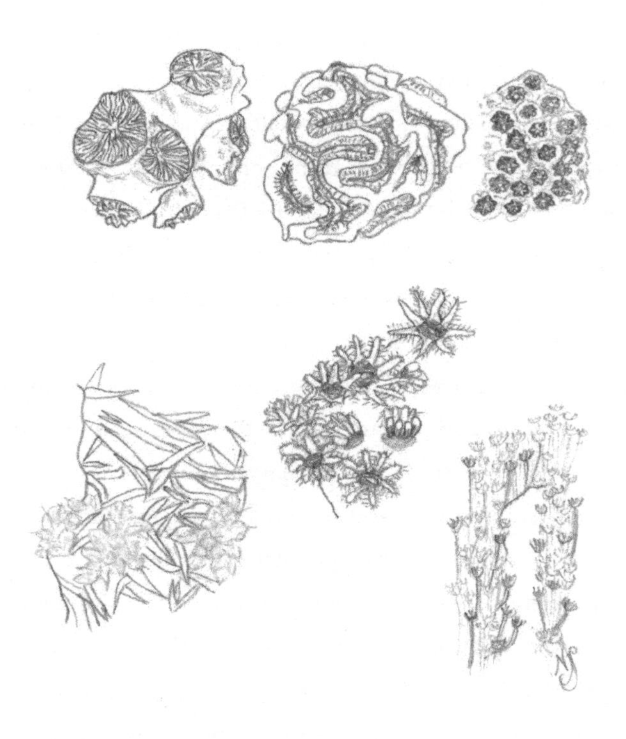

Top row: Lying on the beach - bits of hard coral skeletons show cups which encased each living animal of the colony. Left: a flower coral with 'stalks' surmounted by intricately folded flower-like cups - living tentacles splayed out like daisy flowers. Middle: a brain coral where living tentacles emerged from tiny holes in between hard convolutions. Right: a porites coral has a stony casing of star-shaped cups.

Bottom row: Living soft coral in close-up. Left: visible through the translucent body, tiny skeletal pieces act as an internal skeleton. Middle: emerging at night, delicate crimson tentacles with white feathery edges. Right: a leather coral feeding by day - tentacles held aloft on tiny long stalks.

'CORAL GARDENS' – DREAMING DRIFTERS

At dawn, the beach had been merely pale and the light muted and gentle. As the sun rose, dappled lines of reflections flickered bright patterns across the sandy floor and the corals' true colours came to life. Some were tipped with colour, others entire, an artist's palette of pale lemon through yellow, ochres, orange, bright greens, terracotta, pinks pure and pale or bright magenta, powder blue, purple, white. Some combined colours in artist's complementary shades – floppy pink folded shapes edged with lime green, and blue-centred starry shapes bordered yellow.

Under a clear morning sky with shallows intensifying to an almost blinding brightness of intense turquoise the tentacles of the polyps had vanished within their protective skeletons. They seemed to have reverted to inert coloured sculptures in this bright sunlight but are in fact active and feeding, but invisibly. Inside the thin outer layer of living tissues there are single-celled plant lodgers – zooxanthellae – which like all plants are harnessing the sun's energy forming sugars and starches. These foods are consumed by the host coral polyps: it is an animal–plant alliance, a cooperative. The other side of the bargain is that the zooxanthellae use the waste nitrates and phosphates produced by the animal polyps as nutrient raw materials and they have a protected life inside the coral.

Other sedentary reef animals – sponges, anemones and giant clams – also have this relationship with these microscopic plants. In warm sea water, low in nutrients, this animal–plant liaison of mutual benefit ensures little is wasted; it is a closed circuit enabling the animal to feed on plant products without eating the plant. The elegance of this functional arrangement with these simple plant cells is matched by the realisation that it is they that give the corals and sponges their different colours. Here, functional design and aesthetics seem intrinsically bound together – a potent mix of wonder as one drifts.

With no movement of tide or current we floated past the 'Castle on Fire Mountain' into a large bowl-shaped pool surrounded by a low wall of pink soft corals – it was filled with a slowly gyrating shoal of fish. Hundreds of flattened bodies like a moving mosaic of large flakes of beaten metal reflected palest pink through to blue, changing colours as their slow drift caught the light. They drifted as one, slowly, almost imperceptibly gliding round: each barely moved but for an occasional big swivelling eye. We joined them, floating, spiralling weightless amongst this glittering assemblage of light, feeling a unity with life and the timelessness of being. Was it minutes or hours at a time that we wafted lazily with the movement of fish and shallow water, hanging, waiting... for what? A shoal of sprat-like silversides appeared and joined in.

A grey shadow flashed faster than the human eye could focus. A black fin tip, and it was gone. The glittering throng scattered from the shark's path; the tiny fish that had survived closed ranks. They moved as one twisting and wheeling like a flock of starlings, creating a moving billow of silver one minute, almost disappearing into a dark streaming vortex the next – safety in numbers. It was a stark moment of realisation of the clandestine skill and lightning speed of that most ancient and 'primitive' of fish, the sharks. Large ones eat turtles, but this was a small one. Tiny fish like silversides seem ridiculously small food even for small sharks, something akin to herons stealing tadpoles from a garden pond; having seen both the benefit is presumably quantity. The reaction of prey fish had been at breathtaking speed; far from being creatures with googly eyes and a vacant look, fish learn fast. I recalled my student experiments on fish discriminating shapes associated with a food reward. They had rapidly noticed the difference between a solid square and the same shape subdivided into four. And there was the hopeless fishing expedition during a romantic holiday whim of 'living off the sea'. Rising to the challenge of a large number of edible fish close in to the rocks, I had made an ad hoc fishing net out of our fine mesh shopping bag and a rectangular metal band found on the beach. It only took one trial before the shoal knew what was coming next. Hungry times.

Later in the day, a glittering swirl of silversides was the target of three Blue-fin Jack (Trevally), quite large fish, silvery iridescent blue-green, edged sharp serrated blue with spiky fins. They were hunting from one side when suddenly a long fast streak of a Blacktip Reef Shark flew through from the other side. Whether hunting or cruising by, sharks always took us by surprise, and probably the fish, too, whose sudden disappearance was often the first indication that a shark was on the way. Suddenly, the unmistakable long grey body, line of gill slits, tiny eyes and long, unequal-lobed tail would be right there with us, and we never had an inkling they were waiting somewhere behind us or just outside clear visibility beyond.

On successive days, five times a day starting at daybreak, we swam out to the 'Bowl Pool' and the great shoals were always there, dreamily drifting. Sometimes the silver fish were joined by shoals of Blue-green Chromis, a quarter their size, the backs of both glinting bright metallic pink in the sun but with the dazzling addition of blue-green. Long thin Needlefish came and went, almost transparent and invisibly, and aggregations of Goatfish sometimes joined in, hanging motionless, resting, maybe sleeping in this one place where all the conditions were obviously right, but beyond our perception. We no longer joined in their spiral, a daily target for Blacktips.

'Dreaming drifters' (prey) swimming from left: one Blue Chromis, three silversides, two of an unidentified species, and a Goatfish with its chin filaments for probing sand in search of food. Predators swimming from right: Blacktip Reef Shark, Blue-fin Jack.

'CLAPHAM JUNCTION'

Beyond this dreaming drifter's pool there was a jutting sand promontory with sandy shallows strewn with broken coral and weathered coral rocks. The holes in between created a protective maze for very young fish. The rubble was largely coated with brownish algae and wisps of filamentous weed – visually unexciting but a reliable food source for fish and other small creatures. To many this is an uninteresting zone, inconveniently messy, sharp and lumpy to walk across in order to reach the main attraction. But to tread would be to squash or break, to snorkel is a nightmare of stomach muscle control and 'thinking thin' to avoid scraping injuries from the coral just below while trying to navigate a devious track through a channel maze to deeper water. As we snorkelled over it our passing shadows were tracked from holes and crevices by pin-sized bright eyes straining upwards, perfect miniaturised replicas of the adults in the deeper reef beyond. Juveniles retreated into nursery tunnels and caves; young damselfish darted so fast and so intensely blue, streaked gold that they seemed like momentary luminous lights.

After a few minutes that seemed agonisingly longer there was a gap in the breakwater of piled rocks. This magical place we named 'Clapham Junction'; like a train intersection this was the place of comings and goings. Just beyond was the reef crest where the encircling reef of the island dropped sharply away and coral was knobbly and small, battered by swell, waves and storms. During our time it was calm. Corals and sponges seemed far tighter packed than in the 'coral gardens', holding the reef together. It was a multi-coloured three-dimensional tapestry – lumpy, serrated, tiered, folded, holed, piped, shredded, extended and cupped. Further down the cliff, beautifully fluted cylinders stood out from smooth etched giant brain corals, leafy lettuce-like heads and 'broccoli' forms and in deeper water, delicate filigree fans. Not a gap remained unfilled: fine hair-like seaweeds and bright pink or blue coralline algae encroached and spread, jostling with gaping clam shells. This jumble of colours, shapes and textures reflects the intense competition for living space. The juxtaposed and overlapping edges of corals and sponges are a battlefield where active chemicals and poison darts are aimed and exchanged as each tries to encroach on its neighbour, a coral loser whitening or bleaching as it dies.

Apparently insignificant, the sponges are vital to the reef's life. Their lifestyle is that of an animated filter. A varied texture reflects their pitted surface structure. Water passes through these tiny holes by virtue of repetitive whip-like action of hair projections inside which a flow is created through the surface and on into channels and inner chambers. Sponges extract the nutrients from particles floating in the enormous quantities of sea passing through their body – animal remnants, silt and particles as small as bacteria. Incoming water also brings oxygen, and unwanted carbon dioxide and waste are both carried away with the water flowing out of the top of the sponge, as if from a chimney. Without these activities, sea currents would carry the vital raw materials too deep and too far to be useful to the other creatures of the reef. Having retrieved the recycled nutrients and built them into their structure, the sponges are eaten by others. Few can cope with the crisp crunch of sponge spicules but they are a chosen food of Hawksbill Turtles, and sponge fanciers amongst the sea slugs, starfish and fish.

Two dark eyes following our movement drew our attention away from humps of sponge to a lump of rough texture with frilled outline and trailing extensions which we had overlooked. Careful scrutiny revealed a scorpionfish merging perfectly with its background – totally convincing, camouflaged in a hotchpotch of dull pinkish shades. Its indistinct irregular outline of pectoral fins and flattened body belied its size and the appropriately large mouth, wide and upturned for a fast catch – classic traits of bottom-dwelling hunters who lie in wait, invisible, until their prey happens along. Most scorpionfish (like stonefish, and groupers) open mouth and gills in split second delay sequence creating a powerful suction sweeping in shrimps and small fish. The danger to humans is their poisonous spines, mostly on their dorsal fins.

Other fish 'stood' in wait on level coral tops and ledges, completely motionless and virtually invisible. They stand stable as a tripod, poised like missiles aimed at targets, on extended long pectoral fins at an angle of about fifty degrees. We watched as a long, blotchy brown Lizardfish stood on a sandy ledge, then in what seemed less than a second it catapulted at speed upwards into a shoal of Silversides... and returned with a fish in its mouth. The ambushed shoal distanced and veered away in synchrony as one individual.

This was the first brief glimpse of what was essentially a backdrop. The word 'diversity' needed to be redefined: here was an unfamiliar chaotic world of overwhelming variety. Our eyes were irresistibly drawn from one fascinating detail to another before there was even time to focus on the first. Gradually our seeing slowed to looking, and looking deepened to scrutiny, and a sort of order eventually unfolded.

Every foothold supported small creatures fixed to the spot – sessile beings leading a stationary coral lifestyle, wafting and sieving food from the currents flowing by. As animals they are almost unrecognisable. Many look like plants – utterly alien from a land-living perspective where mobility and all that goes with it is a must for an animal to find shelter, food and water. In the sea, life on one spot is an easy and energy-economic option as it is the food which is on the move and temperature extremes are levelled out. Eggs and sperm can be thrown into the currents to disperse. Without the need to move, a body plan based on forwards and backwards becomes irrelevant. Radial symmetry, like a daisy flower, is a good design and adopted by many sedentary animals.

Corals, sea anemones and sponges share this lifestyle with various worms. The aptly named Christmas Tree Worms, Fan Worms and Feather Dusters live in anchored tubes waving wide circular crowns and spirals of delicately striped feathery tentacles. Barnacles rhythmically brandish giant hand-like appendages armed with feathery fingers as they sieve the sea. Some animals of sophisticated design with beating hearts, kidneys and a repertoire of reflexes and behaviours have relinquished structural complexity in favour of the simple sessile adult life and have taken on a misleading simple appearance. One such group are the sea squirts (tunicates). I knew them from microscope slides, tubes with two openings and something of a headache of lines and planes to draw when squashed into two dimensions. In reality they were unexpectedly beautiful and lively, pulsating, translucent and delicate, in blues or purples, but still basically bags. Only their tadpole-like larvae reveal their true sophistication of complexity with muscles, a skeletal rod down their backs and all the trappings of mobility.

In between the sessile animals in dark cracks and crevices, more recognisable animals scuttled and crept – multi-legged worms, crabs and near transparent shrimps itinerant on threadlike legs. Sea urchins moved slowly, threatening balls of dark spines, sliding and gliding on tube feet. Equivalent to terrestrial insects and spiders these were all foraging for any bits and pieces and even tinier creatures. Many reef occupants have no recognisable terrestrial counterparts at all as it is only under the sea that one can see representatives of all of the different animal body designs that have survived extinction. By contrast on land there are less than half.

Hovering and prodding amongst the corals were small, slim-bodied butterflyfish: round discs reflecting and glittering, smartly striped with black verticals and diagonals. So many patterns seemed like variations on a theme of stripes; zigzags, encircling bands – wide, narrow, cross hatched and linear dots, some with a dash of blue, orange or red while others replaced white with luminous yellow – all sharing the family likeness of neat, crisp and chic. In ones and twos they flitted in and out like busy butterflies, moving and swivelling keen eyes in their search for sessile worms and any exposed coral polyps to pick out with projecting delicate mouths. Like their insect namesakes some species have a false eye spot clearly delineated towards the tail to muddle would-be predators. Above the corals, suspended clouds like silvery snowflakes and floating summer leaves materialised into yet more butterflyfish gathering together with Blue-green Chromis, all feeding on drifting plankton.

Before we had finally resolved these bold geometric designs the angelfishes took over centre stage with sinuous, painted precision of curving contoured stripes. An Emperor Angelfish transforms into an optical illusion as wide blue stripes grade to narrow and the dominant colour gradually shifts from a blue to a yellow background – an insoluble psychedelic riddle as to whether it is yellow on blue or blue on yellow. The more we swam after them and peered, the less clear the dilemma – something like a Bridget Riley painting. The juvenile Emperor was strikingly different – white concentric circular lines rippled over the dark blue-black body as if a pebble had been thrown into a shaded pool. Seized by the enthusiasm of swimming in pursuit of fishy optical illusions we found ourselves near an overhang and under the surveillance of another scorpionfish, or one of its relatives. With so much camouflage potential and so many poison-spined masters of the art this was not a place to touch inadvertently.

Left: Slender jaws and slim bodies of butterflyfish delve into crevices in between sea squirts (top), clam (middle), and Christmas Tree Worms. Right: Two scorpionfish waiting in ambush almost disappear into their backgrounds by virtue of camouflage patterns and outlines made irregular with skin outgrowths. Wide mouths and large front (pectoral) fins aid the lightning speed of their catch.

ALONG THE DROP-OFF

Finning backwards impulsively, the full length of this part of the reef came into view. We were in the main 'swimway' and from further along the reef edge, line upon line of fast swimming, bright silvery fusiliers sped towards us. Four or five abreast, there were over 200 of them in all, dazzling blue, almost iridescent. It was a mass of fish, replicated but differing in their twisting forms, swim angles, swivelling eye sockets as they looked around, their mouths and gills opening and shutting, pushing their pale articulatory jaws out front, gulping zooplankton. They might be seen as grotesque, but to a zoologist or an engineer they were anatomical poetry in motion, ultimately efficient, vacuuming up food, swimming on and on, unerringly into a plankton-hazy blue distance, beyond clear visibility.

Cruising and chasing were Blue-fin Jack (Trevally), streamlined, sleek, gleaming metallic, their predatory intent emphasised by wide mouth, big eyes, bristling spiky fins like ancient weaponry. A large Jack detoured to inspect us, its big yellow lips accentuating its rather disgruntled looking face. Looking up ahead, just beneath the sea's surface, more illusions flickered. Fish or reflections? The streaks transformed into near transparent Needlefish, thin as their name, invisible until one is their subject of interest. The reflecting blue of their backs came into focus as they turned, their big eyes swivelling and observing all.

As we hung motionless, ungainly and incredulous at the surface, all of these species crowded into our immediate vicinity in the blink of an eye. Another large scattered shoal passed through: several species of brightly patterned surgeonfish, some as interested in us as we were in them. As their name suggests, they are armed with forward-pointing, very obvious, blade-shaped spines as sharp as a scalpel – on each side of the body near the tail. They swam by like a themed group: bright Blues, Black Tails, Blue-lined and the more sober black and white Convicts. Intermingled with them were some of their close relatives, unicornfish, brandishing their namesake's strange 'horns'. As we paused, we had a strange encounter with a group of Vlaming's Unicorns, beautiful with subtly tinted purplish sides and gracefully trailing two enormously long tail streamers, half as long as their body. They surrounded us and were joined by other passers-by, Queen Wrasse, 6-bar Wrasse and Orange-lined Triggerfish. This disparate group focused on us and circled us, apparently united in their curiosity. They viewed us for some time before they swam off with the rest. As the last Blue Surgeonfish of the shoal passed it turned very purposefully and threatened a parrotfish swimming nearby, then sped on to join its relatives.

The parrotfish continued on its way. Parrotfish are one of the more peaceable fish of the reef community: flamboyant displays of argument and bickering are one of their namesake's features they seem to lack. However, their colouring is as bright as any parrot's. We tried to memorise the drift from turquoise-green to blue to mauve to shocking pink as a Bicolour Parrotfish fluttered on ahead, a living example of the subtle goal of watercolour art.

There were many vibrant colour combinations amongst the parrotfish. We tried hard to identify all we saw, made more difficult by the many species, juveniles changing colour radically as they mature and adults at the top of parrotfish society changing sex and colour. In the coral gardens we had seen 'teenagers' of pale crimson shading to olive green with prominent diamond scale patterns. Here at 'Clapham Junction' Dusky Parrotfish combined a rich purple body with orange lips and bright red fins; another contrast was orange and Prussian blue, and others touched with purple and with vivid green.

They glided about singly or in groups, fast fluttering between coral heads and rocks. The lack of parrot chatter as they fed, so typical of their avian namesake, was compensated for by a significant crunching noise. Voluptuous lips against plump cheeks barely disguised crushing power jaws which protruded, bar-like. They rasped at filamentous algae, and dead coral chunks simply crumpled in these powerful beaks. Some species also eat living coral. Listening to a group of them at a distance we saw white coral dust floating away on the current. This apparently destructive method of feeding is a key activity within the reef ecosystem, for as they slowly soar away to another feeding site they eject a stream of waste in their wake. This is not ordinary fish excrement, it is coral skeleton ground to a fine sand which floats down in a gentle white shower adding to the sandy bottom and ultimately forms much of the beach. Grating away at algal growth actually helps the living coral in the continuous battle for reef space by preventing the coral from being choked by encroaching plants. Overall the coral community benefits.

Their wide choice of food allows the close coexistence of individuals and several parrotfish species sharing feeding areas without aggression. Their vegetable food sources are plentiful and regrow rapidly so there is enough for all. Their mutual tolerance over food does not extend into their complicated sex life however: rivalry over sexual dominance escalates to fighting between several females under the gaze of the single male, who, if challenged, defends his privileged position.

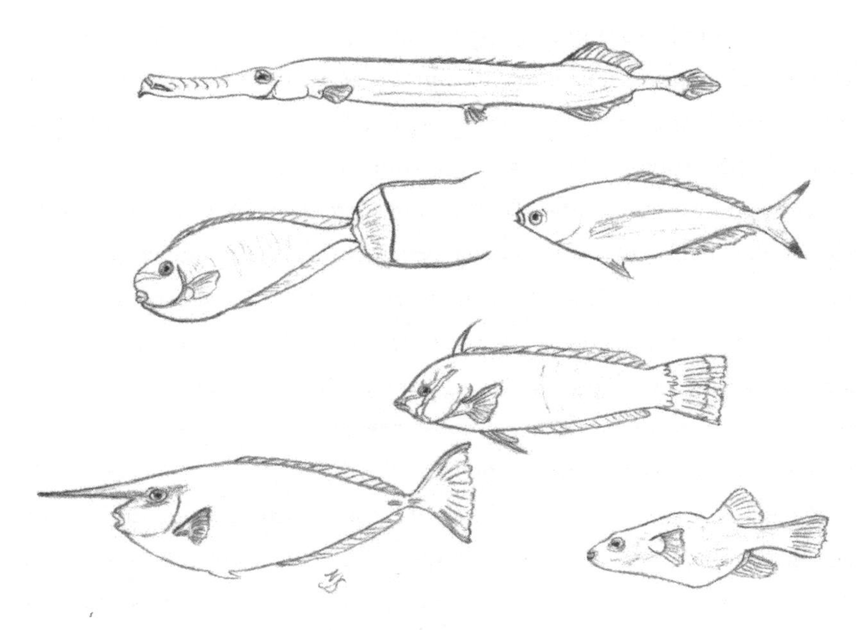

Speeding along the drop-off. Top: A long Trumpetfish above a Vlaming's Unicornfish trailing tail streamers followed by a Blue Fusilier. Below: A Unicornfish with long 'horn', a Queen Wrasse with head stripes, and a pufferfish (deflated).

RELATIONSHIPS – FOR BETTER OR WORSE

Shared activities between related species such as surgeonfish and unicornfish and between the various parrotfish is commonplace and makes survival sense. Further down this road of tolerance and cooperation there are some unlikely bedfellows who have evolved astounding garb and changed their behaviour to fit in with their shared lifestyle. We hoped to catch glimpses of these in little vignettes and domestic dramas as we snorkelled the turtle's circuit along the edge of the drop-off. It was rather like flying over city streets – a kaleidoscope of familiar activities – cohabitation and communal living, partnership and mutual dependence, stealth, fake identities, deception, aggression and courtship.

Eyes appeared and disappeared beneath sea anemones. For a short time, a single enormous anemone showed orange tentacles as bright as a flame with an enveloping sleeve as bright purple as bougainvillea flowers. Others spread their beige-pink tentacles like carpets over the rocks sprawling over the sand. Moving water wafted their stubby tentacles apart revealing dark eyes and mouth – Maldivian Clownfish, and beyond, Clark's Clownfish, resplendent black with white stripes with yellowish lime-green and bright yellow fins, observant and furtive, hovering just above their host. Clownfish do not stray far from the tentacles that protect them from their predators – brittlestars, wrasses and other species of damselfish. The ultimate reliability of this strategy is the lethal poison in the anemone's nematocysts – stinging cells, as in corals. Nestling amongst the tentacles the clownfish protect themselves from sharing this fate, by having acquired immunity to these toxins in combination with a coat of mucus which fools the anemone into not firing its stinging cells. Unmolested, they feed on passing zooplankton, algae, worms and small creatures. They even lay their eggs beneath the tentacles: cleaning the area, sticking down the eggs in clusters and then male and female protecting them jointly. From the anemone's point of view, the lodgers earn their keep as they remove waste and detritus and act as decoys attracting potential prey fish near the tentacles.

The details of the beneficial partnership between an anemone and its clownfish are not immediately apparent to a passing swimmer. Mutual dependence becomes more obvious at a cleaning station, easily recognisable as uncluttered areas of open water often above big flat-topped boulder corals or smooth-domed brain coral. Here animals of totally incompatible sizes and habits gathered in close proximity to each other. Oriental Sweetlips hung motionless, heavy-bodied, longer than a man's arm and striking with wide stripes of black and white, bright yellow lips and eyes and yellow fins boldly spotted black. They just looked. Nearby, a small lavender-tinted Vlaming's Unicornfish hovered. It was a queue, all waiting to be freed of dead tissue, old bits of food and irritating parasites from outside, and inside. With disbelief we watched Many-Spotted Sweetlips arrive and open disproportionately large mouths, projecting their jaws further and further forwards and outwards, seemingly to an extremity of dislocation in order to encourage and facilitate the resident 'dentist/hygienist'. The advantages to the health and comfort of those being cleaned and pampered are quite clear. The cleaner's position is a touch more ambiguous. By the nature of their task, they are very small – picking round scales and flipper folds, delving inside gill slits and picking out rotting food between teeth. They are small enough to become a tasty morsel to their client in one inadvertent gulp. Once away from the cleaning station their clients would do just that, but in the context of the cleaning procedure they desist, resting with vast mouths agape inviting tiny striped Blue Streak Cleaner Wrasse to dart in, wriggle deep inside and streak out. Slower and somewhat more cumbersome on robotic jointed legs and waving long antennae, there were Cleaner Shrimp, transparent but for some barely visible stripes. They scissored and scraped their tiny interlocking mouthparts over large skin scales.

To all these diminutive cleaners the most formidable clients must be the heavy-bodied groupers. When feeding, these draw small fish and crustaceans into their mouths by rapid powerful suction and have jaws, tongue and palate covered with hundreds of small rasp-like teeth to secure their prey before swallowing them whole. A Peacock Grouper hung motionless at a cleaning station, beautiful with dark outlined spots against khaki, but at the same time hideous with wide head and cavernous wide mouth, waiting.

One animal's detritus and parasite has become another's mainstay food: this extraordinary system has evolved to facilitate the exchange. Such a sophisticated and ritualised procedure depends on many disparate species all radically changing their usual behaviours and cooperating within the area of the cleaning station. Such a complex situation is far more frequently encountered on coral reefs than in any other habitat. (It is tempting to wonder how people from widely differing cultures and unable to communicate – say, cannibals and Bhuddist monks – would have adapted their behaviour and resolved their conflicting needs.)

Where there are deals there will always be the double dealer who works the system to his own advantage. The neutrality of the Cleaner Wrasse has been misappropriated and used as a disguise by the Mimic Cleaner Wrasse. This small fish looks and behaves authentically, but then with client in position, darts in and bites out a chunk of living flesh. Without wetsuits during these years, we snorkelled habitually wearing thick woolly tights – in an optimistic hope of an approximation of sun protection. Our woolly clad legs with patches of skin exposed through random small holes obviously bore some resemblance to dark fish heavily infested with pale parasites; wrasse were assiduously attentive 'cleaners' and we regularly felt the tickling caress of tiny nips taking skin morsels. We were never sure which Wrasse was the culprit.

Lower down the cliff we could see more, big red blotch eyes looking at us from the shadows under stones and overhangs – beautiful red Shadowfin Soldierfish and Spotfin Squirrelfish, black traced scales gleaming metallic. Like some other night hunters, they are mostly red, rendering them less visible deeper down: the red part of the spectrum is filtered out by sea water making them near black. The daylight sight of such a vivid pure red against a dark background was sheer joy. If we had had the ears to hear there would have been yet more delight in store. Many species of soldierfish have the habit of communicating between themselves, in grunts, clicks and pops, unfortunately with a frequency so low it is inaudible to humans.

Looking far down, the details of the cliff face gradually blurred into gloom and deeper distance. Bigger fish shapes glided along and out of sight. Suddenly below us we were aware of a slow elegant rhythm of front flippers, hauling a round dark back and trailing back flippers – a turtle. It swam like a bird flapping its wings in slow motion, powerfully gliding, and was soon lost in the opaque blue. The distinctive notched shell edge and pattern of plates combined with the blunt head and hooked bill shape identified a Hawksbill. The rich reef habitat was ideal for its specialised diet of sponges; they were flourishing and profuse – not many creatures can cope with eating their sharp spicules and toxins.

Following the turtle's path and viewing 'drop-off city' from above we caught sight of some of the little domestic dramas we had hoped for. Two pale blue Triggerfish were 'looping the loop' in a chasing sequence – possibly courtship? Further on a young Lunar-tailed Grouper, also known as Rock Cod or Trout, reddish-brown spotted yellow, approached a small morsel with intent. As it poised to open its mouth an Orange-lined Triggerfish pushed in and threatened it. The grouper 'blushed' from brown to a bluish shade and the dark delineated yellow spots turned magenta-purple in front of our eyes. Later, we saw a large vermilion red adult communicate by a flush of colour change. Apparently groupers also change colour according to background and time of day, and use it to surprise their prey.

At the underwater cliff face and in different microhabitats of our island circumnavigation we began to notice we were being accompanied by a strange long floating rigid tube – a Trumpetfish. Its narrow body, encircled with bony rings, and its eyes, extended tubular snout, small mouth and pectoral fins were reminiscent of a sea horse with tail unwound – not inappropriately as it is a distant relative. Cornetfish and pipefish also belong within this group equipped with noses and mouths resembling musical instruments. Trumpetfish are usually brownish, but ours was a yellow variant. Interesting creatures of very ancient lineage from primeval seas, their trumpet-shaped mouth suctions in prey. Singly or in groups, they can lie horizontal and motionless, like floating sticks, or alternatively they swim or hang vertically, head down, invisible amongst reed-shaped verticals, such as corals, pipe sponges, sea rods and sea pens. Either way, beautifully camouflaged, they float and sway passively with the wave action of the water, all the while inching their way slowly towards their prey – small fish such as wrasses and silversides, everyone's handy victim. When they have sneaked up close enough they dart at it rapidly, suddenly opening and shutting their tube-like mouths in such quick succession they create a strong suction drawing the prey straight into their widened mouths. At rest or swimming along unobtrusively like our companion, the mouth seemed small and upturned. In feeding mode, the jaws quickly expand into a gaping circular hole as wide as the body. Another of their stealth techniques is to swim in alignment with other large fish. This is presumably what our bright yellow variant was attempting to do with us in the role of bigger fish. Unprovoked aggressive behaviour also seemed to be part of its psyche; we noticed it had a very prominent presence when swimming in tandem with other fish as cover and threatened them continually. On another occasion we saw possibly the same fish behaving similarly with yellow Rabbitfish – unaggressive vegetarians. Presumably we were inappropriately sized to submit to any threat aimed at us, too valuable as cover for use in ambush, or maybe just didn't notice. Possibly, their social interaction reflects their finely honed stealthy hunting behaviour.

Inadvertently we swam into the territory of a Giant (Titan) Triggerfish and suddenly found ourselves under persistent upward bombardment attacks as she guarded her nest site. She eyed us and zoomed straight up with threatening intent at us or anything else remotely nearby. As for swimming above the precious eggs, only the bravest clad in a thick wetsuit would have contemplated such a manoeuvre – but at their peril, as reports of these fish swimming off with chunks of diver plus wetsuit clamped between their powerful toothy jaws are not unknown.

On a coral shelf further down the reef face there was a scene of domestic bliss – two Peacock Groupers resting peacefully side by side. We were suddenly aware that just beneath the shelf a Blacktip Reef Shark was thrashing about wildly with something in its mouth – only a tail was protruding. After a short while the shark settled in a curved posture and went to sleep. Sharks in hunting action were the most mesmerising and chilling spectacle from the point of view of ordinary humans – as opposed to those addicted to high adrenalin. Although reef sharks are only as long as a man and aiming at small fry, there is still a certain awe at their breathtaking efficiency and speed, particularly with an awareness of their larger cousins out there in the deeper blue, efficient and powerful enough to bite through a turtle's hard shell. Beyond the shark, there was a Clear Fin Lionfish – a member of the scorpionfish family, well-armed with poisonous spines, which was probably far more potentially harmful to us than the chilling face of a shark.

Bumbling along in complete contrast to fast fish elegance there were single pufferfish, stocky, squat, blunt-nosed, some smooth-skinned, some spiky. Dull buff, browns, yellows and bluish, spotted, scrawled or vaguely striped, with elastic big drooping bellies when unpuffed – they are not beautiful fish. Their big googly accentuated eyes stared, panda-like, as we passed.

What pufferfish lack in looks is more than compensated for by their behaviour. The creation of a stunning architectural nest site has been seen recently for the first time. Down on the sea floor, at 24 m (80 ft), a male pufferfish a little longer than a finger painstakingly wriggles and wafts a fin to carve out wedges of sand into deep multi-layered ridges and furrows, like spokes in a giant wheel with a diameter bigger than a man. The geometry is as precise as if devised by a mathematician, the symmetrical mound somewhat resembling a squat traditional jelly mould; and in the moving flow of underwater it needs continual maintenance. Females are attracted and swim over the site carefully – it has been discovered that the more ridges in the circle, the more likely she is to mate. Eggs are laid at the centre and it seems that the carefully sculpted hills and valleys help to reduce the current, reducing the chance of disturbance to the eggs and developing young. During his lengthy building the male even seems to provide for their nourishment in advance by gathering shells, cracking them and placing them in the inner grooves of the structure. All of this was seen and recorded in 2012 off the southern tip of Japan.

Pufferfish are capable of short bursts of speed, presumably to escape predators rather than hunt their prey of Crustacea and sea snails. Their slow speed and manoeuvrability is achieved by swimming with all of their fins, with pectoral fins beating fast and prominent, as in parrotfish. Certainly they were a satisfying fish to swim with as we were not outpaced.

Easily caught with a fishing line, they display an alarming protection mechanism. Pufferfish have the ability to very rapidly increase their size to astounding proportions. They inflate their bodies with water, or air if out of water. I caught one from a rowing boat near a sand bank just off an East Australian shore around the time I saw my first baby turtles in a Queensland bathtub. My parents and I had no idea what this yellow and greyish fish was – we imagined it was edible like the whiting and bream lying on the bottom of the boat. A catch later we noticed this pop-eyed creature had blown up like a balloon with shimmering white tight belly skin. Terrified we scooped it out and back into the sea using an oar, which was fortunate as these fish have hidden thin spines which only become visible when they have reached their puffed-up state. The horrors of the expedition did not end there: in the excitement we had failed to notice the sandbank was part of a channel, the tide had turned and it was going out – and so were we. My parents both rowed with all the strength that terror gives, but we were not even keeping level with the long sand bank, it kept 'moving' towards the shore. With full rowing effort we could not even stay stationary. Always resourceful and brave, my mother leapt over the side of the boat clutching its rope and was soon wading towards the sandbank. Once on it and racing fast enough not to sink into the soft quicksand she pulled the boat to relative safety. I had learnt respect for the sea and its inhabitants. As for the pufferfish with its chameleon-like attributes of swivelling eyes and changing colour to suit its background, the most important outcome was that we did not try to eat it – they are the second most poisonous vertebrate on earth, second only to a small frog.

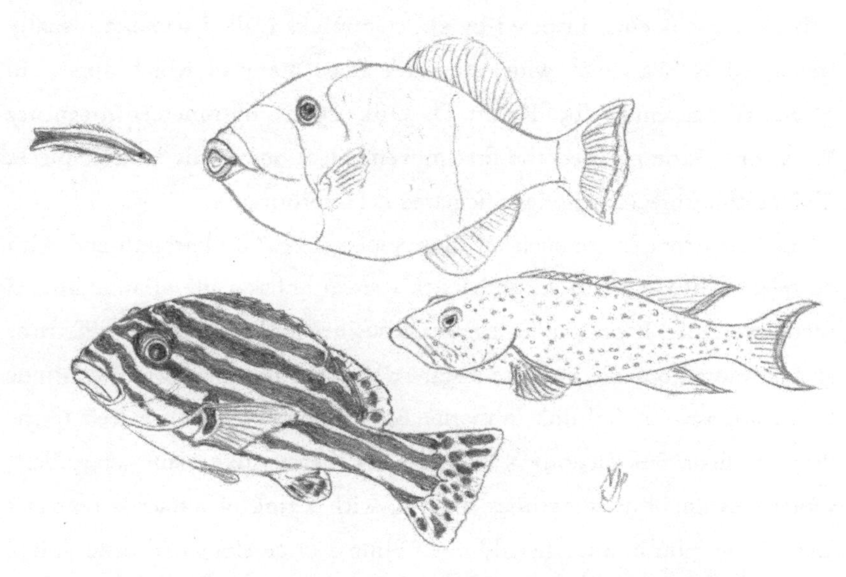

A tiny Cleaner Wrasse faces three clients awaiting cleaning services, including inside their large mouths: a Titan Triggerfish, a spotted Lunar-tailed Grouper and dramatically striped Oriental Sweetlips.

THE LAGOON

It seemed a long, hard swim past areas of rocky walls and coral rubble round the far edge of the island. We passed some sort of grey water drain outlet around which large numbers of fish, large and small, hungrily snapped and grabbed. A sea cucumber, about as long as a fore arm, dangled under a rock hanging by its tail, sausage-like. Easily overlooked, these creatures are the unattractive unsung heroes of the sea floor – certainly amongst European cultures. In Asia they have long been respected and even cultivated as a delicacy and a staple. Before Europeans settled in Australia, the Aborigines of Arnhem Land in the Northern Territory were trading with Indonesian traders to supply the Southern Chinese markets. There are 1,000 Japanese haikus (short poems) inspired by sea cucumbers (called namako, usually translated as 'sea slugs' which they are not): many of which appear in 'Rise, Ye Sea Slugs' by Robin D. Gill, 2003. In nineteenth-century Paris, Erik Satie entitled the first movement of one of his eclectic pieces 'D'Holothournie' (their scientific name is Holothurian).

In sharp contrast to such an illustrious cultural background and with no relationship at all to cucumbers this creature has a life of an animated vacuum cleaner. It goes about the basic business of breaking down detritus and unwanted organic waste to a state which bacteria can further continue to decompose – a vital link in marine ecosystems from shallow reefs to the deep sea floor. Sea cucumbers resemble and behave like giant caterpillars, sometimes knobbly, sometimes smooth, with a ring of retractile tentacles around the mouth. Superficially resembling a large elongated coral polyp, they are related to starfish and sea urchins, all based on a radial body plan. The living *Beche-de-mer* does not have the immediate appeal of a haiku subject or cuisine item: when threatened it has the startling defence of ejecting its internal organs and tubules in a perplexing entangling mass accompanied by a toxic chemical. Straight from the sea, unadorned, they are like extremely tough, salty chewing gum – according to Andrew, our son, who ate them raw for breakfast while 'living native' in Pohnpeii, Micronesia. Our Baros sea cucumber was hanging strategically in the drain flow, grasping at anything passing, part of efficient reef economy visibly in action. We swam a wide detour (round the drain rather than the creature) and pushed on.

At last we reached the big sandy lagoon. As we looked around we had the feeling of floating in infinite turquoise space, dazzled by brightness. The shallows gradually shaded from palest tint to distinct colour as far as the eye could see in any direction. Below us the white sand was dappled with dancing light-lines of ripple reflections. Looking up, the underside of the surface gave an illusion of solidity, patterned with flickering wavy streaks. This part of the island's sea appeared empty after the busy reef, an oasis of peace and calm, even the occasional near transparent fish reflected turquoise as part of this pale monochrome world. White fish shimmered against the ephemeral lacework of ripple patterns glinting and moving with the light, teasing our eyes with the virtual and the real. Just below us a ragged length of fin shuddered as a tiny flatfish, cream speckled, edged deeper under the cover of sand grains; a lone red starfish lay motionless, incongruously vivid. Out of nowhere about sixty Blue Surgeonfish materialised ahead of us, purposefully swimming across the lagoon as if on a mission, and disappeared. Silently we swam through the warm pale haze – a place of illusion and strange reality.

Suddenly there was a group of large, dark bird-like creatures, almost like underwater pterodactyls, flying across our path. We refocused, dazzled by this unexpected beautiful presence of five Spotted Eagle Rays, swimming with graceful slow flapping strokes – just like birds. Their wingspan is 2.5 m (8 ft), comparable with the Brown Pelican. Their graceful movement was totally in keeping with tales of birthing females leaping out of the water to release their young – but it seems that leaping out of the water is more mundane, just a commonly observed behaviour. They swam by, circled round us, trailing immense long tails, more than twice as long as their bodies. One broke the formation and swam to within three wingspans of us. Then, after an incredibly elegant 'dance' motion, off they flew, dark shapes receding against the blurry shine of white haze, disappearing towards the darker, deeper water of the still lagoon.

Skirting round the few luxury chalets on stilts we swam further in towards the shore where concrete jetty piles loomed dark brown with waving weedy growth. Pale sand gave way to shadowy rock heaps and cast-off clutter; ideal cover for diffident secretive species, ambush predators and purple sea urchins. A gloomy contrast to the pale bright lagoon, this was a place for caution – keeping bare skin away from the possibility of venomous spines protruding from crevices. Beneath a fallen concrete pile, a perfect splayed fan of sharp-tipped needles was half exposed, and as we looked, another, and another. Two Lionfish hung motionless in the open, flaunting the perfect geometric symmetry of their enormous pectoral fin fans framing their striped faces – more like a child's depiction of the sun than a lion's mane. Camouflage striped, with notched eyebrow protrusions above moving watchful dark eyes they have the compulsive fascination of extremes – grotesque, beautiful and malevolent. The delicate membranous fins carry sharp poison darts, and their aggression can extend to humans as well as their prey. Lurking stationary they either grab at small fish, or alternatively adopt a more hunting strategy, herding fish into a corner, erecting their spiked fin fans like a giant carnival ruff thus making an effective barrier where the only escape is into the Lionfish's mouth. Twenty young fish consumed in thirty minutes – juvenile snappers, groupers, parrotfish, spiny lobster – illustrates the formidable success of the operation and their enormous appetite to fill their voluminous stomachs. All fall victim to the Lionfish.

Round the jetty, it was a short swim to the zone of 'Coral Gardens'. In the quiet sandy areas between individual gardens we saw a very young Batfish start swimming in a dense shoal of larger silver fish and its rejection could only be described as bullying, an anthropomorphic term but somewhat appropriate. Batfish approach snorkellers and divers closely and readily, without any bribery of food. They just seem to have a friendly fascination, further justifying the term. We watched it swim off into the distance as we turned, now tired, and doggedly swam on towards the inviting shore.

Crossing the lagoon from the right: two Batfish with extreme flattened bodies and fins. Swimming from the left, a Spotted Eagle Ray, and a Blue Surgeon-fish. Below: a sea cucumber is carefully held giving indication of size.

1994 REST AND REFLECTION – 1998 EL NINO AND BEYOND

We had circumnavigated Baros Island, swimming a turtle's eye view through the reef and drop-off edging its shore and across one side of its lagoon. We hauled up, exhausted, onto the white shell sand, dazzled by direct bright sun without a muting veil of water to shield our eyes. We were vaguely conscious of a gentle lap of sea, barely moving, and occasional movement of small tree leaves overhead.

Breathless, but exhilarated by the complexity and intricate perfection of what we had seen, we were also aware that there was so much more out of sight, beyond and little understood. It was the realisation of an apparently familiar green earth world transforming into an extraordinary revelation of blue – something akin to that most famous moment in 1968 when Apollo 8 came out from the dark side of the moon on its fourth orbit and for the first time men saw Earth rise from another world. Cosmonaut Bill Anders described it: *'out of the lunar horizon came this beautiful blue'* – a blue jewel of a living planet suspended in black space. That moment initiated a universal awakening and respect for the extent and significance of the sea.

We felt dwarfed by our close-up experience of this small segment of the planet's blueness, part of an ancient wilderness, still largely intact and self-supporting in spite of the advent of man – it was an immense privilege. Its kaleidoscope of beings had been overwhelming; a living jigsaw of 'eat and be eaten' and 'survive or move on'. But when one considers, this diversity is appropriate to the millions of years during which coral reef forebears have had massive opportunity for experimentation. There have been multiple guises and ploys to outwit the hunters and aggressors which in turn have refined their tactics. Variations and countermeasures have escalated like an arms race and multiplied the diversity and complexity of all parts of the reef community producing the extreme and the bizarre. We had seen it everywhere: in pectoral fins used and modified for acceleration, propulsion, manoeuvring and balance, and in extreme sophistication used as herding and hunting nets in the 'mane' of Lionfish, or, stationary and extended, acting as body props for the poised Lizardfish. We had been completely deceived by skin colour as camouflage by scorpionfish and delighted to see it as a means of communication between Peacock Groupers. Specialised behaviour such as primeval Trumpetfish hanging in mid-water like horizontal floating sticks and vertical corals had made us blink and check again which was which, and we had marvelled at clownfish hanging about immune, amidst barbed anemone tentacles, still only a partly solved mystery of biology.

The efficiency of the reef's 'waste not, want not' economy had been clear wherever we looked, vital in a large community packed into a small sea space where ultimately everything hinged on the cloudy microscopic bits floating by. In this opaque blue were nutrients, apparently lost, fallen to the sea floor ultimately borne up on currents, then feeding phytoplankton of unrecognisable plants – floating and gyrating geometric fantasies. These in turn fuelled microscopic animal plankton; pulsating tiny jellies, larvae jerking by with ripple action jointed legs, rhythmic boat-oar paddles and squirming segmented strands. Waiting for them were the tentacle multitudes of coral polyps, and within them yet more microscopic plants creating food from sunlight. From here the sequence was within the realm of our perception – we had seen this passing bounty grabbed by the sedentary creatures of the reef and shoals of scooping fishy jaws. There was no wanton wastage in any of these transactions for much dissolved organic material and waste particles voided by these was immediately retrieved by the rapid filtering action of the sponges before it could wash down to the ocean floor. Ubiquitous, nestling between the more spectacular corals, encrusting and enveloping crevices and caves, the apparently inert and insignificant sponges were a keystone in the reef economy. Recycling in action had been most visible and entertaining to us at cleaning stations where we shared the timescale of events as they unfolded. Here food opportunities offered extremes of risk, size and incongruity, and mutual cooperation between diverse creatures was vital. Unexpectedly we ourselves had become part of this currency of curiosity and opportunism – many passing fish had noticed us, several groups had detoured and circled and scrutinised us, Cleaner Wrasse had cleaned and fed off us.

We had left our own world and all too briefly been immersed in this apparently timeless world, so different, so complex – another planet. As we lay on the beach in 1994 thinking of the beautiful interlocking of all the pieces of the reef jigsaw and talking of its inconceivable timescales we thought that the reef would ever remain thus. However, nothing is ever static in nature or life. Looking back to this time we were more privileged than we could have imagined.

In the 1998 El Nino event the sea temperature rose enough to kill the zooxanthellae living within the coral polyps. Without the sugar manufacturing plant partner corals lost their colours, bleached, and died. Over 90% of the Maldives' corals were affected with only one third of the reefs recovering.

Since then Baros has become a centre of diver training for Reef Health Checking and surveys. In 2009 a reef propagation and coral rehabilitation programme was begun: fifty guests joined in planting 800 coral 'cuttings'. Visitors to the now fully fledged EcoResort can train to become involved EcoDivers and there is a Marine Centre. Visitors can see marine specimens, browse literature, attend a weekly lecture and snorkel under the guidance of marine biologists who have instigated a strict 'do not touch' policy – underlining the old rule that no shells could be taken out of the Maldives. (Unfortunately there always were and will be those who can't resist or see rules as a direct challenge.) Today wildlife abounds in the lagoon. There are reports of eight resident Hawksbill Turtles, sharks, rays – Spotted Eagle and Mantas. Dolphins and flying fish unexpectedly splash out of the deep water just beyond the reef. The corals vary: apparently there is still a lot of dead coral from 1998 but with a huge growth improvement since 2007 there are many areas of strong regrowth and in 2012 there was a coral spawning.

The island resort itself has radically changed since 2006 to meet the level of luxury and sophistication demanded by today's paradise experience seekers. Basic expectations of an easy-access tropical island 'away-from-it-all' now include the 'with-it-all' of lavish rooms and bathrooms, pampering spa facilities, foreign gourmet imports and the variety of five restaurants, evening music entertainment, gym, snooker and flotillas of attentive staff (not forgetting the luxury market's expectations of private Jacuzzi and infinity-edged plunge pool). A chain of thirty water villas has replaced the handful of 1990s luxury chalets built on stilts over the lagoon. At that time there had been simple, basic and adequate chalets with shower and basic facilities and our simple luxury touch was frangipani flowers carefully arranged on turned down sheets. A dining room served splendidly retro but sometimes challenging school dinner menus including pink blancmange and custard, and there was a small alternative restaurant and a bar. All of the staff were men working away from their family homes on distant atolls. On such remote islands education was limited: advised beforehand, we had brought children's books as gifts which were enthusiastically received.

Modern tourism expectations have raised the stakes of environmental cost, even with the advent of LED light systems, biodegradable cleaning chemicals and heat exchange systems. More than ever wonders and wildlife are in danger of being merely one on the tick list, part of an idle afternoon's pleasant entertainment – reducing them to a fragment of wasted wilderness. Some guests object to the protective reef barrier as it disturbs their view. An optimistic future is in the hands of the enthusiastic and dedicated marine biologists and dive centre managers to inspire guests' interest and to instil environmental awareness.

Top: Two clownfish look out from the top protecting tentacles of a large sea anemone; two more hover at its 'barrel' base. Below: Looking down to the base of a different sea anemone, a pair of clownfish guard and tend their batch of golden eggs, fanning fins creating refreshing currents.

POST SCRIPT

Besides the major events such as El Nino, there have been other less publicised but equally far reaching changes involving survival of marine communities. Two species of Lionfish from the Indo-Pacific have been accidentally introduced into the Atlantic. This foreign invasion began in earnest in 1992 when Hurricane Andrew destroyed a Florida aquarium, distributing its exotic content widely into the surrounding ocean. There were also sporadic releases by a few home aquarium enthusiasts who had become disenchanted with the novel Lionfish additions to their collections which had presumably succumbed as Lionfish fodder. It is thought that this dumping may have started in the 1980s. These Lionfish introductions are now seriously depleting reef populations down the east coast of America, south to Belize, and significantly the naive young fish they consume are an important part of our own food chain and the fishery industry. Stripped of fin barbs, Lionfish themselves make good eating – inspired scuba diving instructors published recipe books in 2011 – a tasty contribution to badly needed population control.

The combination of aggression, voracity and the invasive nature of this species into new areas where juvenile fish are using reefs as their nursery is a matter of increasing concern. As so often happens when a foreign species is introduced to another ecosystem, the invader population thrives to boom proportions – in this case increases of 700% with much greater population densities than in the species' home ranges. One of many unfortunate escapes and introductions worldwide, the Lionfish underlines the delicate nature of marine ecosystems and the catastrophic connection between small and grand scale events.

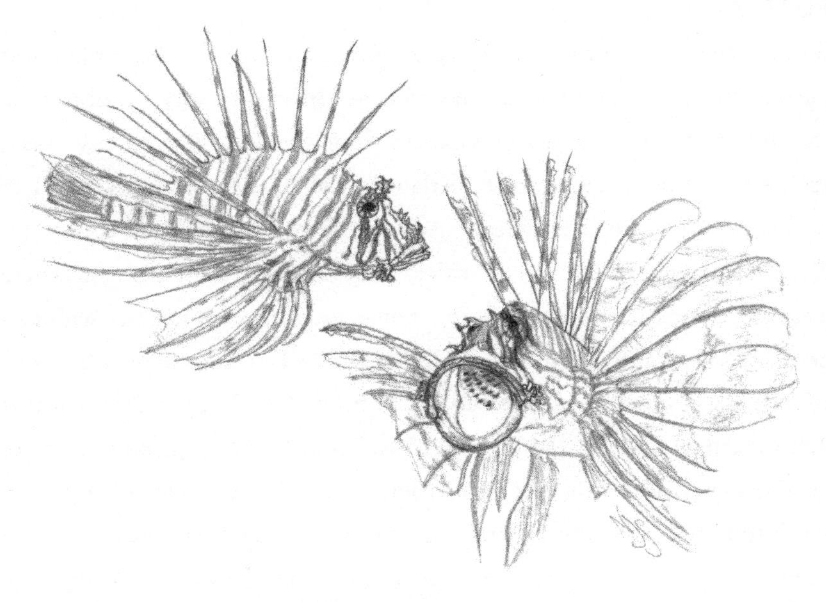

Amidst zebra stripes, a baffling array of spines can be raised and spread into a barricade – the only exit is into the mouth of the Lionfish.

Chapter 5

PARADISE LOST: A JOURNEY TO CHAOS – SUPERTYPHOON

Yap (and Eauripik), Micronesia

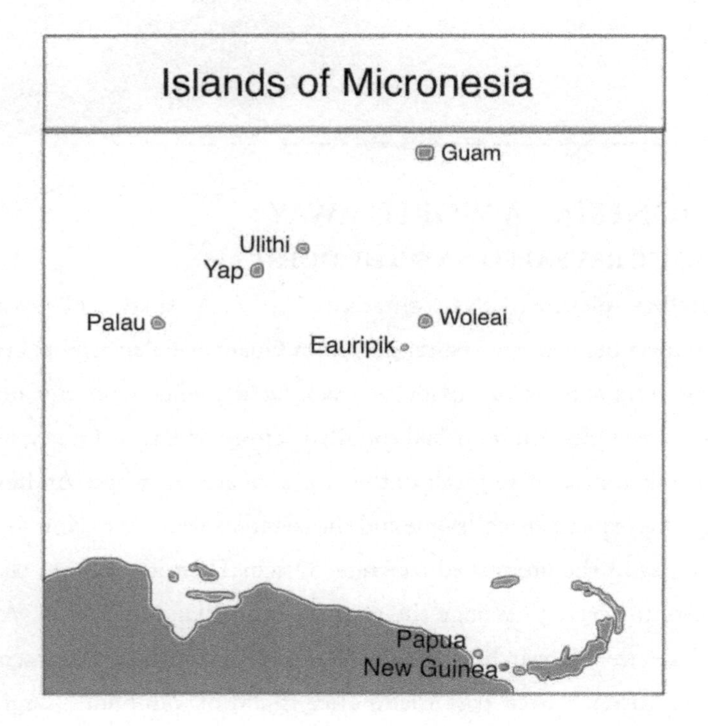

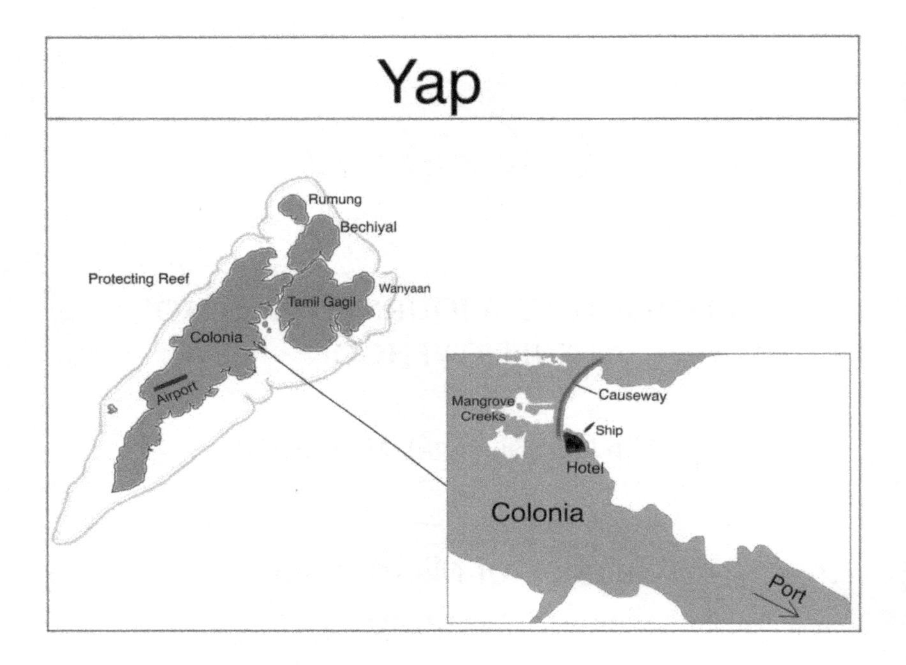

MICRONESIA – A WORLD AWAY

PARADISE REVEALED AND THE QUEST

'... satellite picture... I've contacted Yap...' A snatch of overheard conversation between two passengers from Guam at Palau airport brought chilling recollections of anxiously tracking a typhoon on the internet exactly three years before. It had spiralled across the Pacific Ocean, aiming at Eauripik atoll, a mere speck in the largest of atlases, where Andrew, our son, and his expedition colleague and the islanders were sheltering shoulder to shoulder in the unfinished concrete church. Then it suddenly changed its course to severely damage the neighbouring island of Woleai. A short while later we had watched again on our totally inadequate tiny screen as an angry vortex moved past island after island of Yap State, roughly on the same course as the inter-island ferry carrying them back to Yap's main islands. We were terrified and ignorant as to whether it was ahead of or behind him. Then, as now, April was not the season for typhoons...

So why on earth were we here, in 2004, on one of the Caroline Islands of the Western Pacific Ocean – Yap, north of New Guinea and east of the Philippines? Difficult to explain logically. A lifetime of ephemeral glimpses and images seemed to have imperceptibly fused into a dormant chrysalis of longing to witness, which somehow had imperceptibly transformed itself to emerge as suddenly as a butterfly into a full-blown quest. Remote memories: a child forced to throw a frangipani lei overboard as our ship steamed away – to avert the superstition of never returning to Honolulu; Australian childhood, just that bit too far south; clichés of mission hymn singing; turquoise seas with birds above and fish below – creatures from a zoologist's paradise; laughing eyes and wind-blown black hair decked with flowers; dancing to shrill chanting voices, rhythmic swaying of arms and grass skirts, hypnotic stamping feet; islands clothed in Gaugin-coloured forests, flowers and insects. Then, quite suddenly we had the evidence – the sudden, certain knowledge that this really did still exist, for its own sake, in a remote place, outside of the idyllic dream of 'the beautiful savage' and not as a travel brochure's contrived dream.

Andrew had returned from Eauripik, the smallest inhabited atoll in the Pacific Ocean. For nearly seven months in 2001–2, he had lived as the officially 'adopted' son of a fisherman and his wife in a tiny, close-knit community, one of the most isolated on the planet. He had been renamed 'Fergirang', after a legendary character, and was there by special permission of the tribal chief. His photographs and descriptions of life on Eauripik seemed from a century far back.

Eauripik's hundred people lived without cash or any form of sanitation on this tiny island with a land area of 0.19 square km, (47 acres), one of the outer islands of Yap State in the Federated States of Micronesia. It has one of the highest population densities in the world for a subsistence economy, with a strong reliance on the sea, having fish as the staple diet. There are sixty different methods of fishing, many breathtaking in their ingenuity, based on traditional and practical knowledge of fish behaviour, local environment and the ocean. In the shallow lagoon, some methods required many hands, involving the entire community including children. Out in the open ocean the men used large sailing canoes, one of the last atolls to do so.

In Andrew's 2,000 still photographs grumpy expressions only appeared twice; there was spontaneous singing and dancing for sheer delight and excitement as well as being part of their cultural tradition; lots of giving, and a lot more hardship. Weather and sea often made food limited or scarce in spite of the island's position at the edge of the Indo-Pacific biodiversity hotspot. When good times returned women danced with joy and sang of their men's prowess as fishing canoes loomed into view flying the flag of success – a hundred tuna aboard. A few years previously, the islanders had decided against installing an electric generator enabling them to have a freezer to preserve fish catches in adverse weather. A convenient constant fish supply would have destroyed the social importance of community fishing, and the culture of food sharing between individuals and kin. The installation would also have involved significant felling of coconut trees which they also declined as copra (dried coconut kernel) was a prized food and fallen coconuts helped feed the few pigs they fattened for special communal feasts.

The tropical island dream was alive and well but so was its reality. This was a life of surviving on the edge; living with extreme weather systems; fishing, foraging and eating hand to mouth; putting up with having too little while facing up to difficulties and problems because there were no other options.

Living off a bountiful sea and reef was not a free-for-all. There were lifestyle responsibilities: there were no rules as to fresh water usage but they adapted to not drinking large amounts; personal washing was in the sea and areas of inshore currents sweeping away from the island shore were the latrines. There were strict permanent rules on using natural resources and living within sustainability. Green Turtles could be caught by anyone, but could only be killed by the Tribal Chief; spear fishing at night using flashlights, fishing with gill nets, chlorine and dynamite were banned; coconut crabs caught on the 'larder' island had to be of a minimum size; and coconut cutting could be forbidden by the chief in order to maintain an adequate supply in case of a typhoon emergency. These rules of resource management were an integral part of community life which focused on the sharing of resources within a complicated framework of kinship ties, often between islands.

'2001 Eauripik looks a little different from the 1922 sketch map we unearthed as two islands were taken away by a typhoon in 1975. There are now three islands, Eauripik, Oao and Siting ... on the elliptical reef... which is 7 miles long and 2 miles wide... Eauripik is the only inhabited island... there is one village... of about twenty houses... four canoe houses, the Men's House, the Women's House and two dancing grounds... The centre is the men's dancing ground, a clearing, around which are a very large canoe house which is the chiefs, the Men's House and some other dwellings.... At the four corners of the chief's canoe house are corner-posts of such a size that one is tempted to think they sited the construction on the stumps rather than move the posts... the house is around 60 ft long, 18 ft wide, and 25 ft high in the middle.... Lots of large voyaging canoes, half-hewn timber destined for canoes, fish traps, and assorted gubbins are kept in the house, and the men typically hang around here.'

'All the houses are built on big stone platforms which are surfaced on the top with white coral fragments. The houses themselves are, with the exception of two, all traditionally constructed huts... a steeply sloping thatched roof... generally extended almost to the ground and so to avoid a headful of composting thatch, and indignant geckoes, some stooping is required as one enters through one of the five or six sliding doors with woven palm curtains. The houses are built in a squashed hexagon shape, and inside the floors are of coral rubble with woven palm mats over the top. People sit or sleep on pandanus mats laid on top of the palm mats. Things like fishing gear, looms and coconut graters are stored on the rafters or in the corners of the house.'

'The land around the houses is the most obviously cultivated, and supports a profusion of bananas, small palms, hibiscus, frangipani, spider lily and taro. The main thoroughfares of the village, and the trails outside, look particularly pretty as they are edged with white spider lilies with long trailing petals and huge orange stamens. As regards daily life, things are very much split between male and female jobs. The men go fishing most days (in groups or individually, depending on their quarry) and spend a lot of time crafting their canoes. The women are saddled up with most of the culinary chores, from digging up tubers or collecting fruits right through to serving it up. They also prepare the caught fish, and any meat that might happen their way. Weaving their colourful skirt-like wraps (lavalava) takes up a lot of their time... Men still commonly wear loincloths that do a pretty poor job of covering posterior regions. Not to worry, we're all juvenile enough to laugh about it, quite a lot... it took a short time to learn how to tie mine properly as every man seems to have a different way of doing it, and none of their ways work for me!'

'When fishing the men generally use small paddling canoes... with a Y-shaped prow and stern, and decorated in yellow/red, black and white. These have virtually no draught at all, and in any case can be carried across the barrier reef by one man. There are also quite a few sailing canoes 20–25 ft long, with a gap of 7–8 ft between the outrigger and the hull. The mast and sail are peculiarly curved,

and can be detached from the hull and reversed to switch sailing direction. They can fit thirteen to fourteen people on these canoes. They can go surprisingly fast, and when sailed across the wind the outrigger lifts completely out of the water and the canoe zips along on quite a slant. Having been on a barracuda and wahoo fishing expedition I must say I have the utmost respect for their skills. (I also concurrently wonder quite how they all have five fingers given that they'll happily grab a four-foot barracuda and prise a hook out of its jaws while it is very alive.)'

The risks involved were part of the simple life:

' ...an outrigger sailing canoe that went out this morning capsized, and the mast broke. Having been drifting for ten hours they've just made it back...'

'Other marine fauna such as octopus and giant clams are also caught. The patch reefs outside the Men's House have been cultivated into extensive giant clam nurseries, and so there are piles of them a few metres off shore. Then, of course, there are all the fishing stories... fortuitously catching 700 fish in one leaf sweep and while standing on the reef trying to keep the net under control with sharks, large emperors, 3 ft needlefish, porcupinefish, puffers and giant triggerfish going ape inside... Arguing with a marlin over whose tuna it was and getting sprayed in blood from head to toe when (the remains of) the tuna were pulled in to the canoe... Watching fishermen hand feed hooks to the shoals of jacks as they're so tame... (I was) diving down in the bottomless blue with nothing but shafts of dazzling sunlight and a turtle being wrestled by a loin-clothed fisherman to be seen in any direction.'

'There are a variety of fishing methods used. For kite fishing some men go out to catch a shark (preferably 8–14 ft tiger shark), and once dead they bring it back into the lagoon and land it on the beach. They then butcher it, and remove the spinal cord which has an extremely sticky substance inside, and so is beaten and teased into a network of little threads. This tangle is then attached to the tail of a kite made of breadfruit leaves and flown over the seaward side of the reef so the shark nerve grazes and skips along the surface of the water. Needlefish are attracted to this, and spear

it with their noses, and get entirely stuck; so it is then simply a matter of reeling in the kite and pulling off the needlefish!'

'Oao is the larder island of Eauripik, although it is densely jungled, most areas have been carefully planted with palms, breadfruit, papaya, efooch, banana, taro, etc. There are also large bright-blue coconut crabs, turtle nests and plenty of birds (and nests) such as fairy terns, frigate birds, tropic birds, petrels, etc. When returning on a canoe from Oao the sailing canoes look quite spectacular with produce such as live crabs, small canoes, coconuts, etc. suspended from the outrigger platform ... Turtles and turtle eggs are eaten, but not very often (by special permission from the Chief), which doesn't bother me as turtle fat has a very strong smell which is not altogether pleasant! (When you're handed a cooked flipper that's just been hacked off a cooked turtle there's a reasonable bit of dissecting to do.) Food is generally fish, fish and fish, with a lot of (imported) rice, and some preserved breadfruit, taro and cooked bananas. They also make very nice candy from copra and various coconut syrups and such...'

Aspects of real paradise food emerged from his diary: being presented with fish recooked five times on successive days to stop it putrefying in the heat, having to eat raw baby frigate bird, prolonged extreme constipation, meal after meal without protein when fishing was impossible, three-day-old stale fried doughballs for breakfast, diarrhoea, and a menu where the only variation was the type of fish.

'The reefs... are almost untouched, and have a profusion of species... The marine fauna is given over more to shoals than individual fish, and you often come face to face with hundreds of needlefish, tang, ... parrotfish... coral encrusted vertical spires and drop-offs, walls with huge forests of different soft corals and vertical pinnacles so crammed with corals, sponges and clams that they are tipping off the sides like an overloaded banquet table. Also there's the time we were snorkelling a deep reef and suddenly bumped into large tuna that had come into the lagoon... There is a pod of dolphins, plenty of transient whales and from time to time... manta rays around the

edges of the reef.'

The reef also harboured wrecks, old and recent, perched at crazy angles on the coral. Sadly, makeshift rafts, straws of hope for fleeing refugees, added to their number during his stay, complete with battered domestic bits and pieces and human corpses. The new wrecks sometimes were a source of raw materials and bounty for the islanders. Against this background of a reef's plenty as well as dour realities life was full and enjoyed.

'They had a party... everyone collected in the (Chief's) big canoe house ... and after lots of speeches and hilarity we progressed into local chants and songs ... and local dances... Some dances were plain motions and others were quite flamboyant with people jumping around beating sticks and generally doing Micronesian Morris Dancing! This continued longer than I could stay awake, and so I dozed with the breathtaking stars above, the crashing surf behind and the whirling, singing dancers all around.'

His journey to Eauripik had also been as if from an earlier century: permission to visit not a matter of accustomed visa bureaucracy, but permission from the Council of Chiefs on Yap after extended preliminaries. The voyage from Yap was on a converted 1960s freight ship which sailed a seventeen-day circuit of the outer islands on an irregular basis, depending on possible engine problems, fuel shortage, or untimely deaths requiring transportation of deceased and mourners. Return dates could not be forecast and there could be three months between island visits.

Some of his adopted kin lived on the more accessible Yap. Here was our opportunity to catch a real, albeit sheltered glimpse of this very different world.

Eauripik dug-out outrigger canoe with pandanus and coconut palm ropes: the unfixed mast allows switching bow for stern. The rag flag signals a bumper catch of a hundred tuna. In the distance a shipwreck lies stranded on the encircling reef.

ANTICIPATION

After two years' planning and a year's postponement Peter and I were at last in Yap, a tight cluster of four islands, 100 sq. km. (39 sq. miles) of rolling hills, 9 degrees north of the equator. Thoughts of typhoon talk were pushed from our minds by the sight of a pale turquoise lagoon snaked around with reddish sand in the late afternoon light as our plane came in to land. Customs consisted of a smiling lady festooned with frangipani. Behind the barriers there was a man wearing a thu, a cotton loin cloth with long trails, and a young woman sheltered from the rain. She too was wearing a traditional dress of Yap and Eauripik, the lavalava: a wide strip of cloth wrapped around the body covering from waist to knee and nothing else. Traditionally Yapese men and women are bare above the waist, although the ubiquitous T-shirt had crept into everyday dress in some places.

We had a great sense of relief after the long arduous journey from London and were full of anticipation of a wealth of new experiences. Our thoughts were a kaleidoscope of excited anticipation: waking to the sound of a gentle sea under a bright blue sky, the sensual freshness of tropical breezes, exuberant animal and plant life, snorkelling pristine reefs with maybe a manta ray in the distance, and hymn singing on Easter Sunday a few days hence fit to lift the tin roof off the church with its spontaneous joy and uninhibited total belief.

On a more practical level, there was the immediate anticipation of food and a cooling drink available on board the ship permanently moored by the hotel – which was to assume enormous relevance later. We walked along the angled wooden walkway linking hotel ashore to the moored ship: a massively heavy nineteenth-century Indonesian lumber vessel, 45 m (145 ft) long with a superstructure akin to a pirate ship, something of a fantasy come to life. The sea by our feet was quiet, gently lapping between the ship's hull and the shore. The night was calm; tropical shrubs and flowers crowded the narrow shoreline of garden in front of the hotel. The overheard conversation belonged to another world.

Next morning the view from our balcony was out to the moored ship, her heavy hardwood structure looking even darker against pale sea and sky as grey and gloomy as an English winter's day. Below at the water's edge the luxury rooms' terrace decks were deserted, with large pot plants and giant green sunshades looking superfluous without blue sky and a bright sun. Even so, the heat was already intense and promising to be uncomfortably clammy. During breakfast on board men were carrying new white ropes and lashing down everything in the bow, but we thought little of it.

It was in the manager's office that we caught the whiff of what was to come.

The manager was one of Andrew's contacts from 2001 and he greeted us warmly. We innocently enquired about Easter celebrations and the possibility of a guided bird walk. He directed our gaze towards his computer screen. It showed the projected path of an imminent out-of-season typhoon, Sudal, which was forecast to pass well away from Yap in the night. Horror and annoyance – the overheard conversation was real. Other guests had gathered; one was an oceanographer who explained the basics and we learnt that typhoons and cyclones were the same thing, named according to which hemisphere was the host. His interpretations of Sudal's forecast were optimistic – it was to be a mere 'banana' typhoon – it would only bring down the banana trees.

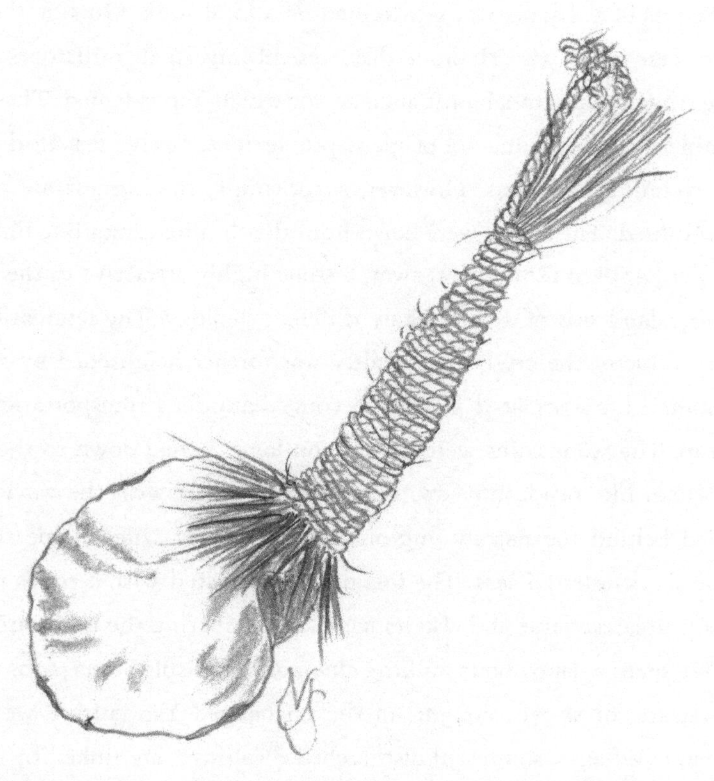

Traditional Yapese money – 'small change': a pearly shell, pierced and mounted on a handle intricately wound round with handmade string of plant fibres.

APPREHENSION

All day preparations continued on the ship: three extra ropes tying her to the road causeway across a neighbouring mangrove swamp as well as to the hotel shore; lashing down the roof of the cabin; battening down hatches; tightly binding the flag to its staff and stowing outdoor chairs and tables. Determined to see something of the vicinity before the storm robbed us of a day or two, we decided on a local walk. Outside the hotel there were some whitish stone discs resembling small millstones. These were stone money, much of it ancient, for which Yap is famed. These were humble in size as some are of giant proportions, twelve feet in diameter and weighing five tons. However, surprisingly, the biggest are not the most valued. The stones were hewn from the shining crystalline limestone of Palau, 450km (280 miles) away, a stone highly attractive to the Yapese whose island was of a completely different geology. The fascination and rarity value of the crystalline quality was further heightened by the loss of human life associated with each coin's hazardous transportation back to Yap. The stone coins were 'strung' on logs, carried down to the shore, and then, like pendulums swinging unpredictably with the waves, were trailed behind the narrow dug-out canoes as they sailed home through fickle shark-infested seas. The loss of life associated with a coin's journey gave it greatest value and also its name, remembering the lost mariners.

We spent a happy hour walking along one of the old stone paths nearby, a foretaste, or so we thought, of the unchanged Yap culture we would see later. Villages, some still of thatched dwellings, are linked by ancient cobbled paths, often lined by the stone money discs of the ancient village 'bank', many too heavy to move so statically changing in ownership for traditional transactions. Andrew had described impressive long sequences of these along the edges of these ancient thoroughfares, and had advised us if walking less-frequented paths we should observe the traditional etiquette of carrying a leaf as a sign that our visit was peaceful. As our path was near the edge of the main town of Colonia rather than linking remote villages we gathered this courtesy was unnecessary.

Winding uphill, our path was as wide as a town pavement, with a central trail of large, carefully placed, smooth stones, flanked each side by a jigsaw of less worn smaller stones encrusted with moss and tiny plants. The path was edged with lush green hedges, some neatly clipped and spattered with red starry flowers. Beyond the hedges there was a wall of every shade of green blocking out the sky: tall bamboos, many sorts of palms – betel nut palms, coconut palms, mango trees, ficus plants and great spreading dark breadfruit trees giving a delicious shade from overhanging branches. Their trunks and branches were festooned with small ferns and aerial plants dangling roots in mid-air hovering over various types of bananas, pawpaw trees, white and pink frangipanis and red hibiscus, and below them, crimson-flowered ginger, lilies and taro patches. A beautiful black and yellow birdwing butterfly flitted in front of us and was gone. Invisible birds continually called to each other as they worked their way through the treetops; two Red Cardinal Honeyeaters crossed our path in a blur of speed.

Amidst this tropical exuberance hurried footsteps sounded above homely sounds of chickens scratching amongst logs and distant competing cockerels. It was our hotel manager, on his way home to lunch he said, but it transpired he was about to board up his windows and close his house.

A voice came from behind: 'Hey you guys, do you have a problem? Are you lost?' A young woman appeared with a large cluster of white flowers in her hair. I avoided admiring the flowers – earlier in the hotel I had exclaimed at a frangipani lei crowning an immaculate woman scrubbing the floor. Introducing herself as Kathie she had smiled, removed the tightly woven band of palm leaf and flowers from her hair and had presented it to me regardless of my protestations. We now explained we were exploring; Mary introduced herself and as we chatted she grinned at Kathie's lei in my hair and gave me her flowers. She consented to have her photograph taken as a memento and we left, now festooned with scented flowers given by smiling strangers.

Lunchtime was surreal. There are very few places to eat on Yap, maybe because traditionally men ate separately from women and different castes did not eat together. The tiny Indonesian cafe which Andrew had recommended was deserted but not silent. On the walls were 1940s newspapers of VJ Day in the Pacific, the battle of Palau and faded war-time photographs of Yap under Japanese administration. The radio was at full volume giving loud continuous broadcasts as to safe evacuation structures, concrete schools, churches, and Colonia's supermarket. It was as if we had entered a 1940s time warp and were expecting an air-raid. The reality was that these were instructions for people in every village on their nearest shelter from the coming typhoon. The cafe proprietor appeared – a World War II veteran, called Mr. Lucky. He proudly put on a competing American video of compilations of 40s and 50s Pacific War footage and turned up the volume control in competition with the radio. Pathe News war clips were a ghostly memory for me, having lived in relatively close-by Australia during the Indochina and Korean troubles. We ate our lunch to a barrage of gunfire and optimistic proud commentary from the video and the insistent urgency of the voice on the radio. Mr Lucky's eyes were distant, smiling inwardly at personal war-time memories: on the wall by our table was a very faded curling photo of three Yapese men, used as slave labour, building a runway with shovels for the Japanese. By the side was a letter written in stilted English by the Japanese man who had taken the picture asking if Mr Lucky could trace the three men; he had tried hard he said, but had not yet succeeded. As he turned the gunfire yet louder we assured him there was no need on our account, but to no avail. Maybe muzak does have its good points...

Outside it was raining hard and the sky was heavy with grey cloud. Banana trees were already falling like blades of grass. Back at the hotel the oceanographer was getting more and more excited as typhoon predictions were updated and prospects worsened. At 1 p.m. the typhoon was apparently in the region of Ulithi atoll, 191 km (119 miles) to the north-east and by midnight was expected to be passing 40 miles north of Yap. Snorkelling prospects during our three-day stay on Yap now looked grim – but bearable – as we were booked to fly to Ulithi for a five-day stay on the shore of its enormous lagoon, a holy grail of underwater exploring.

The evening atmosphere on board the hotel ship was one of partying, anticipation and making the best of things – easy gestures over full glasses of wine and plates of hot fresh food. Everyone had navigated the walkway to the ship in driving rain, carefully hanging on, its treads now a slippery stream. At 6:45 the *frisson* of excitement at the screaming wind in rigging and streaming rain down windows turned to startled apprehension. The metal roof of the walkway was banging and ripping as it lifted free. From then on through the night there was incessant hammering and shouting as men laboured trying to keep the walkway to the ship intact. Safely ashore, excitement turned to horror as the latest satellite pictures and computer projections of the typhoon's changing path carved through carefully planned itineraries and holiday daydreams. It had shifted and would pass not north, but 40 miles south-west of us at 3 a.m. The oceanographer told typhoon tales, theorised and calculated speeds, path and times, relentlessly and loudly, finally reassuring us we'd all be snorkelling and diving as if nothing had happened by Sunday – so all not lost yet. In blissful ignorance of future developments, we all resolved to set our alarms for 3 a.m. to witness this unavoidable bit of Life's Mixed Pageant. When we returned to our room, our balcony furniture and potted palms were already stowed inside.

Weather satellite picture: the sidewall of the eye of the storm was positioned over Yap for over twenty-four hours. (Photograph from the US National Oceanic and Atmospheric Administration.)

REAL AND SURREAL – SUPERTYPHOON

THE FIRST NIGHT

By 8:30 p.m. mains electricity was off and the hotel generator joined the cacophony of sounds of squealing wind and great gobs of spattering rain hurling down against our windows. Now, reliant on a generator, it was essential services only: a couple of lights and sometimes the ceiling fan.

All through the night men continued trying to stay and prop the walkway from underneath. By midnight it was at a crazy angle to the ship. Three hours later the ship was being blown closer in towards the hotel:

only a narrow band of turbulent water showed beyond the tossing shrubs still attached in the garden strip on the retaining wall below us. At 5 a.m. the ship and its walkway parted company and splintered planks and limp electric cables were engulfed by waves. As we watched, the remains of the walkway swivelled sideways and the ships stern pushed closer and closer to the hotel wall. Finally, at 6 o'clock the walkway collapsed sideways completely and disappeared into the heaving sea of wreckage whilst the ship lurched almost onto the shoreline wall directly below.

In the relative safety of our room the water had gone off at 4:15 a.m. and an hour later the generator had stopped as well. For hours we watched, mesmerised by the squalling wind, water being jetted in horizontal sheets and layers of rain rivulets streaming down our windows creating fractured multiple images of the rocking mast and uncontrolled spinning ship's wheel. It was a strange feeling. Neither of us said anything about being afraid: neither of us were – we felt almost no conscious emotion. It was as if we were disconnected as we watched, riveted, bemused, in a state of suspended disbelief, just waiting for what might happen next. We were no longer in control, we had become part of an unreal world of melodrama on a wide screen, but now we were inside the screen and the disaster movie was happening before our eyes and it was soon to be all around.

When our fly screen was ripped off and away, the outside glass door continually opened; we jammed an upturned chair to keep it shut. With the balcony door securely closed, the curtain in front of it still billowed into the room like a fluttering flag. We stood well back from the glass. The wind screamed, sea, silt and rain sprayed through every sealed window and door joint, a small waterfall cascaded over electric sockets and down the chest of drawers onto the sheet of water that was now the floor. The soles of our shoes squelched as we emptied the drawers of their contents into carrier bags. The water spraying in was as if for a carwash – as Peter said, *'This is like being in a washing machine'*. Heavy ceramic roof tiles were flying and smashing, and with sounds of breaking glass we closed the curtains and propped the furniture and palm tree against them to slow things up if the glass door broke. Cold practicalities and keeping vigilant against dangers left no space for thoughts of fear.

When dawn lightened the sky we peered out through wooden blinds and could make out vague silhouettes of streaming ribbon-like palms tossing on the opposite headland. The wind was pushing white-topped waves inland towards the road causeway and whipping off shimmering plates of horizontal spray. We could make out refrigerators, bedside lamps, kayaks, bits of dive shop and beds sweeping past on surging brown waves below our windows. The ship twisted away, then back yet again, stern tight into the hotel wall and nearly onto our balcony, her cabin roof in line with our window on the second floor. With a real danger now of the ship smashing our balcony and room we got dressed and threw a few essentials of medications, cameras, left over water bottles and snack food into carrier bags and put them by the door ready to run. I jammed basic bedding and the presents for Andrew's friends and kin into the wardrobe. At 6:30 a.m. the telephone rang and we were evacuated from our room.

PEOPLE DISCONNECTED

Downstairs people were gathering in reception. They were coping with the night's drama in their very different ways. A quiet Filipino lady sat in the corner with a toddler and a young child; she smiled, and we discovered later she was the manager's wife. There was a group who knew each other, obviously a tour group, a few of whom we had met over the typhoon forecasts the previous night, but their attention was focused into their communal huddle while some quipped and made hollow jests. An inappropriately preened matron, like a self- appointed queen bee, presided over them all from the only comfortable chair – in fact her grasp was expanding over the whole proceedings. Her chief attendant was an equally manicured woman, glamorous, blonde and tough. She behaved like someone in authority but we were not sure of her exact context as she fluttered between the queen bee and the hotel staff and ignored all the other guests. The queen bee bore the privilege of her luxury bedroom's dramatic damage with pride; she relaxed back her head elegantly with closed eyes, waking to arrest each passer-by with the challenge of had they heard her windows pop.

Tightly packed next to me on a cane sofa, a young couple seemed oblivious to the whole proceedings as the escalating passion of their writhing embraces left no doubt as to the nature of their response to thrilling physical danger. We boring British, by contrast, busied ourselves with practical details – keeping splitting plastic carrier bags and spilling contents together and out of the growing puddles. Rain was spattering in with sudden fierce gusts forcing open the securely closed doors. A shy English member of the Dive Shop team was cutting microtome thin slices of banana bread more suited to a vicarage tea party on an immaculate lawn; she offered a slice together with a welcome small bottle of water for each guest. A French family appeared to be taking it all in their stride, occasionally peering at the typhoon's progress through the swinging outside doors.

In this part of the hotel sounds were intense and different. There was a continuous shrill squealing, so loud one had to shout. It was wind whistling under doors as we had never heard before. On the other side of each flimsy door the full force of the wind now raged unchecked; most south-facing windows had been blown in with an explosive bang around

6 a.m. The doors were now the only remaining barriers against wind and rain and the force was too much for them. Sounds of urgent hammering heightened the noise as baulks of timber were hammered across doors and frames. The relentless wind still screeched through the remaining gaps, like a crazed demon transforming doors into giant threads vibrating in an unearthly Aeolian harp.

We decided to ring Andrew to set his mind at rest as he may look at a Pacific weather website to see our holiday prospects. We were ushered to a seafront downstairs room still intact and with a telephone. Unknown to us, Andrew could hear the sea thrashing against the large window and the noise of surging detritus outside, a sound he knew all too well. After the call he logged on to Yap airport weather information and had an uneasy night when all went silent for 6 hours. On Yap, just after our phone call, all contact with the outside world was lost.

The last typhoon path predictions had shown the night's events were just the warm-up. The real thing was still on its way towards Yap – a supertyphoon with 200 kph (130 mph) gusts.

Two hours later outside the front door, tall bamboos streamed out in horizontals and tossing branches, uprooted trees and heavy roof tiles crashed down with the squalling rain. Oil and petrol drums rolled about like marbles leaking out their contents. Parked cars and vans rocked, buffeted and dented, windscreens and windows shattered. On the other side of the road the corrugated iron roof of the Chinese store was beginning to heave and strain, banging backwards and forwards and starting to lift away.

At the same time on the sea side of the hotel, the ship's bow had moved closer in towards the terrace decks on the ground floor. Standing back at a safe distance we peered through a plate glass door; the ship was only a few metres away, rocking in a high sea. Tall patio trellises disconnected as a frothing white wave surged up over the terrace and hit the glass in front of us. A large shade shelter collapsed and disappeared. Twisted and cockeyed, the trellises bounced away into the stream of wreckage coming from the dive shop. Waves sprawled and slopped over the raised deck floors and panels pitched and heaved in all directions as they and their pier supports began to break free. With that the elegant terraces had now completely gone. The central concrete Jacuzzi pool might be left, somewhere down there under the murky surge. The thick plate glass door in front of us, now leading to a non-existent terrace, shook as each brown and white wave hurled at the glass, turning it momentarily into a room-height aquarium view.

Seeing this we judiciously moved ourselves and our wet belongings onto the first floor and made an encampment by the stairwell with a couple of chairs – uncomfortable with people going up and down stairs and squeezing by. Further along sat Julie, the receptionist, quietly making betel to chew, worried stiff about the fate of her daughter and grandchildren in a distant village. All the corridors around us were lined with suitcases, ready for a sudden exodus. Most of the passers-by were from an extraordinarily expensive cruise tour, and were rounding off their yachting/snorkelling exclusive round the outer atolls with a few days of Yap's manta rays and traditional culture. Some were never quite sure which islands they had actually visited, some were numbed silent and wide-eyed, looking totally shell-shocked, but all unanimous in their immediate requirement of an exclusive undamaged suite in which to rest undisturbed... with room service. We, the few other guests and the Yapese staff, squatted in the corridors amidst hammering, shouting and the noise of ongoing destruction, sometimes thinking of a drink of water. Below us, the sea had begun to creep under the downstairs doors, seeping through improvised towel dams and trickling into corridors.

Outside, the roof of the Chinese store opposite finally succumbed and ripped off with a loud bang and the four walls stood like a stark island in a lagoon of sea, which a short time before had been just a grassy sward. The wind shifted round to the south-east. The ship was being pushed hard back yet again, dragging its four 5-ton anchors and swivelling with the force of the waves. Her stern was now level with our vacated balcony and gradually moved back and back perilously close to the corner of the building. The sea became wilder, its surface undulating murky grey mounds capped with white, sometimes barely visible through the driving rain and spray. Slowly the ship was pushed further back towards the road until her bridge was opposite us with the stern hanging over the causeway. She lurched over onto her port side at what looked like a catastrophic angle as spray broke over the bowsprit.

Indoors, water slowly seeping into the ground floor corridors transformed into a flow as a slowly escalating tidal wave burst through the downstairs windows. It surged through the hotel, engulfing bedrooms, the office, reception area, souvenir shop, dive photography and workshop and swept out of the front doors. The ground floor was now flooded with dark brown stinking water swirling about with a viscous surface of the shimmering rainbow colours of escaped oil. Looking over the banister rail made one feel distinctly sea sick, with ripples slurping and slopping as more black waves laden with sewage surged in with every movement of the sea outside.

Looking tentatively out of a window, cupboards, shelves and boxes were bobbing about in the car park outside the front doors as the car park, road, causeway and the creek were transforming into one continuous racing sea, brown with silt and fuel oil. Swept along in the turmoil were half boats, complete boats, branches, coconut palms, fuel drums, twisted corrugated iron, kayaks, a fridge, roof joists, bits of walls and windows, animals and coconuts while car roofs and windscreens stood out like islands. The sea was now on all sides of the building as well as through it. It was 12 noon.

We and our carrier bags were above water on the first floor, but our passports and money were below in a safe in the hotel office. Peter ventured downstairs. The office was dark: desks stood out like murky islands around which papers, printout and computers and telephones bobbed about or sank into wet darkness. Under there was all manner of office paraphernalia, like a submerged assault course. As the surface swirled about like a choppy miniature sea, electric sockets were exposed for a few seconds before being slurped over and concealed once more. While Peter let the slurping subside between surges, it occurred to him that electric currents might still be live... but then other people were wading about nearby without harm... He grabbed our torch, rolled up his trousers and waded in. The water was up to his groin. Beneath his feet oozing piles of papers squelched into the stinking sludge of sewage and he could feel it creeping up between his toes. The safes were still above water and only needed the one key to open. Our passports and money were unharmed.

Tiles were still smashing down amidst sounds of breaking glass and the stench of petrol had become overpowering all over the hotel. We returned to our room to escape it, but that too smelt appalling. We put face wipe tissues over our faces to act as air filter masks and to cover up the sickening smell. Water was fountaining through the window joints onto the drawer unit making a pool. We tried to use it to wash an apple and it transpired that the decorative marbled pattern on the surface beneath was not meant to be there - it was reddish silt brought in with the driving rain. We peeled and ate the apple and kept the core in case things came to that level of desperation. We had been up for the last thirty-two hours – with only a brief night's rest in between three previous days of travelling without proper sleep and with jet lag. We were hungry and thirsty. We rested for a while trying not to sweat and to conserve energy ready to remake the bed with the damp salty bedding which we had fortunately stowed well away from the windows so it was not actually sodden. Foul water was everywhere and we faced the exhausting task of somehow cleaning up our room enough to live in it a while.

Our immediate task was to try and mop up the water from surfaces and floor; the loo badly needed flushing so we decided to combine both operations. We mopped up water with a towel and squeezed it into a carrier bag in the hope of finally filling the cistern, but as we trickled water in it dribbled straight through the cistern and out again. Peter decided to go scrounging and returned with a dustpan for scooping up the floor lagoon and soon filled an old paint bucket with which we bypassed the cistern – victory! I unpacked for the second time in two days and sorted things into survival and non-essentials. With all this physical activity the room was beginning to steam up, it was 100% humidity and the floor remained thoroughly wet. The wind was still roaring so windows could not be opened beyond a crack and the ceiling fan was not working. We had long since finished the small bottles of water we had been given early in the morning, so we sipped the little left in our hand luggage from the flight.

Having achieved a very damp floor and a slightly damp bed in a sizzling hot room with no prospect of electricity or water, we took stock of our situation. We were under no illusions that the next few days were going to be an assault course for two over 60s somewhat restricted in activity. Our goal was basic survival. The hotel's supplies of drink and food storage were in the ship marooned on the rocks; apparently one of the hotel staff and the manager's wife were trying to improvise a makeshift feeding set-up. We had seen the one local shop lose half its roof so it could probably be discounted. We had some food oddments of cereal bars and compressed fruit brought for our planned snack lunches with a packet of salty crackers, two apples, six carrots and a box of pineapple juice bought on arrival which, at a pinch, could take us both through a few days. The water situation was more serious. We had a few small bottles from the journey. We still were in total ignorance as to whether there was a desalinator and whether electricity was a prerequisite for the hotel's 'highly efficient water purification system' or if the advertised 20,000 gallon water storage tank would be sanitary when and if water came out of the pipes once more.

If we were unable to continue our journey to Ulithi as planned, our final flight out of Yap was eight days away. On an island with no clean water, no electricity and not much food, it could be a long haul; hardly the paradise of our dreams. It was a grim prospect in the company of a tour group more used to prodigal luxury than hardship. How long would the obviously scant supplies of bottled water last? How long before thirst, hunger and irritability affected people adversely?

Peter went on a sortie to see what was going on in the corridors and returned with the information that the tour group were ensconced in their quiet suite and having cups of hot coffee and cookies brought in on trays. Those who shouted loudest obviously got. With hunger and thirst gnawing at us we had a choice of either depleting our emergency rations or following suit and asking the hotel for food and drink. Being a true British gentleman Peter was in favour of not bothering the hotel as they were preoccupied with cleaning up; being of Australian inclination by upbringing and never travelling without ultimate emergency food and water I was all for holding back our rations in case things got really dire, and reminding the hotel that there were other guests out there.

Peter set off once more under duress. On the ground floor and in the corridors, hotel staff and the few young divers were sweeping water and mud and mopping up mess. Others, like us, were salvaging their rooms. Many seemed to have had supplies of Coke and crisps – not a great combo for surviving dehydration, but they were young and energetic. Half an hour later Peter returned having smelt food, whereabouts at present unknown, and continuing along the trail, sniffer-dog style, he located a first-floor room with a small kitchen hastily furnished with low coffee tables, a few odd chairs, picnic plates and oddments of cutlery. The wonderful smell of food salvation was Spam (sort of fried), tinned cocktail sausages, some tepid tinned spaghetti and meatballs, eaten on a single knife or teaspoon depending on availability. The tinned food and juice had just been bought at the wrecked Chinese store opposite: as someone put it *'Open to the rain and open for business!'* With rain still blasting horizontal I could only risk poking the disposable underwater camera around the edge of the fire door to get a photo of these heroic proprietors standing, apparently smiling at the opening of their remnant shop, one clasping a calculator in a plastic bag while the other was sweeping wet detritus into forlorn piles.

The lukewarm Spam and cold spaghetti with two mini meatballs were delicious in spite of being the remnants left after the luxury party had already had the pick and retreated to their allocated suite. It was becoming apparent that the hotel management was so totally preoccupied with trying to salvage the ship and haul it off the rocks that domestic arrangements had slipped to a low priority and were on an ad hoc basis. There was no crisis plan or rationing of food or bottled water and no indication of if and when food might be available again. It was first find it, then first come, first served: survival of the fittest. In the face of competition from fellow guests, some of whom might charitably be described as 'life's professional survivors' it might be imagined as a stage set for a *Lord of the Flies* scenario or a 'murder weekend', a particularly vivid one, when a group in isolation find their backs to the wall. Yap telephone and internet communications had been lost and our part of Colonia was totally isolated from the outside world; it was just hotel guests with limited and fast diminishing supplies of water and food.

Feeding, watering and keeping vaguely sanitary were everyone's priorities. People were on the defensive, and now some became stealthy, quietly sidling into rooms, hopefully unattended, as if to plant evidence – but their target seemed to have a more practical bathroom-oriented purpose. Our first uninvited guest was the oceanographer. He burst in without knocking and on seeing us hesitated, then loudly launched into details of supertyphoons. This one had behaved inexplicably contrary to the norm of travelling north from the equator in the northern hemisphere, and had abruptly changed course and swung south and encircled the island. To us, in our sleep deprived state, he seemed to be jabbering and capering with accelerating excitement – to the point of incoherent jargon. With the stranded ship and ravaged island visible out of the window behind him, the interlude was approaching the edge of a surreal caricature of *The Tempest* in which he could only be cast as Caliban. Maybe in reality he was not heading for our bathroom at all, and had come to view the ship or to educate us further in the ways of typhoons.

Soon after his exit, another member of our impromptu cast entered unannounced. The door opened slowly and furtively – in a better theatrical production it would have creaked and groaned – and the very vague male member of the tour group sidled in sideways towards the bathroom door. Earlier, intent on photographing the typhoon outdoors he had been oblivious of the danger of high-speed flying tiles, and now he was equally unaware he was being observed as he moved with intent towards the lavatorial facilities. We intercepted and his exit was one of bemused disappointment. There was obviously some opportunism afoot as few guests had had cause in their previous lives to understand the working of a lavatory cistern let alone had to improvise flushing. Our latest visitor in appearance and behaviour was suited to a Transylvanian scene and he assumed a starring role in our little drama as the 'phantom crapportunist'. It was at this point we deemed it sensible to always lock the room during our short absences.

Eventually we slept through sheer exhaustion until hunger and thirst woke us at 10 p.m. We 'midnight feasted' like naughty school kids on a small snack bar each and some water – 'dinner'. Out of the window, the wind was still blowing hard, but headlights were moving tentatively on the opposite shore.

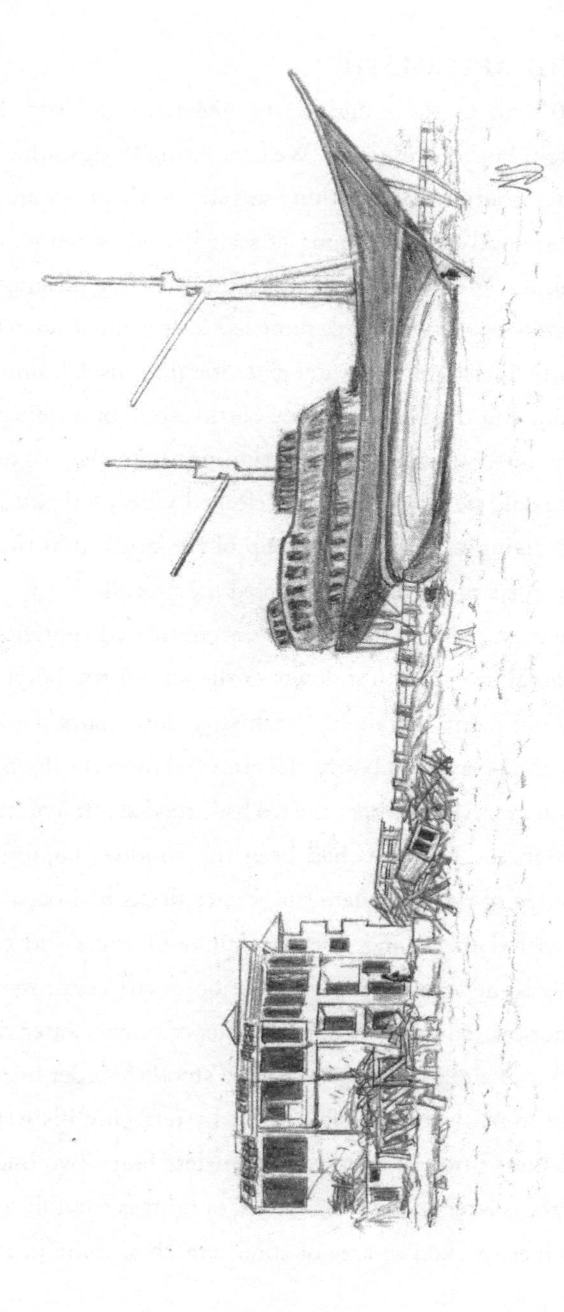

Seen from the sea, the beached ship and derelict hotel with a few roof tiles remaining, dive shop in splinters, and remnants of terraces and the walkway between ship and building. The stern overhangs the causeway road and the deck is tilted diagonally; a man standing under the bow gives scale.

EXISTING IN THE AFTERMATH

We woke at 5:30 a.m. to the sound of the generator and very limited electricity – one light but no ceiling fan. We kept losing things, which made us more irritable, more fatigued. Everything was sticky with salt water which had continuously sprayed through joints of sealed window frames – chair cushions were soaking. We 'washed' using a mini travelling cleanser cream and one ball of cotton wool – only three more left for the duration, whatever that might be. Early 'breakfast' was water and vitamin pills. Cleaning teeth consisted of first dipping the brush into one bottle capful of drinking water between us, applying toothpaste, then spitting out onto the lavatory seat and basin so they could be wiped over and cleaned with toothpaste (albeit second-hand) like diving masks. Another dip of the brush into the cap of water followed by an energetic shake completed the process.

The next project was the lavatory and its accumulated contents. Peter embarked on a foraging expedition down to the site of the hotel terrace which yielded an old paint container. The luxury downstairs rooms were now accessible, with the typhoon barricades removed from the doors. There was silt and filth on everything where the sea had stood about a metre deep. He stepped through the hole that had been the window, hoping to dip for water at the edge of the sea where the terrace decks had been. Newly exposed pipes, twisted metal and uneven chunks of stone and concrete obstructed his way so he transferred his attention to the gaunt remains of the Jacuzzi. It was now reduced to a concrete box of brown water rising in absurd isolation out of a relatively calm sea and stood shoulder high above him. He managed to reach its accessible water by retracing his steps back into the hotel and out through another windowless hole. Two bucketfuls up two flights of stairs later and we had lift off, or more accurately a flushed loo. Antiseptic wipes, packed in case of coral scratches, came in for hand cleansing afterwards, and in anticipation of the continuing procedure all wet wipes were cut in half so there would be enough for cleaning hands before eating. When these ran out we planned to substitute loo roll moistened with perfume and aftershave, expensive but at least solvent based and better than nothing.

As it became lighter the gloom of the grey scene came into focus: limp remnants of isolated palm trees amongst fallen trunks; contorted iron roofs tilted, upended, dented, torn, and relocated; boats on land, roofs in sea. The ship looked colossal, now high up the shore, heavy stern overhanging the road causeway. Her flag and flagstaff were gone and, as if in substitute, the waves had flung coloured rags and torn plastic over her ropes. They hung limply, draped like grotesque bunting. Around the ship, splintered wood, planks from the ship's walkway, tree branches, oil drums and kayaks formed heaps of detritus and cars were creeping a slow meandering obstacle course. People picked up pieces here and there, clearing the way – like moving a haystack one straw at a time. Distant figures and groups moved slowly amongst ruins, unsure, disbelieving, dazed at where to start. The sky turned bright and the day started to heat up under a heavy haze.

Sniffing sorties revealed breakfast – black tea or hot water, Spam stirred into scrambled eggs and warm toast. There was a treat of banana bread, that is, if one was quick off the mark and grabbed both courses in one go. He who hesitated with the niceties of separate courses went without. Fair play, sharing or rationing had no place here.

Some of the tour group, having had the first pick, talked excitedly amongst themselves of hopes of being evacuated in a military plane, and of bargain paintings and ancient artefacts in a local gallery which had weathered the typhoon. In another corner, three European guests worried over a seventeen-year-old son who after two days would still not get out of bed and was refusing all food and drink as a protest that he was not having his diving holiday as promised. No bottles of water were available which confirmed our suspicions it was every man for himself over the road at the dwindling storehouse of the Chinese shop.

Here the floor was awash, being swept and slopped out along with wet, unsalvageable stock. There were shelves of bilious bright pink trinkets, cheap toys and Chinese lanterns, now superfluous in competition with equally bilious pink tea and pink watermelon drink. We bought some of these in spite of the colour, their saving grace being the water content. All straight bottled water had already gone. Some biscuits and chocolate bars completed our meagre stores which would have to last until who knew when.

Outside there were shattered blue roof tiles blown from the hotel roof 50 m (55 yds) away. Palm trees had been remoulded by the south-east wind, some with fronds standing erect at extreme angles unnatural to growth, as if caught on film in frozen motion. The road and the causeway were littered with broken timbers and detritus, from which a name board protruded – *Microspirit*; this was the all-purpose ferry on which Andrew had travelled to Eauripik. The *Microspirit* herself was half a mile away up the bay. Everywhere there was a filthy brown blanket covering ripped remnants of the lush vegetation of two days before. Silt coated the rubbish, all now strewn with bits of plastic and glass, splintered planks, protruding nails, twisted iron, road and shop signs, an occasional toy. A one-eyed ET, threadbare with loving, lay filthy in the road amongst torn plastic bags and muddy chunks of coral.

At the roadside a large spreading tree, carefully dressed with bright blue uniform strips of cloth and plastic, was now further festooned with multi-coloured plastic rubbish, caught in a twiggy net. Rubbish and tree dressing had closed the full circle. Chickens scratched amongst the rubbish and pecked at broken coconuts – how on earth had they survived? Here and there traditional coconut palm roofs remained intact, albeit often tilted off centre.

The heat and humidity were intense, held still by a solid roof of grey-brown haze. We dripped sweat under panama sunhats that felt like heated helmets. Regardless of the heat, everywhere there were sounds of chain saws freeing house remains from tree trunks, hammering of salvage back into useful shelter and machetes swiping at branches and brash. Men shovelled mud, women prepared food al fresco with their homes scattered in pieces around them. People gathered unspoilt fallen coconuts and walked from the remains of the hardware store precariously carrying new primus stoves full of fuel. Amazingly, and in keeping with Yapese etiquette, everyone greeted us with friendly smiles as we walked by, and each other. A pretty young woman with flowing black hair, a Gaugin-like beauty, was swinging serenely chatting with her friends and smiling at us as if she were on the classic Fragonard swing – but hers was an old bicycle tyre hung from a branch over the quagmire of a mangrove swamp thick with rubbish and debris. I longed to capture this incredible moment on film – it illustrated everything we were learning about Yapese attitudes and culture, but we knew enough to know that to take a photograph would have been a gross intrusion of privacy and the depth of bad manners in her eyes. She must remain an unforgettable image in the mind, along with all the people of that morning. Photographs of their devastated surroundings taken well out of their range must serve as reminders of their presence.

We were looking for a particular house, a pink house apparently, or its remains maybe, belonging to Andrew's Eauripikese 'uncle' so we could deliver the large parcel of gifts. We picked our way carefully round the rubble and heaps obstructing the road. Drivers were also tentatively navigating the tortuous route and smiled and waved thanks with Yapese etiquette as we stood back out of their way. We squeezed along the car queue outside the one petrol station and everyone greeted us as we passed – a macho looking guy in bright purple and pink T-shirt and headband, and a 4WD cheered with bunches of pink starry tinsel from mirror to dashboard; men in mud-stained T-shirts, a woman in clean dazzling white, a pedestrian dressed in thu and flip-flops, a large lady reminiscent of Queen Salote with green and white orchids tucked behind her ear, most of them chewing betel, all able to smile warmly.

On the causeway the cars stopped abruptly. Something was happening beneath the colossal overhanging stern of the stranded ship. People lifting detritus from the road had also stopped and turned away. A European voice shouted in erupting anger, 'If you come back tomorrow I'll have the themed T-shirts for you...' The obstruction dispersed: the luxury tour group removed themselves and their intrusive eighteen video cameras off the road; the waiting cars then continued threading their way through and those clearing rubbish continued their miserable task unmolested by prying lenses.

Inland from the causeway, the creek stank stagnant with more than a hint of sewage. Between the arches of mangrove roots there were movements of fish. A mental picture conjured by Andrew flashed across my mind – an eccentric male relative who stayed at his 'uncle's' bungalow habitually sat on the veranda chewing betel while taking wild pot shots at the creek fish with a rifle. His success rate was somewhat impaired by the occasional intake of an entire large jar of instant coffee in one day – the resultant shaking hands reducing his accuracy of aim to nil, but he persevered in hope and inadvertently ensured the other members of the household were always totally awake. The fish were small and camouflaged with dark brown blotches, almost as if finger-marked by the grasp of a clumsy fisherman. These were Banded Archerfish, with the ability to see through the water and up into the air above, somehow taking into account the bending of the light as it passed from one to the other, which was beyond the capability of the human aiming the rifle.The fish are 20 cms (8 inches) long. They can accurately aim at an insect resting on foliage up to 3 m (nearly 10 ft) above them and spit a jet of water to knock it out of the air to drop into their open mouths. The force is such that at close range, drops hitting a human face cause a stinging sensation. New studies have revealed the fish can change the speed and stability of the droplets by opening and closing its mouth at different speeds. Adults almost always hit the jackpot first shot; juveniles have to persevere and learn – maybe these were the inspiration for the misguided optimism of the armed man on the veranda. I remembered this incredible fish from a childhood book of the 1950s, *The Strangest Creatures on Earth*, and smiled at this incongruous sighting which was the realisation of a childhood ambition. Amongst stench and chaos there was still a touch of underwater wonder.

On the low hills behind which had been our green paradise walk of two days before, there were a few untidy piles of wood and corrugated iron which had slid down crabwise and straddled leaning trees – all that remained of Mary's house or her neighbours. The Micronesian Starlings and red nectar-eaters were silent – if they were there. Mr. Lucky's cafe had lost part of its roof. The windows and door were well boarded up – it looked for all the world as if it too had become part of the Pacific War still raging within its walls. By the creek side there was an orange bungalow which unbelievably had gained a second roof, all cockeyed, while precariously perched up behind it were the crumbled roofless walls of its rightful owner. Household furniture was stacked about to dry and in the midst of all this, two large ladies were hacking turtle meat with cleavers, one clad in the ubiquitous T-shirt, the other, bare-breasted, in traditional dress of a dark blue and white striped lavalava and an extravagant hair clasp. They cheerily returned our greetings, smiles reddened with betel chewing, and we continued our quest for a pink house.

Eventually we discovered they were our destination. Their surprise at our reappearance was predictable. It was difficult to know how to begin, so I settled for *'Hello! We are the parents of Fergirang!'* In reply, came open-mouthed amazement, then laughter and wild gesticulations from the lady in the T-shirt, translating in rushes to her companion who gasped, gazing at us in disbelief. Tears of joyful memories trickled down her cheeks, she exclaimed incomprehensibly and rushed to grasp our outstretched hands, but suddenly remembered the turtle blood and hurriedly washed under the rain water tank, repeating *'Fergirang! Fergirang!'* She clutched our hands kissing them. We had never had such a welcome in our lives: it was our golden memory of Yap. It transpired they were the sister and sister-in-law (Jo) of Andrew's 'father' on Eauripik. We gave them gifts from Britain and agreed to their invitation for an evening meal when they sent word that Andrew's 'uncle' was home. As harbourmaster he was heavily involved on the Disaster Committee dealing with the post-typhoon chaos.

We picked our way through mud and puddles back to the hotel. I noticed with relief that the heavy stone money coins stood unharmed by the wall. The heat was now indescribable but the hard work on the road clearing since we left was impressive – cars could drive in direct straight lines for short distances and verges were already stacked high with debris. Timber reusable for ship repairs had been carefully removed and splintered remains were already being recycled by new owners. We were dripping all over with hot sweat and fantasised about dripping with fresh cold water, but nothing in our room had changed except complete loss of electricity so no fan or water.

The heat and smell of sewage was attracting insects and flies and our gauze door had been blown away. Was it better to keep the door shut to keep out insects, but get hotter and hotter in an airless room running further into dehydration? Or was it the lesser of the evils to open the door for maybe a slight movement of air and risk bites and contact from insects known to carry dengue fever, and now probably a lot else besides? We opted for the latter and located our strongest sickly smelling insect repellent.

There was a good smell of lunch in the corridors – beef stew and rice. People had been groping about in the darkness in the marooned ship and located freezer contents which were presumably rapidly defrosting. There was no water and still no thoughts of water allocation. Mains water pipes were broken, as were sewage pipes, and Water Board workers were understandably working around the clock to establish some sort of roof over their heads. Our hopes for tap water from emergency sources had rested on the hotel generator working to power a desalination plant. However, questioning revealed that there was no such plant, only the 20,000 gallon standby water tank. The most frightening news of all was that this was totally dry, and there was no standby supply. It had been emptied the previous week, having not been used up fast enough and had not been replaced as the transport truck went into maintenance the same week and was still there.

Things now looked extremely bad. We were definitely beginning to show signs of dehydration after two days of minimal water intake in the extreme humid heat. Our tongues were furry brown and tasted disgusting. We were both irritable and felt vague and were continually forgetting and losing things. Ridiculously and incomprehensibly we were both peeing volumes – it seemed as if we were passing more than we drank in spite of losing so much water by sweating. Unfortunately my student zoology course never included such useful physiological insight. We decided to work out how much fruit drink, tea and water we had and work out some sort of daily ration based on a maximum length stay. Three times we added five figures and divided the total by the number of days and managed to get different answers every time. Eventually we managed the definitive answer – it was a shock: if we were unable to fly out to Ulithi we had a week ahead of us in Yap on half a litre each per day, and both of us sweating uncontrollably. The very real horror now was slow dehydration compounded with sewage-transmitted disease following in its wake. It was frightening. I wept with terror and thirst, resenting the wasted water loss of every tear but unable to stop.

Faded memories of physiology lectures prompted me to think that our ion absorption and water balance was disturbed so maybe we should use the rehydration sachets we had with us in case of diarrhoea. The measured dose would use a lot of valuable water in one stroke, but it seemed sensible, and furthermore if we asked the catering manager for a measuring jug for the purpose it would focus his attention on the deteriorating state of the hotel guests outside the tour group. It worked; there was no measuring jug available but later in the evening two bottles of water were delivered to our door unexpectedly! I have kept the paper with our ration calculations as a record – too grim a reminder to be classed as a souvenir.

Temporarily we felt better for the rehydration powders, but were totally possessed by feelings of thirst, overwhelming heat and sweaty discomfort. We decided we must double our ration and hope that there was a breakthrough in the water crisis before we ran out completely.

Peter was heroically braving the heat, regularly checking the immediate vicinity for drinking or utility water, or anything useful to put it in when it came. At tea-time he stumbled upon a party going on in one of the wrecked bedrooms. It was the tour group celebrating the imminent arrival of the US Federal Authority military aircraft to inspect the airport damage and assess the possibility of civilian planes landing 'blind'. The control tower had been blown away, so pilots would be landing aircraft visually, World War II style. For them the end was in sight. They had been due to fly on to Guam next day and if visual landing and take-off were cleared by the authorities, things looked good. Failing that, they were convinced that a military plane would evacuate them from the horrors of a hotel without maid service or flushing lavatories. Peter politely declined their offer of Coke or wine, but as he left he noticed a pink plastic waste bin by the door which he quietly scooped up as he left – for a future water carrier.

A little later, a brief expedition down the corridors to catch any snatches of information or supplies was richly rewarded: some buckets of water appeared at the stair well. It was drinking water from the Water Board. At last, a long, long drink, bottles refilled, and then to make life sheer bliss, a slow-turning ceiling fan. The earth might have moved. In fact, on our return to Britain we found that at 5:35 p.m. it had. There had been an earthquake on Yap, 5.8 on the Richter Scale, which we had not even noticed. Such is the power of thirst.

Three hours later it became obvious that the precious buckets of drinking water were being squandered. The tour leader sauntered down the corridor in crisp white bathrobe and hair in a white towel, turban-styled. She just needed to sing 'Gonna wash that man right outa my hair' for *South Pacific* to come to life. From then on she featured in our surreal drama under the name of the film star, 'Mitzi'. Faced with such blatant prodigality we squared up to the free-for-all philosophy and followed suit, but with as economical usage as possible. Our half-full pink bin washed both our hair, ourselves, our clothes and then the floor and flushed the loo

– a feat of recycling which occupied us for the next one and a half hours as our basin didn't have a fitting plug and the only other container was the decorative baby clam shell soap tray. For the first time for two days we could clean our teeth and use half a glass to swill our mouths out – bliss! Well-watered we went happily to bed and slept.

GHOST HOTEL

It was Easter Sunday. We woke to a grey sky at dawn, followed by wonderful refreshing rain which gradually washed the sky blue. Breakfast was a joy: just us and the manager who reappeared for the first time for two days, having spent all his waking hours clearing rubble and assessing the state of the stranded ship and how she might be shifted. He had also been happy to keep out of range of Mitzi's demands for her clients.

On the forecourt below, her tour group were clad in their unofficial uniform of crisp white socks, trainers that never trained, safari shorts and hats. They clambered into the storm-battered bus to set off for the unknown. Their plane was not due to arrive until early afternoon but apparently they intended to sit it out at the airport, which at the time of their incoming flight had rated as more comfortable than the present state of the hotel... but no one had seen it since.

No one knew the state of anything beyond down the road. Yapese hotel staff, stranded or sheltering during the typhoon, had returned to their villages at dawn Saturday and had not returned. It was doubtful if many of them still had homes, but no one really knew. The state of everything and everywhere was unknown. It was not certain if the Guam flight would materialise. The state of neighbouring islands was unknown. Had the typhoon veered east or west? Was Yap near the eye of the storm? There was no way of knowing how badly our next day's destination, Ulithi, had been hit or if our Missionary plane could fly or if it was transporting casualties rather than passengers.

Over breakfast we discovered that Mitzi had been totally undaunted by the disastrous situation faced by the hotel staff and the Yapese, and had demanded regular meetings on the availability of creature comforts, maid service and luxuries. The divide separating the cultures of luxury tourism and locals could not have been demonstrated more painfully. The unintentional black comedy of the man who asked for maid service mid-typhoon and had to be reminded that there was no water could only be surpassed by an American twitcher (bird spotter) we met a week later in Palau. He was on a 'full house' quest, aiming to tick off every bird species unique to particular islands and was totally unable to grasp that Yap was not a place to visit if one had not pre-booked accommodation and made contact to check the room still had a roof and four walls. On being told that any stray birdsong would be swamped by chainsaws and there were not many trees left for the birds to perch on anyway, his eyes glittered with resolve and anticipation. '*Aah, that's even better, it means they'll be much easier to see!*'

Of the twenty-nine rooms in the hotel eleven were lost. On the ground floor a tentative glimpse through half-open doors revealed dark cavern-like interiors floored with brown mud from the tidal wave. Here and there on areas of roughly wiped floor tiles were sleeping bags and signs of hurried habitation – maybe staff were camping there.

We were now the only guests in the hotel, which brought a huge sense of relief and a strong feeling of unreality. As they departed for Guam our kind German neighbours had offered the Coke and water they had left unfinished in their room. Their room, the Mandarinfish room, was one of real fantasy, with a glorious hand-dyed bedspread which did justice to the vivid colours of these tiny fish – a potent reminder of our ill-fated plans of seeing them in reality. Our room was the turtle room: its beautiful images of turtles swimming through colourful reefs would also have to remain an unachievable ambition for now.

The sun was relentless and the temperature rising. The quest for a cooler room and a new found sense of freedom and curiosity took us from one themed room to another: seahorses, octopus, clownfish, Manta Ray, shark, Emperor Angelfish, all as dazzling as the reefs themselves... nearly. The quiet of so many empty rooms had an aura of the *Marie Celeste*: a derelict dwelling where the occupants busy with everyday survival had suddenly been interrupted and hurriedly left, time indeterminate. Flung bed linen and empty drink cans personalised the emptiness. Best of all, a forgotten jar of anti-wrinkle cream in the glamorous Mitzi's room proclaimed she was 'worth it'. At least her skin was human.

At the south end of the building, facing out towards the wide bay to the distant barrier reef and the open sea, the luxury rooms were derelict. Big picture windows had blown in and the partition walls leaned, broken. Carved wardrobes and chairs lay overturned and broken, or hurriedly stacked and left. Vestiges of drapes fluttered fitfully at window spaces or hung limply round elegant four-poster beds. Sounds usually unnoticed magnified to the sinister – unsteady creaking, occasional flapping. Outside, the pale grey lagoon was completely still with reflections of remnant palms and trees – beautiful but for the overpowering smell of oil. The feeling of unreality was intense; it was a strange incongruity of luxury and dereliction, outside of time and place. The feeling intensified into a reckless adventure as we came across some abandoned necessities of life: candles, four cans of juice and some chocolate – we felt like Jim in *Empire of the Sun*, free from the normal constraints of measured civility and manners. After the challenge of survival largely in competition with many fellow guests we felt a joy in the emptiness, not desolation.

Our thoughts were interrupted by a Yapese lady who had come to sweep up all the broken glass. Her young daughter and baby grandchild accompanied her, but she was tearful as to the fate of others in her family. Her home was largely gone and they were being fed by the hotel. We gave her the canned drinks and chocolate to give to her kin.

Around lunchtime the sight of a pile of luggage in front of the hotel wiped the smiles from our faces. Had the tour group returned? Could the airline have actually flown in more guests, knowing the state of the airport and island? Yes, the airline had flown in more guests without warning them of the situation. Worse still, some of the replacement guests were already proving to be more of a challenge than their predecessors. Far from being middle-aged to elderly, pampered and out of their depths when faced with stirring whitener into their coffee themselves, these were young divers, up front, aggressively demanding fulfilment of holiday promise. They did not seem able to grasp, nor want to, the severity of the typhoon damage and its exhausting aftermath. Their expectations and demands were projected with boundless energy. The reality was no dive boat pontoon, dive shop completely in ruins, dive boats wedged in amongst mangrove trees in the shelter of the creek and staff mostly gone to find if their families were safe.

We now gathered from hearsay that water was just available for two hours per day. As regards our next destination, Ulithi, tourists would be wanting to leave there; unlike Yap it was an atoll with no natural springs, so water availability there could be far worse. Most alarming of all would be the uncertainty of a return flight. It was a pity that we had not gleaned this information earlier along with the fact that there had been spare seats on offer on the morning flight to Guam. We decided there was no other option than to leave Yap as soon as possible and start our time in Palau,

420km (250 miles) away ahead of schedule.

The head of the hotel had also flown in from Guam. He was another of Andrew's contacts from 2001; Peter introduced himself. Guam and the outside world had seen the satellite pictures of the typhoon's progress. There had been sustained winds of 185 kph (115 mph) as the sidewall of the eye positioned over the island for over twenty-four hours; on Good Friday Typhoon Sudal moved just south of Yap and peak winds were estimated at 240 kph (150 mph), the strongest typhoon to hit the island for over fifty years.

It was noticeable that hotel life and facilities, such as they were, suddenly became organised and efficient. Up until now, there had been no indication of when and if there was a meal, which when it happened was essentially an ad hoc affair and pretty basic and we had assumed that the price would reflect this standard of necessity. Now, suddenly there were place settings and paper table napkins round the carefully placed coffee tables: there were enough chairs, all placed, a noticeboard with mealtime menus and prices, and a waitress with pencil and odd scraps of paper in hand. Some staff had returned and the hotel was back into the world of commerce and enterprise.

There was now some water in large plastic vats in the corridor, but also signs it was undervalued by the new arrivals and disappearing fast. With no fitting plug in the basin I raided the corridor cleaning cupboard and found a plastic bin of empty cans which I emptied and appropriated for its water containing potential and bagged up the cans ready for a surprised cleaner. In the corridor outside the water was down to a few inches – definitely the time to keep a few inches of water stored in the bin just in case, and to leave the island.

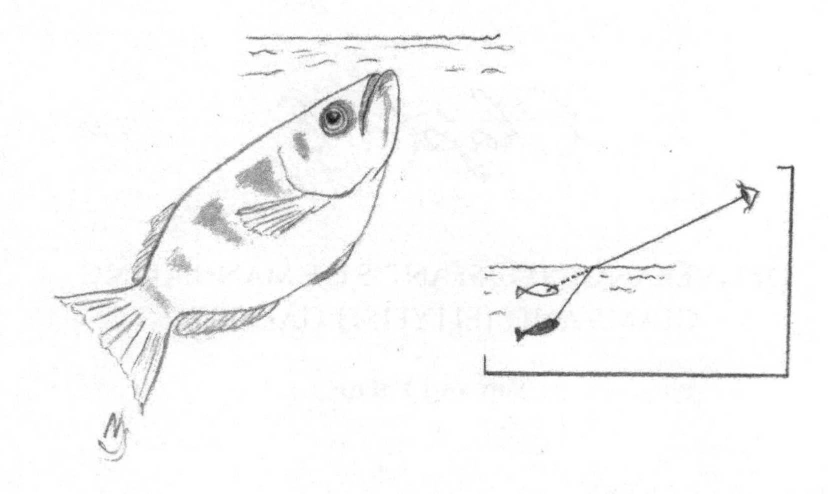

Target practice. The very mobile eyes of the Banded Archerfish can be directed upwards, sideways, and backwards. Within the projecting lower jaw, an odd-shaped tongue assists aiming a jet of water at insects in the air above. Fish persistently practice to achieve the skill of taking aim and spitting water at a speed to shape it into a blob just before impact, so knocking its prey down into the water. Their aim compensates for the distortion of light passing through air and water. Inset: On the bank a local eccentric habitually aims his rifle at fish below the water... without compensating and without success.

Chapter 6

DELIVERANCE TO ISLANDS OF MAN-EATING CLAMS AND JELLYFISH GALAXIES

Yap and Palau

THE DAYS AFTER...

The drama of Supertyphoon Sudal had passed. The steady climb for people and wildlife to continue life in the devastation left in its wake had begun.

KINSHIP FROM EAURIPIK

We were awakened on Easter Monday by a loud knock at the door, followed by a pause then a Yapese accented 'Good Morning'. Bleary-eyed, in my nightdress, I opened the door. A well-built man clad only in shorts towered in the doorway, extravagantly waving his arms: *'I have come to take you to Ulithi!'* He introduced himself as Serphen (Andrew's 'uncle') and was amazed when I stammered, totally embarrassed, that we had decided it was too risky an undertaking and hoped to leave Yap for Palau as soon as possible. I invited him in as Peter draped himself in a towel and we offered him the last can of apple juice acquired on our explorations the previous day. His surprise at our decision, given he was a very important local personage and on the Disaster Committee, highlighted the extent to which we were all totally ignorant of the post-typhoon state anywhere – on or off the island.

Serphen decided we must all go to the airport and discuss things with the missionary pilot who lived on site. We dressed in five minutes, and joyfully sat in his air-conditioned 4WD truck – it was the first time we had been cool for four days. We now saw the far end of Colonia bordering the lagoon and it was a shambles. The small concrete mall – the improvised typhoon shelter – remained intact with its boarded up windows and doors. Stacked up against its walls were vestiges of torn trees, and bits of the hardware store from the opposite side of the road which looked as if it had been unzipped into two parts.

En route to the airport the scenery was devastated: browning trees and remnants of a few small houses and shacks, all of which had looked so idyllic and lush on our arrival. But nothing prepared us for the airport. Uprooted pandanus trees lay everywhere; scrawny dogs sniffed round heaps of rotting vegetation; the control tower was no longer there, it had been blown away. The high-peaked iron roofs of the airport building, inspired by the traditional shape of a Men's House, had been torn away and were flapping loudly with electric cables and lamps hanging limp from exposed girders. A tiny shack advertised cool drinks and ice cream to a deserted silence. It was like an eerie set for a post-holocaust movie.

The pilot emerged from a little bungalow just beyond the airport building. He was unable to fly anywhere, even for casualties, as the force of the typhoon had buckled the aircraft hangar door and it could not be opened. Amazingly, the door had not caved in thus saving the planes inside from being blown out of the back of the hanger. He described how during the peak of the typhoon a 50 by 100 mm (4 by 2 in) joist was blown from a building 15 m (50 ft) away and went straight through his office wall like a missile, and out the other side. In his thirty years in the islands he had never witnessed such a typhoon. Strangest of all was the thick fog which had blanketed the island earlier in the morning. It still clothed the shore areas we could see below the airport – he had never before seen a fog on Yap.

Serphen drove to the port area where large containers were strewn across the roads as if thrown by a child in a tantrum. Unbelievably, the sea had picked up a huge metal barge full of fuel oil and dumped it high and dry above the road. Here was the chief source of the sickly stench of fuel which hung over Colonia. There was a ship which looked as if it had been in a breaker's yard, but it was current and in use. In the distance at the head of the inlet the strange morning fog still hung over the top of the hill which was as brown as Britain mid-winter. At the water's edge was the hotel, dwarfed by the great hulk of its stranded ship. It was not until that moment that we realised the great size of the ship and how far she had finally moved away from our balcony and her original mooring.

We returned to the hotel, too late for food or water; a fifteen hour wait for water was hard to contemplate. Peter's shoulder was now aching badly after carrying buckets of sea water up the stairs for loo flushing. We were hungry, tired and demoralised with calamities, devastation, irritations and the realities of living on what was essentially a rubbish dump with an overpowering stench, which we had paid thousands of hard-earned pounds to reach. After two years of planning, saving, anticipation and a year's postponement this was anti-climax, to say the least. We resolved to try and retrieve just a few hours of our planned underwater adventure. We had originally planned a day's taxi trip further round to the east of the island to Wanyan Bay to snorkel its Blue Holes. Maybe this would still be possible as there now was a precedent: dive boats were already out on the reef.

Against all odds the newly arrived young divers' demands had been met. They had put their energy to good use and helped to clear up the mess of the dive shop, the dive boats had been retrieved from their safe haven jammed amongst mangrove branches and roots, and a rival dive pontoon used from across the bay. It seemed vaguely incongruous that a boat, driver and dive master could be off on a jaunt when there was still silt and mess to be cleared, but there was another important consideration. The divers had led the way and the hotel was functioning on a commercial footing. One way to benefit local people who had lost their houses and possessions was to give them money through employment so the hiring of boats and staff was all to the good.

The charming Yapese dive master, Theo, who had met us at our arrival, lived in a village north of Colonia and had sampled the roads. I explained that this disastrous week was in reality our one and only chance to travel to the other side of the world for what had become something of a holy grail. Unlike the young Guam divers, age and finance didn't offer a 'next time' to see the island ten years on – when trees would have regrown, traditional houses been rebuilt and hard corals reappeared in profusion once more. He understood completely but the only access to anywhere was by sea. He went away to see if he could organise something so we would have some positive memories of Yap and returned with the joyous news that a boat could take us next morning. The life we might see was open to question, but looking down from our balcony there were a few small fish hugging the new shoreline just visible through the dark oily shallows; the amazing ability of wild creatures to hang on and survive was encouraging in this sad, browning landscape.

A further degree of normality was returning as we heard a rumour that there was a flight out of Yap on Wednesday which immediately became the focus of the afternoon. There was no telephone link in existence between Yap and Ulithi or between Yap and Palau. It appeared the only communication was by radio to Continental Airlines who were only flying to Guam. We decided the only thing to do was to ask Andrew to organise our exit arrangements from the London end. Again we seemed adrift in an unreal world that was repeating itself – exactly two years before we had been trying to extricate Andrew from here in extreme circumstances. We set about contacting England, but found the line to the UK was down. We were close to despair. Fortunately, out in the corridor Peter saw the head of the hotel, and told him of our fruitless attempts to contact the airline. He stepped into the breach and organised our flights by personal contact. We had no paper or reference number to prove it – we could only trust and hope.

The sea was flat calm at sunset, with a sky like a Turner watercolour but for the eerie menace of sickly lurid yellow and the visible oil slick. For us, the most significant details in view were the returned dive boats, somewhat battered, but watertight. Life now took on a new turn with the prospect of a few hours of seeing surviving reef life and imminent departure. More immediately there was our fish feast with Andrew's 'family' in the evening.

A fish feast in Eauripik under sprawling tropical trees – fish portions are laid out on banana leaf platters on mats of knotted palm fronds. Children fan leaves to ward off flies; the boys wear thus.

Fish feast – the words evoked memories of Andrew's 2001 pictures of feasts on Eauripik. In the shade of extravagantly lush trees, a long line of banana leaves was laid out on the sand, each leaf 'plate' with portions of fish, banana, taro and coconut cream; flower-bedecked children fanned leaves to fend off flies. Yap 2004 could not have been a greater contrast with the all-pervading smell, wet silty mud beneath our feet, brown limp leaves hanging overhead, stacked wet furniture and a loud generator. The consistent factor was the celebration of kinship and the generosity of our Micronesian hosts. On the naked chopping block in front of the fire area stood two plates piled with delicious fried fish chunks and whole green coconuts, cold straight from the freezer – a loud generator had its advantages. Our hosts drew up plastic chairs for us and watched us while we ate, continually urging us to eat more. To our embarrassment, they ate nothing. Optimistic cats and dogs were shooed off the chopping block, but one filched a morsel as it escaped.

As Andrew had said, one was never quite sure who was who or who was related. Distant relatives and friends were all part of the extended family which seemed in perpetual flux. The complications of adoption were a norm, and a clan structure as well as a tradition of formalised obligations and responsibilities. Various ladies came and observed our small gathering, all traditionally bare-breasted and wearing lavalavas, and a boy, obviously of Indian ancestry, whom we could not place in Andrew's approximate family tree. His English speaking 'aunt', Jo, was the attentive hostess. Noticing our profuse sweating she fanned us with a woven palm fan, commanding the boy, Rami, to decapitate a coconut with his machete. He did so with one swipe and I savoured the unaccustomed feeling of a cold, cold drink. Even my thirsty fantasies of the last few days had not ventured to the realms of real coconut juice. There was a tirade of disapproval and gesticulations towards the boy who grinned, embarrassed: Jo explained, the machete was still coated with fish and turtle guts. A cursory look confirmed it was dirty, but then so was everything. How could things be otherwise given the circumstances, and how could one refuse such open generosity in adversity? We both knew we were taking enormous risks but acceptance of hospitality was a diplomatic necessity. Rami vaguely wet his fingers from the rain water butt and ran them along the edge of the blade.

We talked of the typhoon until Serphen returned from his disaster meeting. His laugh and his ebullience and his lack of wrinkles belied his age. I brought out my camera and they all whooped at the recent pictures of Andrew dressed in a city suit rather than a thu. Serphen wanted to see what had happened to the ship during the typhoon – he had helped to moor her. Rami was appointed to accompany Peter back to our room to pick up the video, hesitating and politely removing his flip-flops at the door. All eyes were agog at the images of the great hulk emerging and disappearing repeatedly from a curtain of rain, wheel spinning.

As we left Jo presented me with two beautiful baskets, intricately woven and decorated, from Indonesia and New Guinea. They were embarrassed and explained how everything they had suitable to give us was spoilt by rain and mud, and these were the only gifts they had. I knew from Andrew that far from being something to carry shopping, baskets in Micronesia are important and treasured possessions. Custom-made baskets, miniature to colossal, function in every aspect of existence: trapping fish, catching crabs, cultivating shellfish, cooking rice portions, serving meals and storing food, cradling infants and food gathering. An island saying is that you can tell which island someone is from when you see the contents of the basket they carry. They all accompanied us back to the hotel and as we said good night Jo slipped the palm fan into my hand. I treasure it, with the baskets.

During the night we were awoken by the noisy engines of a military plane. At home it would have been a source of irritation, but now it was a source of delight – everything needs to be seen in a different context before it can be judged. A fleet of ambulances passed by with sirens wailing, no doubt evacuating all of the hospital patients, some injured by flying glass, who had been surviving somehow without a roof over their heads for three and a half days, with improvised tarpaulin cover and scant liquids. With such thoughts in mind I brushed aside my stomach discomfort and indigestion.

SEA SPRAY AND BLUE HOLES GHOSTS

The sirens and heavy plane engines faded into the night. We were awakened in the small hours by what sounded like a musically dyslexic deep bongo group at their first practice. Waiting for the next bang was a sure antidote to sleep. Peter described it as 'subliminal awareness of bad wind'. It was old oil drums hung with ropes round the ship's hull. They had been attached in a vain attempt to float her off at the turn of the tide, but she was far too hard aground for that.

There was a sewage pollution warning to divers in the area. We could only hope that Wanyan, 12 km (7 miles) to the northeast was far enough away from Colonia, the source. Our snorkelling trip began: the joy of being on a moving boat became an intense feeling of elation as we accelerated, the air movement on one's face and sea spray giving the illusion of a cool wind amidst hot airlessness. Theo and the boat driver seemed to feel it too. Our little part of the nightmare seemed at an end.

Ahead there was a sky of pale blue and sea of vivid aquamarine, green and pale turquoise streaks. Below us, a glittering net-like pattern of light shimmered across pale yellow, ochre and turquoise tinted sand and corals.

Behind us our wake of uncurling white spume lengthened into patterns of watery lace. Far behind, receding from sight and mind, was the dirty grey pall hanging over the browning hills of Colonia, presumably a fusion of oil and water vapour hovering as fog over the hot reflective land. Between us and the open sea was the far-off white noise of waves battering the barrier reef. This had provided a protecting rim for the islands during the impact of the waves.

The boat skirted round shadowy corals and through tenuous twisting channels. These men were expert boat handlers who knew their island waters intimately. It was a good time to talk. The boat's driver, who spoke no English, came from Rumung, Yap's forbidden island which had chosen to remain aloof, traditional and closed to visitors. He had crossed the short Yinbinaew Passage separating Rumung from the main island by boat to Bechiyal and journeyed on by road across the several bridge-linked islands to the hotel in Colonia. He reported, via Theo, that Bechiyal was completely destroyed, a tragedy for Yap as well as its people, as this seaside village had not only opened its doors to overnight guests, but had become the window on traditional Yapese life – a sort of unofficial cultural centre for locals and other Micronesians. As in Eauripik, people wore traditional crowns, necklaces, arm and ankle bands of palm shoots, skirts of palm fronds over their lavalavas and garlands of flowers – a spectacle of greens, yellow and red. Above all there was dance, very much a living and treasured art form done by men and women for celebrations and communicating island history down the generations. Visitors could arrange to see palm and pandanus plaiting and the ingenious multi-purpose weaving of baskets and life's essentials. We had sought permission to see these activities, having heard Andrew's descriptions of traditional life.

Sea life motifs inside a Men's House, Yap, 2001.

As in Eauripik, and all Yapese villages, the Men's House was the centre of traditional male life – planning fishing trips, educating young boys with skills of sailing, fishing methods and crafts, and simply as a social centre for telling stories, settling differences and drinking. The elongated hexagonal house had stood on a high stepped coral stone platform with sturdy tree trunk pillars supporting a towering steep-pitched roof with the end peaks overhanging at each end. The sides of such houses were sometimes completely open or partly panelled with palm fronds in between the timbers, and the roof was 'tiled' with partly plaited palm fronds which allowed cooling air passage, but not water. At Bechiyal the massive gable end overhang had been beautifully painted with sea motifs. Between shore and reef there were two ancient V-shaped fish traps which isolated bigger fish in the narrow end when the tide went out enabling an easily caught meal; we wondered if the traps were still there. The peak of the Men's House had towered nearly as high as the surrounding tall trees and coconut palms – it must have been these which had smashed it and all the village houses before the sweeping tidal wave scattered further destruction. Structures and people had weathered many typhoons in the past but this had been the strongest in fifty years. The sea side of the barrier reef in this north-east corner was badly damaged. Later it was assessed that from 6 m (20 ft) down to 30 m (100 ft) more than half of the hard corals were heavily damaged.

As we skirted along the coast the scene was mostly leaning, torn and uprooted trees. On the shore, two ancient Men's Houses, long abandoned, had been tilted, with peaked palm roofs stove in and timbers broken and disjointed by fallen trees and surging sea. A sad sight made even sadder when Theo told us that Men's Houses all over the island had been completely smashed or swept away and that the traditional knowledge and skill of their intricate construction without nails had died with the last generation of elders. These two remnants were all of the traditional architecture of Yap that we were destined to see.

Theo told us about the devastation in his village in the south of Tomil Gagil island which we were now passing. Most people had taken their children to grandparents or relatives sheltering in designated schools and churches. When the warnings were broadcast on Thursday morning Theo had spent every spare moment sawing down the trees surrounding his house in order to lessen the damage from falling timber. His house had been slightly damaged, but he was lucky as his village had a spring and the stream ran near his house. In villages all over Yap repairs would be slow as supplies of basic building materials were non-existent and further supplies would be slow arriving and at a premium. The supply of nails had run out and for many there was a lack of cash. Where the tidal wave had inundated the village gardens of taro, bananas, mangoes and passionfruit, the earth could be salted and spoilt, just as it had been during the 2001 typhoon affecting Woleai and Eauripik. On that occasion it had been estimated that it could possibly take fifteen years for the natural productivity to recover.

We heard how in another village a husband and wife had sat across their table with a basket of their essentials between them ready to dash. Suddenly they had found themselves engulfed by a wave and swimming, no time to grab the basket or each other. In another place a very young child sheltered under the table at the mother's feet. When the wave hit they were swept away separately and the child was lost. It was the same desperate story for an elderly couple who had not managed to surface and swim the wave.

Theo was tired, surrounded by human tragedy and faced with salvaging and constructing shelters for relatives and friends with rapidly dwindling supplies of materials. Amazingly, he still had a delightful open smile, eyes sparkling. The two Yapese chewed betel as they talked – it reduces hunger. They refused to share our packed lunch of slices of banana bread.

Zigzagging in between areas of dark blue and leaf-green sea we arrived off Wanyan Bay. Theo carefully waded ashore through Turtle Grass to call at a house standing amongst a few shredded trees on the beach. Yapese custom required asking permission to snorkel in the 'blue holes' 90 m (100 yards) off the beach. The quiet of the place was intense compared to the sounds which had become our norm. Against a background of the sound of the sea and a quiet roar of the waves way out on the reef there were soft bell-like calls of birds coming from the land – the first we had heard for four days. It was a sound picture of stillness.

Theo returned and we slid into the cool sea, a sensation all the more delicious for having been postponed. The 'blue holes' were dark violet areas where the shallow floor of sand gave way abruptly to deep coral-walled holes large enough to shelter an occasional Manta Ray. Andrew had described the holes as magnificent – a feast for the eyes of colours and forms, myriads of corals, fish and sharks. Our first view was of a pale brown world. Silt covered pieces of broken branched coral were lightened by a few passing parrotfish. Two Moorish Idols, chic fashion fish in black and white, trailed twirling white boas of long dorsal fins. Theo dived for a cowrie, shiny with beautiful dark spots, and a three-inch bivalve shell to show us, then carefully replaced them. Three pale straw-coloured pipefish and a Cleaner Wrasse completed our sightings. Any hope of a young Manta Ray sheltering below us was in vain, for they, like all of the bigger fish, had swum or been swept to the deep open sea away from the coastal turmoil. A large coconut palm had fallen in across the hole along with bits of the corrugated iron roof it had smashed – 90 m (100 yds) away. The second hole was also coated in the yellow-brown silt, but the handful of fish and molluscs we had seen gave some hope for the future. The coral would eventually regrow and a reef community would slowly return.

Things looked better in the shallows near the outer reef, with miniature underwater islands of coral gardens in the sand: tiny turrets, columns, bumps and folds, smooth and sharp, spikes and branches, in pastel greys, pinks, orange, lemon, mauve, blue and dark lavender. A few soldier fish were hiding under the coral; a group of small pale-blue fish darted about, and beneath the sand there was another bivalve. We could have stayed much longer, drifting with the swell as this little world unfolded further, but our two Yapese companions were very cold; apparently the water was much colder than usual. The trip had been useful for them as they had assessed damage to this area and the extent of returned sea life. This eastern side of the island was hardest hit and the outer side of this area of barrier reef was heavily damaged with about seventy-five per cent of the coral damaged or destroyed – a vital statistic in the diving equation as visiting divers are a mainstay of Yap's tourism and employment of local people.

Back at the hotel the afternoon held the unexpected pleasure of the arrival of mains water for two hours. As our shower remained faulty and all the undamaged rooms were now full we arranged to shower amidst the ruins of a luxury south-facing room. Picking a path to the shower through broken glass and stacked furniture was a surreal experience, but the joy of cool water dribbling down one's body was totally real.

During our last evening of packing I began to feel bad, too nauseous to nibble the slice of cold, soggy pizza which was hotel supper. It soon became apparent I had a virulent gut infection. My misgivings of the previous night had been well founded. We were indeed leaving Yap just in time – doctors and medication would be more available in Palau. Peter tucked in to a plate of prawns, frozen from some distant sea healthier than the expanse below our balcony. He went to say thank you to Serphen's family and made my excuses.

Next morning, we wondered how the hotel charges were going to be sorted out given that circumstances had precluded basic room servicing beyond the first night and there had been minimal food and even less to drink. Much to our horror we were presented with a very large bill commensurate with a week's luxury, high living and a regular cornucopia of culinary delights. Here was a dilemma, but how could we question it when many of the Yapese staff at the hotel were without a roof over their heads? Afterwards we read that the hotel was feeding forty staff and their families, so we felt that we had done the right thing in paying a luxury price for the worst week of our lives.

As we left our room I hesitated, with Kathie's now dead frangipani lei in my hand, unsure if the superstition of never returning demanded its return to the sea or if the land would do. I couldn't bring myself to throw such a carefully made object into the filthy water below, so I draped it on the lampshade and left. Downstairs there was an air of bustle and action. Post-typhoon clean-up was swinging into action. Yap had been officially recognised by President Bush as a disaster zone and throbbing transport engines had joined the regular sounds of the night. Newly arrived American soldiers were being billeted in the hotel – experts on sewage pumps and emergency water supplies. Their confident swank was gladly forgiven by those who were tired, bemused and battered by the typhoon.

Theo, the dive master, drove the bus to the airport. For us the pressure was off as we thankfully looked forward to seeing green again, breathing fresh air, and having enough water for regular showers and clean clothes, and sleeping undisturbed in dry bedding. Our discomfort had seemed interminable but it had been a mere week. We felt a sense of desperate loss and regret to have glimpsed these caring, open and smiling people having to try and rebuild their bit of paradise from stinking chaos, when they were still recovering from the previous Year's Typhoon Lupit. Their release back to normality was a long way off. We wondered if Ulithi, our special goal, had been badly hit, and Eauripik: incredibly vulnerable being a mere 1.5 m (5 ft) above sea level, with its one little village of Andrew's friends and adopted kin.

RETROSPECTIVE FROM THE FUTURE

Later, we found out that Ulithi had not suffered nearly as badly as Yap:

700 of Yap's 1,700 homes had been destroyed and 900 were damaged. Two weeks after the typhoon 500 Yap residents were still in the island's eighteen shelters, with hundreds more staying with relatives or sleeping amongst their remnant possessions under the stars. The oil in the harbour and swirling through the hotel had come from several ships being sunk by the combination of waves 6.7 m (22 ft) high and storm surge of 3.7 m (12 ft), and this was the magnitude of force battering the coral reefs along the coast. During the fortnight after the typhoon there were twenty-three flight missions with emergency supplies and 20,000 gallons of water, although relief was disrupted by the airport's damaged runway. As I had surmised, within days of the typhoon, the presence of sewage and lack of clean water had created health issues of dehydration, sickness and gastrointestinal problems and people who washed in oil-contaminated sea water suffered skin irritations. As in Woleai in 2001, salt water intruding inland destroyed almost all of the food crops on the island.

At our destination, the island of Palau, there was an official collecting point for Aid to Yap – anything useful that people could spare for their fellow Micronesians. Every gift, even down to a set of toothbrushes, was painstakingly recorded in a large notebook. The spirit of concern and sharing was everywhere. It is these and the social traditions so doggedly continued in Yap which support the islanders through adversity. Throughout Yap's contact with the outside world it has resisted losing its old values and particular culture regardless of the pressure of early Spanish missionaries, foreign traders or administrations. In the mid-nineteenth century, other Pacific islanders could be tempted to trade by the explorers' standbys of novel coloured cloth and glitzy beads. However, the Yapese were not impressed and continued to value their own traditional hibiscus cloth and grass skirts more highly. The only barter which they valued enough to give their trading commitment was the transportation of their newly quarried traditional stone money from Palau, traditionally by canoe. Subjugated during the first half of the twentieth century by the Germans, then the Japanese, the vastly outnumbered and dwindling Yapese population was forced to build air fields and military installations in the run up to World War II – as we had seen the photographs in Mr. Lucky's cafe. Punishment for non-cooperation had been carefully aimed at the very core of their culture, the enormous stone money coins. Many of these treasured relics were hundreds of years old, standing in important places and lining village paths. They bore the iconic names of the lost mariners who had perilously transported them from Palau in dug-out canoes. In 1929 the Japanese civilian government had recorded 13,281 stone coins by village pathways, but when military might became the priority many stones were smashed as punishment of the Yapese, and their humiliation was multiplied when they were sometimes forced to use the broken pieces as mere road fill.

At the turn of the millennium the Yapese remained the one Micronesian culture mostly resisting Western ways, retaining their customs and traditions, undiluted. In the forbidden islands and outer atolls like Eauripik, traditional ways remained strongest. In Palau, there was worry about the typhoon losses and human hardship, but also universal concern as to whether Yap would be able to attend the impending Pacific Festival of Culture. It was chiefly the Yapese who carried the torch of traditional Micronesian knowledge for the future. To an outsider it seems the strength of this culture lies in the values and priorities which have become unfashionable in the West: the discipline of an expected standard of behaviour, responsibilities, obligations, and courtesy and manners based on consideration and a tradition of team effort and sharing. Population pressures and tourism have not yet degraded the culture or the environment.

Our quest had brought us much more and much less than we had sought. We had seen nothing of the tropical exuberance of sea and land and the ancient culture we had crossed the world to see. Instead of our expected isolation in a peaceful paradise of plenty without insistent telephones, news, intrusive media and commercial pressures and trivia, we had come to understand the reality of isolation from all of this modern communication – but in adversity and in need. We had witnessed one of the most ancient and elemental forces on the planet, but in the privileged circumstance of a safe building. We had experienced extreme misadventure with diverse people all of whom responded to the challenges of physical threat and stress in very different ways – both personally and culturally. Most of all, we had, to a small extent, shared this extraordinary event and its unpleasant aftermath with Andrew's friends and kin, who, like their forebears, expected life to be close to Nature's bounty and its destructive power.

We had encountered few sea creatures, but we had had an enormous encounter with the sea at its most destructive.

YAP REVISITED 2009

Andrew returned to Yap in 2009. Young trees were growing and old deformed survivors had sprouted afresh. There were Men's Houses with neatly painted traditional fish motifs which tourists were encouraged to see, and there were some divers' reefs which had escaped major damage.

There were, however, other very sad changes: Serphen and Andrew's 'father', Manuel, had both died, the latter at a young age. Unexpectedly he found his 'mother' and many of his adoptive relatives and friends from Eauripik were now living on Yap – Andrew explained:

'They had left the atoll as sea level rise was causing salt to leach into the fresh water aquifer on the island and was killing the vegetation. Older members of the

community had remained. The islanders are amongst the first victims of climate change and their rich cultural heritage is likely to pass away into the history book within a generation.'

A Yapese Men's House, 2001, remaining traditional and remote from visitors and outside influences. Constructed of wood and woven palm fronds from the surrounding hills, it stands above a still brackish creek lined with thick mangroves. These make a valuable habitat preventing erosion during storm surges and sheltering boats (such as during a typhoon). Their visible stilt root systems and tree islands dissipate wave energy, bind sediment and make a sheltered nursery for juvenile reef fish.

A WORLD BEYOND

EXTREME ISLANDS – PALAU

We were looking down through shallows of dazzling brightness and clarity: water of light viridian and emerald green. The remains of an aircraft lay on the palest of sand. It seemed small for one vulnerable person, particularly when one considered the magnifying effect of light refraction through the water. For a moment we were re-entering Mr Lucky's domain of World War II in the Pacific which we had glimpsed in Yap during the typhoon build-up. During that war this submerged fuselage was one of Japan's most lethal aircraft and had succumbed, probably after a dogfight, in 1944. Palau, midway between Guam and the Philippines, had featured prominently in the battleground of the Japanese and the Americans. Our small boat had just passed by an island slightly larger than most of the 250–300 tiny islets of this extraordinary archipelago. This was Peleliu, at the tip of the island cluster, with a steep wooded coastline. Here thirty-four Japanese soldiers had remained, surviving secretly and still continuing their side of the hostilities in March 1947, eighteen months after the war had ended in 1945. The caves and strange geology were ideal cover for clandestine operations. These dislocated ghosts of the past gave the place a strange aura, but this was also a physical world unlike any other.

The smaller Rock Islands stand like green-topped mushrooms on concaved stalks of limestone, which are continually gouged further by sea erosion and nibbled by chitons, sea urchins and molluscs. They are a group of ancient relics of coral reefs, a complex network of ridges and dips, lifted up by violent geological forces – some are as high as 207 m (680 ft). In places the islands are like a maze, so close together that the sea in between forms narrow convoluted channels. The rising sea level from the last Ice Age flooded fissures and valleys in between steep ridges, creating the channels, and filled depressions within islands to form little lakes of sea. Between tightly packed islands the water alleyways are cloudy turquoise, carpeted with thick white rock clay as the meandering current does not carry away the rock flour. To the touch it is a glutinous and viscous slurry, but more granular than porcelain clay which it superficially resembles.

There is a strong current flowing through eroded passages such as 'Soft Coral Arch', a tiny island split apart making a humpback bridge. Under the shading arch the current runs fast and food laden, enabling unearthly soft corals of deeper dark waters to thrive just beneath the surface. We duck-dived through tangled trailing strips of bladder seaweed into a surprise world. The soft corals waving with the water flow looked delicate and vulnerable compared to their solid hard-coated cousins. Colours were muted, and some intense. Oranges, reds and greens encrusted walls already festooned with semi-transparent miniature 'trees' in palest pastel shades of cream and pink. Wispy lemon 'bushes', intricately branched, were topped with globular grape-like clusters – fragile and shades of grape colours, yellowish-green, lavender and dark purple. Through the arch it was a world of sponges: their diversity completely covered walls dotted with sponge 'vases', some purple outside, white inside.

By Ngerchong Island, the hard 'Coral Gardens' were so prolific that the scene resembled a tablecloth dotted with a repeat garden design. Miniature island landscapes with 'trees' and 'vegetation' sheltered fantastical coral 'buildings' and caverns – a Gulliver land crowded with life. Sitting or creeping slowly about the coral tops were the stealthy and the small – a hermit crab in a beautiful spike-edged pink shell, a diminutive pink-striped fish, as still as a statue; a dominant dwarf fish aggressively acting the role of big fish protector, brandishing a prominent yellow and purple dorsal fin as it strutted and swam about a band of lesser individuals. Black thin-branched growths vied with squat ones – like chilblained cold hands of bluish pink and white with sawn-off macabre fingers. Young coral mounds grew perfect and uniformly dotted with prickly tips: bright pinks, blue, purple and yellow. Vertical plate-like corals undulated between piled tall pinnacles, but all were dwarfed by enormous coral brains, and red and white whip corals as tall as a man.

This profusion was a backdrop to white wafts of 200 and more Pyramidal Butterflyfish, aptly named. Their place was subtly usurped by myriads more, yellow and long-nosed, as transient as their namesake butterflies. Blue-green Chromis followed in clouds, intermingling with fluttering finned Bird Wrasse and parrotfish. Themes of stripes passed by: blue and yellow fusiliers, white and black butterflyfish and Oriental Sweetlips further embellished with gold. Deeper down, a stiff bright blue starfish sheltered under an overhang, and red soldierfish hung immobile with their scale outlines etched and watchful eyes, big and black. The ultimate showstopper was a magnificent large Emperor Angelfish with psychedelic shimmer of blue and yellow stripes hovering over a vivid red coral 'tree' which thrust out of a vertical naked rock. Amongst this plethora of colour and movement – milling about, feeding, threatening, viewing – the big fish cruised with confident purpose, reef sharks, Giant Trevally and khaki camouflaged grouper.

Nocturnal feeders. By day, soldierfish and squirrelfish, red and with big eyes, shelter under an overhang.

'MAN TRAPS'

Giant Clams are prolific in these clear waters. Seven of the world's nine species live here, many aged individuals as big as armchairs. The shells were beautifully sculpted forms in their own right, but the living creatures within surpassed them in ravishing texture and colours. The gaping shells faced open to the surface, exposing their soft mantle skin spilling over the shell rims. Like stretched textiles, they flexed and moved as water was being sucked in through a siphon tube visibly opening and closing. Their variety of vivid colours was totally unexpected. Background shades seemed almost themed and coordinated with decorative details as pure and bright as if embroidered – pink with beige and salmon; pale green, flecked pink, darker green and blue; turquoise on blue and vice versa. Blue-green circles crowded together into impressions of sprawling iridescent colour – akin to the jewel glimmer of peacocks or shimmering blue Morpho butterflies. Spattered bands of intensely coloured spangles and dots followed undulating edges of the shells, creating detailed patterns like draped strings of bead necklaces – and no two animals looked alike.

In the world of the 1950s and before, Giant Clams, like most extra-large creatures, were seen as a terrifying threat to innocent humans. Their alternative common names were 'Killer Clam' and 'Man-eating Clam', and they were depicted as loathsome animals of ambush, just waiting to grab the next swimmer by the feet and snap shut in the manner of an eighteenth-century man-trap. The death of a diver 'caught in the jaws' of a Giant Clam was recorded in the 1939 history of the 'Pearl of Lao Tzu', the 'Pearl of Allah'. The pearl was discovered inside this criminal bivalve shell and was the largest known, weighing 6.4 kg (14 lb). The diver was found drowned, his hand caught between the closed shells of the clam. He had been looking for conch shells and was unaware of the presence of the clam which was partly hidden amongst coral rocks. The caption of the photograph of the undersea 'murderer' stated it was not unusual for a diver to be caught as Giant Clam jaws 'clamp shut with the suddenness and strength of a bear trap'. In fact, the shells close too slowly to seriously seize a person: a limb dangling or hesitantly reaching between the great shells would be gripped, rather than grabbed. Reputable science publications and practical (US Navy) diving manuals of the time included details on where to cut clam muscle to extricate oneself.

Over and over again, we swam furtively near several Giant Clams to look at their detailed colours and forms, and carefully positioned ourselves beyond creating any shadow. But all too often, the shells closed as we approached. If we had been the eagerly sought-after prey we would have escaped every time. What is the life story of this gorgeously clad, sedentary 'killer monster'? As always, its colours, structures and habits are focused on its own survival and successful proliferation. But the sequence of ingenious ways and means of achieving this goal is as enticing as the trail to the 'Pearl of Lao Tzu' and the story shrouding its human owners and events. And both human and animal stories have mysteries still to be resolved.

The animal's carnivorous aspirations extend no further than the minute life of floating plankton. Pairs of tiny Pea Crabs, large in comparison to plankton, live within a clam unmolested. Water is drawn into the clam through an inhalant siphon, microscopic food is filtered out and water is expelled through a second siphon. This provides but a small portion of its food; most of its sugars and proteins come from resident microscopic plants – zooxanthellae – as in the reef-building corals. It is the same scenario of mutual benefit for plants and a sedentary animal: plant products for the clam and protection at an ideal sunlit depth for sugar-making plants. The Giant Clam provides extravagantly advantageous accommodation for its lodgers – extra space in the form of delicate tube extensions of its stomach and roof windows of pale clear patches to facilitate light passing through the covering mantle skin layer. This extra-large colony of illuminated plant residents allows the clams to live and thrive in the more barren areas of sea where plankton food is sparse. In conditions of plenty and multiplying plant numbers, the clam consumes some of them, a relationship verging on farming.

The fabulous Giant Clam colours are also part of the liaison. Like all green plants, the zooxanthellae have pigments to absorb sunlight for their food production. Some colours of light are unusable and reflected, giving a reddish-brown appearance. To increase food production, the plants can convert less useful colours into useful ones by using extra pigments which reflect and fluoresce creating different colours. The clams themselves create still more pigments and more optical illusions by making sunscreens. They and their valuable plants, like us, are susceptible to damage by excessive amounts of ultraviolet light. The skin of the clam has built-in light reflectors: bundles of pigmented cells with stacks of reflective platelets. Acting as sunscreens, these create the iridescence of the jewel-like spangles of turquoise, blue and green. It is thought they may also benefit the clam's vision. Besides these reflectors, they also have chemicals and colourful pigments which have a sun block effect.

This wide range of plant and animal pigments can mix to create an endless array of colours – an incredible artist's palette, still under investigation. The range of patterns and variation of individuals is extraordinary and enigmatic: causes and effects remain obscure. Genetic controls, the type of zooxanthellae, long-term changes in light intensity, and extra nourishment have all been investigated, but inconclusively – there is a lack of consistency. The beautiful variety of Giant Clams seems to be endlessly variable.

With their two shells open to benefit their plant lodgers, the colourful Giant Clams are visible, meaty, static and without defences – ready meals. The only protection for themselves and their valuable plants is to withdraw their soft mantles and shut their exceptionally hard shells. They need to be aware of approaching predatory fish and divers. As we swam near we had been under efficient surveillance from the dotted pattern of the mantle and the dense 'necklaces' along its borders. Several hundred or even thousands of watchful eyes nestle in the glittering pattern of spangles. The sensitivity of this warning system presents a dilemma. Food production needs an open shell for light but is adversely affected by a shell closed against an approaching predator. If warning of danger is too sensitive the shell would over-react, continually closing and opening, reducing light. The animal only needs to be aware of movement nearby rather than detail of the mover. The clam's solution is in the myriad of small dark dots, a simple version of a snail type of eye – pinholes which are simple cup-shaped intucks of skin, lined with cells sensitive to light and without a lens. Their simplicity limits vision to mere awareness of movement of a dark object – a sudden dimming of light and movement at a distance. Experiments have shown that the dimensions and array of this apparently unsophisticated system are just enough to alert the animal to approaching danger of appropriate sizes and speeds, even if no shadow is cast over their body, allowing just enough time for it to quickly retract its mantle and close its shells. Trying, unsuccessfully, to sidle up to them unawares, our encounter had been a particularly one-sided affair. Rather than a man hunter, the Giant Clam is something of a diffident monster – or maybe not so diffident, as they can aim a surprise squirt of water from their siphon.

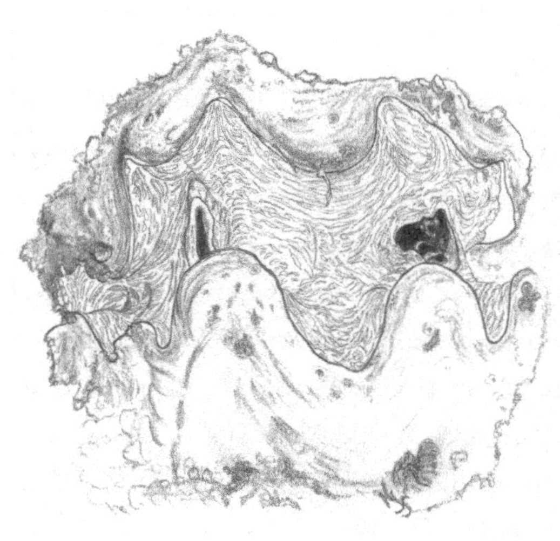

The rough-surfaced shells of this Giant Clam are encrusted with limpets, barnacles and algae. The open shells expose undulating folds of its soft body, patterned iridescent turquoise and dark blue due to its plant 'lodgers'; its two open siphons are pumping water.

'FULL FATHOM FIVE...'

The delights of shimmering shallows contrasted to the deepening blue and drop-off of Ngemelis. At the top of the reef, it was a swim past of myriads of fragile butterflyfish and sinuous fins of Moorish Idols. Black and white pyjama-striped Oriental Sweetlips were hanging about being their lugubrious selves; black Clown Triggerfish, white blotched and gold 'crazy-paved', appeared and disappeared. Scattered along the plateau of the cliff top there seemed to be diagonal leaning lines, like a field of blown canes, static sticks suspended mid-water, drifting slightly with the ebb and flow. Suddenly the close ranks broke and they all became horizontal, lying in parallel with each other, then they all transformed into a dishevelled spreading heap in all directions – these were the aptly named Cornetfish, wonderfully camouflaged and flared mouths, ready to suck in unsuspecting passing fish. We soon identified several 'no go' areas as our shadows passed over nest sites of over-zealous Titan Triggerfish which accelerated upwards towards us with serious intent. It was difficult to disengage from this immense moving canvas and focus on details. There were many: such as little Reef Squid, golden with pale blue eyes swivelling to view us as they passed by, beating little propelling fins, and clownfish backing abruptly into the protection of their anemones' tentacles.

Looking along the top of the cliff, this was a place of traffic. Wave after wave of long lines of hundreds of iridescent Blue and Yellow Fusiliers, Yellowtail and Scissortail Fusiliers were flashing by. Vast drifts of plankton feeders floated above and below – Red-toothed Triggerfish, with their distinctive triangular fins and lunate tails accentuated with long lobes. A quick glance almost gave the impression of hanging bats. Unicornfish competed, with so many streaming graceful tails they almost united into long undulating ribbons. Larger fish drifted past, gliding, invisibly propelled; others moving with curving bodies and tails in elegant S-shapes. Surface shafts of light etched round the sleek grey bodies of the bigger jacks, making them seem almost more than three-dimensional, with far more heavy presence than can ever appear on a TV screen. Their look was almost like solid polished metal, possibly iridescent layers in their scales. As we swam towards darker blue, a shoal of vivid green parrotfish veered across and led the way, spilling away out of sight over the edge, deep and steep below, dropping deeper to infinite vague gloom.

Out beyond was ocean rather than sea. We had ventured deep many years before, but in the cosseted, air-conditioned convenience of a viewing submarine. Then, sitting in a line of people looking through glass had been a little like looking at an enormous all-round screen, with a certain divorce from reality. Our present uncluttered view was watery reality on an enormous scale. Even so, the submarine view had been an incredibly memorable sight, and as close as a non-diver could get to this bigger, deeper version of sea life. Deeper down, the colour and variety had become sparse as the sunlight filtering down from above grew dimmer. Coloured corals had become conspicuously absent without enough light to sustain their plant lodgers. Hovering above a monochrome sandy floor, there had been nothing familiar in sight – eerie and sparse. From this apparent desert, thin, dark, wire-like growths emerged, some curling and spiralling. Deeper, at 46 m (150 ft), the light dimmed further and I remembered the shiver of cold down my spine – or was it a shudder of fear? Peter, a professional submariner for a decade, had not been enthusiastic about this alternative way of underwater viewing. I knew he had been quietly noting the boat's structure and escape facilities, and even I knew that the captain's safety speech of reassurance on how twenty-six people would be retrieved from that depth without giving them the 'bends' was not the glib operation he had outlined. Peter sat with white knuckles and I too was mighty relieved when we ascended towards colourful life. Aged 12, Andrew had sat wide-eyed. His teacher had said he was a changed boy afterwards: he always seemed to be somewhere else in his mind. It eventually surfaced years later, in 2001, when a brief email had come from Yap… *'I have just had a Manta Ray swim six inches above my head. Oh, did I tell you? I have qualified as a diver.'*

Andrew later followed us here to Ngemelis, and, hooked on to this cliff, had the privilege of a Marlin swimming right by him, its sail fin full spread high. This cliff was indeed a pelagic highway. It was a place of grand scale, the 'Big Drop-off', stretching down out of sight. Out of sight was way below the 1990 tourist submarine depth. More accurately it was 274 m (900 ft). To either side was the vertical sheer wall running the length of Ngemelis Island. Life all around seemed scaled to match the majestic size of the place. Beneath us big rays undulated fin wings, large Whitetip and Blacktip Reef Sharks glided slow with heavier grey relatives whose identity was blurred by distance, and two Grey Reef Sharks slept by a ledge. In the depths, we watched as five individual turtles flew past, rhythmically see-sawing their flippers like intent birds. Fish merged into glittering masses, hanging and dangling, darting in the blue 'ether', between long shafts of light, spotlights reaching down, seemingly bottomless. This was another planet, another dimension.

View towards the surface with Red-toothed Triggerfish (dark silhouettes) trailing and twisting long lunar-shaped tails. Beneath, a khaki camouflaged grouper watches, thick-lipped and wide-mouthed ready to suck in prey. Below its belly between its pelvic fins a tiny Cleaner Wrasse is visible.

FLOATING GALAXIES

A well-anchored rope strung between trees helped us scramble and haul ourselves up the side of a steep island using tree roots and jutting rocks as steps. The tree roots scrabbled and scraped their living across lumps of sharp pitted limestone – this was no place to trip. The jungle was thick, green and lush. Fleshy green climbers straddled trailing hairy loops of lianas; Strangler Figs knitted aerial roots into imprisoning nets – the antithesis of delicate ferns around them. Bare areas were a warning: the domain of a local tree, apparently so poisonous even water drip from its leaves caused fearful skin reaction. Here and there were rare Ironwood Trees – the name said it all – traditionally used for spears and the intricately carved story boards, recording myth and history of these Pacific Islands. Over the crest of the hill we descended steeply down the other side. Here the trees abruptly changed to Black Mangrove which created a tight tangle of humped roots at the edge of a lake. Walled in by rocky heights covered with such dense tall trees, the water was green and opaque, dark and shadowy round the edge. It had an aura of the unexpected and the strange: a new lake, 12,000 years old, in an ancient island, but isolated enough to have evolved its own unique animal community.

There are about seventy such isolated marine lakes amongst Palau's Rock Islands, each with its specific environment and resident populations. Jellyfish Lake on Eil Malk (Mecherchar) Island is connected to the surrounding sea lagoon by three tunnels through which tides come and go, but the lake's depth (30 m, 98 ft) is such that this tidal flow never thoroughly mixes down to the depths. We wondered if we had witnessed tide flowing back into the sea while snorkelling along the steep-walled shoreline. The wall was encrusted with lush yellow, orange, lime-green, terracotta and purple growth, with corals emerging in tall orange pinnacles and unfurling layers of leaf-like plates, and through it, there was water tumbling out of a 'subterranean' hole. The juxtaposition of Pennant Bannerfish and Christmas Tree Worms gliding and waving elegantly by an underwater cascading waterfall seemed more like something out of an aquarium fantasy, but more realistically, was possibly part of the island's tunnel system.

The surrounding forested limestone wall, over which we had climbed, effectively stops any wind from ruffling the lake's surface and mixing of water. Being so near to the equator, daily temperature variation is too slight to cause any mixing between layers. The result is a lake that is permanently stratified in two halves – the top half, slightly turbid, containing oxygen and able to support life. In the lower region the oxygen level is zero: a layer of sulphur bacteria thrives and forms a shading dark 'skin', under which the lake is dark and clear and dead. Hydrogen sulphide, ammonia and phosphates are in concentrations high enough to poison a diver through the skin.

After the effort of the steep climb and descent in beating heat, dense vegetation encircling still water offered a cool oasis. The feeling was confirmed as we submerged. Spiky finned Orbicular Cardinal Fish hung about under the jetty. As our eyes became accustomed in the shadows, dark mussels materialised on the dark mangrove roots, and ephemeral outlines of sea squirts. Amongst them were small pale sea anemones, elongated simple animal sacs, recognisable polyps, fixed to the spot and waving their rings of long thin tentacles. They looked far too delicate to survive, but their small size, simplicity and beauty belied an efficient killer. They are the major predators of the millions of creatures which inhabit the lake – their much larger relatives, Golden Jellyfish. Their other relatives, the coral polyps of the surrounding sea built the substance of this and all of the Rock Islands. Jellyfish are, in effect, single anemone-like polyps turned upside down and floating free. We were in a small, polyp-dominated universe.

We swam from the jetty shadows into sun-drenched water, scrutinising the middle distance hoping to meet them. At first, nothing. The opaque water beneath created hazy shafts of light, emanating from the surface like an underwater version of 'God's fingers' in a sunset sky. Then an occasional tiny jellyfish, about as small as a little finger nail, drifted into focus out of the green gloom – pale, vague opaque forms. As we swam towards them, almost imperceptibly there seemed to be more. We blinked to confirm they were really there. Their shapes were slowly revealed, like the 'Alice in Wonderland' Cheshire cat. As they floated through descending shafts of light the sun touched their bells, shifting from near transparent to a reflecting surface sheen, and an occasional glimpse of whitish structures illuminated within. Eventually we were surrounded by Golden Jellyfish of all sizes – it is thought there could be five or more million of them – some as big as an outstretched hand, like toadstools, upside down, upright, gliding, umbrella bells pulsating, throbbing. They had something of a lampshade look, hung with heavy shading tassel drapes, or maybe even exotic chandeliers. They were as ephemeral as their colour: that 1930s hue in between pink and gold, trimmed with coffee lace. The salmon colour shaded more intensely down to the stubby tips of their dangling arms.

One accidentally bumped by me – their perception and their control of direction are very simple – its umbrella was soft and firm, like rubber. Such a touch from a jellyfish in the sea beyond could be painful, as they have the same stinging cells, nematocysts, as corals and sea anemones. In the special conditions of this lake, the Golden Jellyfish do not need stings to immobilise small fish or to protect themselves. Like the Giant Clams they gain food produced by gold-coloured microscopic plants living within their tissues which give them their name. Their diet supplements are Copepods – tiny, shelled animals of the lake's plankton, somewhat resembling diminutive woodlice, caught by a slight sting. Only the most sensitive skin of our lips can feel it, but it does exist; their evolution into being stingless is a myth. Copepods also feed the lake's million carnivorous Moon Jellyfish, which stay out of sight in deeper waters and whose sting is not powerful enough to pierce human skin

The moving mass of jellyfish was not an accidental event. They combat the threat of the anemones lurking along the shadowy edges of the water by a spectacular behaviour particular to this lake. As the sun rises they begin a 1 km (0.6 mile) long daily migration from the western basin of the lake to the furthest sunlit edges of the eastern basin, arriving by mid-morning. When they reach the edge of the shadows they stop and congregate, well short of the lake edge, thus remaining out of reach of the carnivorous anemones. Throughout the day they are in the sun near the surface, swimming and rotating counter-clockwise. By doing this they maintain an even exposure to sunlight. Their contained plants gain protected perpetual transport to the light, optimising their sugar manufacture. Early in the afternoon the jellyfish slowly pulsate in the reverse direction, to return to the western basin by mid-afternoon. Here they remain through the night, moving up and down within the oxygenated layer absorbing nutrients for their valuable algae.

Looking far distant through the water, there was green nothingness, just sun glinting creatures wafting by, continuously passing on their way through, on and on; on and out of sight, a seemingly endless stream of life, like a slow moving galaxy of stars. The shafts of light filtering down accentuated the cosmic illusion. Below, was the total eerie silence of this underwater universe. Above, in the earthly domain of the wall of trees, there was the monotonous booming of Fruit Doves, the shrill shriek of insects and singing small birds. Black Terns passed overhead, the underside of their wings reflecting a metallic sheen, and a group of White-tailed Tropicbirds floated upwards and out of sight. The feeling of being at the boundary became overwhelming with one ear tilted above the water, the other below. We were between two contrasting green worlds.

Looking up towards the surface, bright sunlight spotlights Golden Jellyfish structures from many angles – radial symmetry, dangling arms around the mouth, and the tiny golden plants crowded in their tissues which give them their colour and their name.

ROCK ISLANDS POST SCRIPT

Surrounded by millions of creatures in a protected habitat on a remote island one is tempted to think that their continued presence is stable and permanent. Six years previous to our visit, in 1998, they quite suddenly disappeared. Access to Jellyfish Lake was closed. The most likely cause was probably the weather event of El Nino at that time (which also affected the reefs of the Maldives). It seems the water temperature rose, causing the zooxanthellae living inside the Golden Jellyfish to increase their rate of photosynthesis, so producing more oxygen. At a certain concentration this becomes deleterious to the host which ejects the cause. Without the algae and their products of photosynthesis available in their tissues, the jellyfish starved and died. The population did recover slowly and the lake returned to normal. However, it is an illustration of how a subtle natural change can have a dramatic large effect. There has been another dramatic decline in their numbers in 2016 accompanying extreme El Nino weather conditions; the outcome remains uncertain at the time of writing.

The other marine lakes are closed to public access for conservation reasons. The Rock Islands are a World Heritage Site, greatly valued and protected in Palau. Here is a microcosm of the wider world. The influence of tourism is always a delicate issue: policing the rules of non-interference and undesirable means of achieving today's tourist's all-important photo opportunities is difficult socially and practically. Dive and boat tour operators come from a range of cultures having different standards in attitudes to animals, respect for the environment and awareness of mankind's ultimate dependence on it. And their clients have equally diverse personal reasons for visiting, whether to see, experience, understand, touch it, or photograph it – or themselves victoriously in front of it – or tick it off the list. In 2004 some boats blared loud muzak across the reefs, disgorged twenty-five people or more at a time, organised them into a circle, heads in, legs radiating out, while dispensing large amounts of leftover human lunch at the centre to attract fish and photographers. With two trips a day and many boats this apparently innocent incentive soon snowballs. Several decades ago, feeding fish was an accepted norm. On my first snorkel in Buck Island in 1973 my biggest smile had been for a large Technicolor Miracle fish that deftly took hard-boiled egg from my fingers – the boat's crew had given us the remains of lunch to attract fish. Now the memory brings not a smile but a frown of concern. In the years since, research has shown without doubt that feeding fish on bread, eggs, chicken bones, burgers and chips causes them digestive disorders and ultimately death – their digestive systems are not designed for remnants of human lunch. Worse still, the overall effect of the starch and fat of land lubber's fare upsets the subtle balance of the reef's own very intricate system of nourishment and decay. It is, in effect, a slow insidious form of pollution interfering with a subtle resources roundabout which has been perfected over millions of years. Many people still misguidedly believe they are doing the fish a favour. Unfortunately feeding fish human food, as opposed to special fish food, is still common practice in various parts of the world, even with dive and tour operators. It guarantees the promise of an 'awesome' photo opportunity. Choosing a tour operator with care allows selection of exceptionally knowledgeable guides sensitive to unique habitats and privileged areas of biodiversity.

Large gatherings of small fish feeding attract larger fish to feed on them, and on up the scale to large predators, particularly within close proximity to deep water. The delight of being in the centre of myriads of glittering fish can render one blind to the less attractive possibility of being mistaken as another morsel of lunch. Through a misunderstanding, early on in our snorkelling adventures we found ourselves left in deep water over a wreck diving site. I had never stepped over the side of a boat into deep blue water in my life. Below, the frail frame of the wreck was barely visible, rhythmically appearing through a slight swell. Some large fish sides glittered now and then. Aware of our isolation at this wreck site we snorkelled with some apprehension after our boat had disappeared into a dot and people on the beach looked like distant ants in an aerial photograph. Myriads of small fish began flocking around us as I was armed with the remains of breakfast, crammed into spare bra space in my bathing costume, still ignorant, like most people, of the deleterious effect of human food on fish. Peter kept motioning to me not to feed them, but I had felt like an underwater version of St Francis of Assisi. Peter was not clairvoyant on fish digestive physiology, more trying to ensure our survival unmolested: unknown to me, there was a gathering shoal of large silver Barracuda a few feet behind mine and eager for the small fish. In fact, this disconcerting habit of following divers and swimmers is typical Barracuda behaviour. Peter was remembering the stories from Buck Island about Barracuda teeth, so sharp they could shred your fingers off just by passively shutting their mouth – even if an open top jaw dropped shut over one's hand while retrieving a hook after the fish was dead. True or false, it did not matter; as predators using the element of surprise they just looked like malice aforethought, and that was enough. Snorkelling far out in deep blue water with Barracudas, it was a relief when the brash *Jolly Roger* fantasy pirate ship appeared, flying skull and cross bones – just in case there was any doubt – and spilling out happy tourists in scores for the quick snorkel segment of their day trip complete with pirate rum. It was the only occasion ever that we positively welcomed a mass influx of very modern man complete with accessories into the ancient quiet of the underwater.

It is a salutary thought that casual fish feeding was cited as one of the main causes of sharks attacking five snorkellers in the Red Sea resort of Sharm el-Sheikh in the space of a few days in 2010. There had been 'small fish feeding' activities from a pier which in turn encouraged larger predatory fish and there was a deeper drop-off not far away. There were also organised dive activities of feeding sharks with prey fish, which, although a natural food, artificially alters their behaviour and local population size – in some instances leading to attacks on humans. In the blink of an eye the sea can become a dangerous place for land beings.

Curious or on the hunt? A pack of Barracuda, efficient predators with powerful large tails and sleek streamlined bodies for fast swimming, large mobile eyes and forward projecting lower jaws.

Chapter 7

THE PAST WRITTEN ON A VIKING SHORE – SEALS, SHELLS AND A WHALE
Scotland

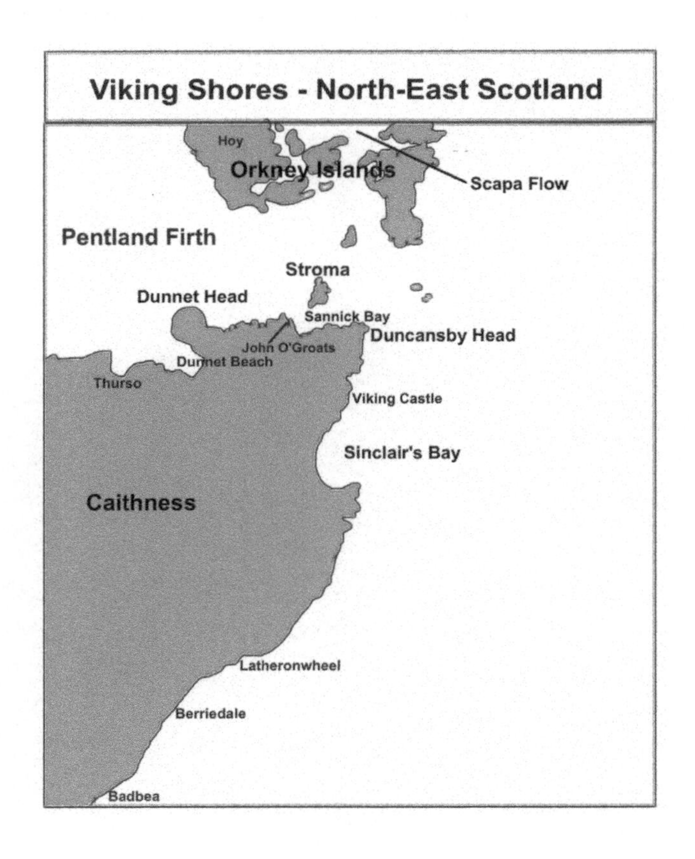

STROMA – AN ISLAND INTERLUDE

The farmer's rich voice rang out, far across the encircling streaked sea and into a vast sky bordered with pale duck egg blue. It is the colour of the far north. His Gaelic song was of the flowers of the wild moors, addressed to us, the sea birds and the diminutive purple Scottish Primrose at his feet. He was standing in the centre high spot of his tiny island. To the north were the sprawling islands of Orkney, like grounded elongated clouds of blue-greys, receding to the horizon like layers of shadows. At the western end was the island of Hoy, with barely a sign of human presence – sharp stepped cliffs topped with reddish moorland and finalised abruptly by the sharp pinnacle of the Old Man of Hoy. Here and there, on some islands, there were reassuring homely patches of green and pale lemon fields. Across choppy swirls and the white horses of wind-whisked waves to the west was the mainland with the imposing flat-topped cliff of Dunnet Head, the most northerly tip of the British mainland – and the cold North Atlantic. To the east, the jagged jutting face of Duncansby Head heralded the North Sea. It was an evocative and changeable sea space under racing smears and wisps of clouds strewn sparse by the strong wind. Tricks of cloud and light could spotlight the high cliffs of Hoy and Dunnet Head, giving them such clarity as to defy distance.

The farmer's island is a tilted slope of turf rising out of this petulant sea where ocean currents meet. The wind denies the existence of trees. Cliffs border the western side, packed with ledges and flutters of white seabirds. Below them, shallow swirls of waves sweep across flat pavement-like plates of sandstone, angled and potentially dangerous: places for seals rather than people. The sea surrounding the island is visibly treacherous. There are ever present and unpredictable races: swells, whirlpools and eddies of the Pentland Firth – the Witch's Cauldron, the Merry Men of Mey and Hell's

Mouth. At the tip of the island is 'The Swelkie' whirlpool, its name derived from the Old Norse 'Svalga' – 'the Swallower'. According to Viking legend this part of the sea's turmoil is caused by a sea-witch turning mill stones to grind the salt to keep the seas salty.

This north-eastern part of Scotland was under Norse occupation for nearly 350 years, ending in 1231. Here, tales of seals shedding their sea skin to assume human form, enter the shady realm of near belief and folk memory. Seal people, 'selkie-folk', were irresistible to village lads and maidens (and vice versa) but to return to the sea they needed their magic skin – if lost or stolen they were doomed to remain on land. Such stories of tragedy and intrigue abounded in Iceland, the Faroes, Scotland and Ireland, and the stories travelled further with emigrants.

This particular part of Orcadian selkie-folk country is wild, eerie, romantic, threatening, breathtakingly beautiful, dour or downright dangerous by turns. While high numbers of seals flourish, human life here has been on the edge, even in modern times. Such a sea becomes a moat, isolating an island community in an impenetrable fortress – or a prison. Many crossings between islands and mainland have ended in disaster; drowned grandparents, parents and siblings are still part of island life. Looking across to the islands of Orkney, inviting low hills offer the shelter of more peaceful water. One does not immediately think of shipwrecks here with large scale loss of life. It was not always a peaceful quiet place – a marked sea grave remembers an intentional sinking. The protective ring of islands around Scapa Flow was artificially completed with barrages and was used as an enclosed haven for the British Fleet in two World Wars – five brothers, childhood friends of my mother's, lie there with over 800 others in *HMS Royal Oak*, torpedoed in 1939.

A traditional isolated life depending on sea crossings relies on the health and strength of the young staying in the community. As is so often the case all over the world, modern life offers ease and plenty, and it is the ageing population that remains. The domestic fields of Stroma are now deserted. As we wandered, we saw a silent church and sparse lines of houses, left as if on hurried impulse. In some, old wedding photos and magazine pictures remained pinned to walls, unretrieved, and rusting chain and spanners lay neatly laid out, mid bicycle repair, in a lean-to shed open to the sky. The entire community left in the late 1950s, the island put up as a prize in an American lottery, withdrawn, then sold to this local Caithness farmer who had spent his boyhood here.

In summers he transported his sheep and student shepherds from the mainland to the fine grazing on Stroma, crossing the narrow strip of sea in an old ex-military landing craft. For land transport there was a powder blue 1950s Morris Minor, rusted and worn to the point that the car floor had rotted away in several places. The impression of speed was enhanced by looking down between the accelerator and clutch pedals and cables and seeing the pebbles on the track racing by beneath the car. Behind the steering wheel our chauffeur was a ten-year-old boy, thrilling with power and laughter as he accelerated down the hill towards the narrow jetty. Slowing and braking was achieved by extending his feet through the hole in the floor and walking the car to a standstill. In retrospect across many years, the short journey to and from the centre of the island vied with the Gaelic song for the most vivid memory of the day. In the strange way of coincidence this boy's path and ours crossed again decades later. We were at a deserted harbour on the mainland coast, not far from the old mooring of the Stroma landing craft. This stone jetty jutted out a long way across rocks skimmed by a shallow low tide; a place rich with curlews and oystercatchers. We walked to the end of the jetty and heard a tractor arriving on the shore behind us. As we turned, it slowly reversed along the jetty towards us. The tractor was not wide and neither was the jetty. There were a few inches to spare – not a large margin given that the driver was a small boy. A man of about 45 was sitting on the mudguard, back-seat driving, passing on his childhood Stroma driving skills to his son.

ON THE BEACH

VIKING SHELLS – ANCIENT AND MODERN

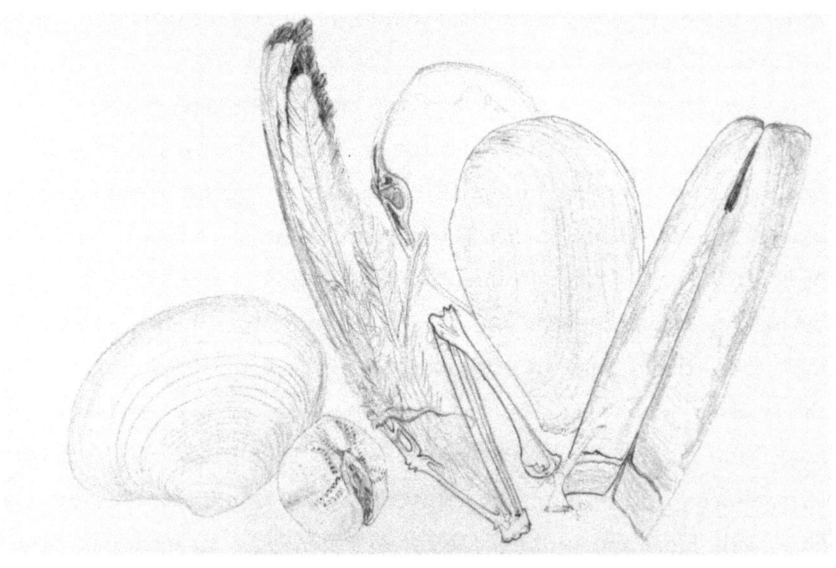

Beachcombing finds. Bird's wing – the 'arm' bones are long; feathers are still attached to elongated 'wrist' and finger bones. Two Otter Shells – paired shells are separated to show the hinge of one. Elongated Razor Clam with its two shells still firmly joined. On the left, one shell of an Icelandic Clam: its growth rings age it at only 126 years old. Sea Potato – a very different animal design based on fives.

Across the strait from Stroma, the mainland shore is a place of busy trading – ancient and modern. John o' Groats is the northern goal of tourists, record seekers and fundraisers – driving, riding, cycling, walking and even canoeing. It was always a busy shore; fish and shellfish abound for seals and people. A shallow shelving rocky beach nearby is littered with the detritus of fish processing – not a modern prodigal monstrosity, but biodegrading refuse from Viking times. The surface is a loose, deep uneven carpet of white lumps, bumps, spikes and broken edges. It is a discomfort in bare feet or soft soled shoes, but stunningly beautiful as an uninterrupted expanse of spirals and curved sculpted shapes – remains of Common Whelk shells, in large numbers, and many others. Archaeological digs have revealed that the Norsemen who settled in the area had a lucrative trade of exporting shellfish and dried white fish as far away as Europe. It was a particularly valued commodity during Lent when eating meat was forbidden. Broken and whole shells of various whelks, several types of clams and fish bones remain easily visible here, stacked tightly in shelly layers beneath the turf overhanging today's beach. For 800 years or more, rabbits have burrowed in the soft sandy bank, waves have battered the weakening edge and loosened the layers. Shells from the distant past mingle with those recently abandoned by foraging sea birds.

Sea shells are the most obvious signs of animal occupation of any shore and an irresistible magnet for people with a love of wandering quiet beaches to discover the unusual and beautiful as well as the edible. I had become entranced by shells on the Australian east coast and when very young I had been given a handful of shells from more northerly tropical waters. They were delicately coloured and as glossy as the lustre of high-fired porcelain, some with flared mouths, some extravagantly fluted and spiked. The eccentricity of these beauties had been inseparable from that of their collector. Esmé was one of that intrepid, now regrettably past, breed of solo lady traveller who ventured into the wild dangerous places that still remained. Dynamic and enthusiastic, she was in the mould of past artist explorers, Margaret Mee and Marianne North. In my eyes she fitted the enticing title role of my book *A Woman Among Savages* as she visited remotest New Guinea – in 1950 a destination only for tough explorers and scattered government officials. She photographed remote tribes and their dead ancestors, green, stiff and folded to fit their cave storage racks, and for me she had collected shells. I always thrilled for my own searches but without her associated extras.

Beachcombing along these northern shores, particularly Dunnet Bay, the shells were very different from those of Britain's more frequented southern beaches. The shells are mere inert remains; the animals which created them hold a greater fascination of their own, with innovative solutions to the problems of life under the sand. They belong to the 'soft-bodied' group of creatures – the molluscs, fancy and extreme versions of garden snails and their kin. The molluscs have a very significant and prominent foot, muscular and fleshy, which in practical terms translates as good food potential. The group is ancient, possibly one of the earliest to move about on the primeval sea floor and many of its members have featured on menus since humans started hunter-gathering. The Latin title of the snail version translates as 'stomach-foot' which is an apt description. With a relatively insignificant head, these are the Vikings' whelks and limpets and, in warmer waters, conches. Another very edible group of molluscs have two shells and no head – the bivalves, translating as 'two waves' – the Viking's clams, cockles, scallops, oysters, mussels and, in warmer seas, geoduck. The most fascinating mollusc group are the 'head-foots', cephalopods, which have big alert eyes, brainpower and attitude, which makes for memorable encounters with humans. Having developed the soft body design to an extreme, these animals – squid, octopus, cuttlefish and nautilus appear to have little in common with scallops or snails.

These very different creatures all share the single, large edible foot; a basic structure which has been commandeered for diverse purposes and beautifully illustrates the 'lateral thinking' type of design so frequent in the natural world. The molluscan foot comes in many shapes and sizes according to how it served its original owner: pulled, stretched, squeezed, reinforced or twisted during its reinvention for different uses. In snail types it is a broad and sturdy slider gliding on lubricant slime; in limpets it is a suction disc; whilst the conch variant digs a pointed sickle-shape tip into the sand for a hopping molluscan version of pole vaulting. Bivalves bore, dig and burrow the foot into sand and mud. The elongated Razor Clam (Razor Shell or 'Chinaman's fingernails') goes for a high-speed dig involving distinct stages of shell opening, closing, hydraulically inflating the powerful long foot, deflating and squirting water, repeated cyclically. The 'head-foot' has transformed into supple flexible tentacles and arms fit for ingenious manipulative use. Regardless of means or speed, forward movement via a foot needs eyes, another shared feature, and a nervous system to process the image. The system is simple in many, such as Giant Clams, and advanced in the squid and its relatives; the alien mollusc body design is one of potential sophistication.

Octopus on the move. This animal's head was coloured and textured to match its background of beige, dull pinks and greens of seaweed encrusted rock; its eyes are set high in protruding 'humps'. In octopus and other 'head-foots', the foot is wrapped around the head and is divided into flexible manipulative arms. This alien appearance elicited gesticulations and shrieks from an approaching onlooker... at which the octopus rapidly changed to white, unfurled its arms, spread itself 'larger' and then exited at lightning speed.

The decorative and protective shell, treasured by people and molluscs alike, is created by a covering skin – a mantle – another feature they all share. This mantle skin cover can, like the foot, morph in many ways. Folded into a simple tube it can create a siphon transporting water with oxygen, as in the whelk. Equipped with chemosensors it can smell, taste and suck up food like a vacuum cleaner. The octopus version can power an eye-blinkingly efficient means of propulsion by expelling water. Siphons are snorkels for those that burrow – the Razor Clam, Otter Shell and Icelandic Clam. The Razor Clam stands vertically, just out of sight, with short inhaling and exhaling siphons exposed whereas Otter Shells can live in much deeper mud or sand needing immense siphons to match, extending two or three times the shell length.

The shape of Otter Shells is accentuated by delicate concentric sculpted lines, showing periods of growth, similar to tree rings. In the Icelandic Clam (Ocean Quahog) these very obvious lines have become enormously significant in studying climate change. On a few occasions, Dunnet Beach was transformed into a wandering trail of these shells and little else. They followed a gentle wave line as far as the eye could see. Vikings and early hunter- gatherers possibly recognised the potential of these very thick and strong shell 'spoon' scoops. Dished deep enough to be useful as a small bowl, we had collected them as useful containers for years, unaware we were reducing breathtakingly special objects to the mundane.

The young clam larva is taken by the currents until it finally settles on the deep sea bed. It grows shells and burrows ready for a life of filtering plankton food drifting down from above. Far northern waters are cold and they grow and age slowly — very slowly. This species – called the 'tree of the sea' – claimed the world record for animal longevity when an individual was dredged from a depth of 80 m (262 ft) in north Icelandic coastal waters in 2006. Named 'Ming', the shell was aged at 507 years, assessed by analysis of the shell's annual growth lines and confirmed by carbon dating. Something like the seasonal rings of trees, these reflect the conditions of each year's growth, capturing variations of temperature, salinity and food availability. Where shell timelines overlap it becomes possible to see the sequence of such environmental events. As a result, these unassuming molluscs form a vital chronological link in current research on climate. Colonial corals, also long lived, show such variations, but are only indicative of climate in the much warmer seas where they live. A member of the Icelandic Clam research team explains the accurate time records within the shells:

'One fascinating aspect of this work is that we have been able to cross-date the patterns of growth increments from one shell to another, so constructing long chronologies that extend beyond the life span of any individual shell. We are now approaching 2,000 years in Icelandic waters and able to reconstruct very detailed records of changing seawater temperatures from chemical changes within each annual increment. This clearly shows variability in the temperature of waters around Iceland, relatively warm in the Medieval period, very cold in the Little Ice Age between the fifteenth and nineteenth centuries, with a marked recent warming since then. These are key data for constraining model simulations of North Atlantic circulation and assessing the impact of human-induced climate change on the oceans' (James Scourse, School of Ocean Sciences, Bangor University).

The shell chosen from my collection of Icelandic Clam 'dishes' for the sketch was also checked for age. It was investigated in optimism as it was particularly large, but was in fact remarkably young. It was only 126 years old, born in the same year as my grandmother, and had obviously had a life of plenty in the fast lane. Cod, seals and wolf fish eat the clams, as does man. They are commercially fished, to the point of wiping out some populations. 'Ming', born in 1499, was fortunate in living in an area of few predators and minimal fishing.

Along the beach there were other remnants. These were fragments of creatures from the deep, the shore, land and air, and from distant places and the distant past. Remains of crab skeletons lay half-submerged in the sand: their archetypal multiple eating tools of variously sized claws usually dislocated from their body shell, but still making an intricate fit for meticulous action. In the lacy edge of receding ripples there were occasionally animals scooped in by the tide, such as soft Moon Jellyfish passing by in a passive drift.

The arrival of such animals and remnants on the tide is not random. Like the Eider Ducks, Pintail Ducks and Great Northern Divers out in the bay, they have their particular times of the year. Different tides and strong gales bring with them extremes in types and numbers of sea creatures and relics. Even the distribution along the beach of left and right shells of bivalves such as Icelandic Clams can be the result of left and right shells catching the current differently; such distributions are measurable. Sometimes we saw a 'tide' of Otter Shells almost exclusively; at other times Banded Wedge Shells dominated, or Thin Tellins, many with two valves still joined, like flutters of little pink and yellow butterflies, stranded on the sand.

POTATOES, WORMS AND FLOTSAM

'Sea Potato tides' were an unusual event: a wide band of fragile white empty shells stretching along three miles of beach. Not a mollusc, but a type of sea urchin, the Sea Potato is covered with short yellowish spines when alive, and belongs on a very different animal planet based on radial symmetry, often in fives. Starfish, sand dollars, sea stars, brittle and basket stars, and sea cucumbers all belong to this group – the echinoderms. Their body design has another strange aspect; a fascinating hydraulic system which works thousands of tiny transparent tube feet. They are the animal's very visible means of movement. They can sense prey, can clamp on to and prise open a closed mussel shell, or pass food particles down to the mouth. The Sea Potato buries itself in the sand at about a hand's depth equipped with extra-long tube feet to reach for food particles lying on the sand above. The empty shell sketched in 'beachcombing finds' shows the arrangement of tube feet visible as double rows of apertures arrayed in star symmetry.

The long reaches of Dunnet's smooth wet sand are dotted with little coils of sand, like tantalisingly neat twirled cake decorations on the surface, each beside a perfect circular depression – ornate miniature sand pyramids and ponds. At low tide, the wide flat expanse is peppered by thousand upon thousand of them, all regularly spaced. I stood looking into a distant spray haze and their multitudes receded beyond sight to the end of the beach and down to the creeping edge of lapping waves. The wet sand and mounds were the subjects of rapt attention from groups of seagulls, Oystercatchers and Common Ringed Plovers. This is a world where life tries to hide beneath from the threat from above: each bird species feeds on life living at the depth of its beak – worms, molluscs, crabs and many more.

The orderly array of pyramids and ponds hid multitudes of extraordinary secretive creatures living in U-shaped burrows below, not soft-bodied molluscs but lugworms. Even theoretical lectures of student years and chalk drawn diagrams on dusty blackboards had never dulled the wonder of the movements of these animals according to a strictly regular rhythm. The lugworm is an apparently humble and unprepossessing worm, a popular fish bait. It is built on a railway carriage plan of sequential segments, looking very like an earthworm but with three slightly differing regions. The middle section has visible bristles for anchors to assist movement within its burrow. It seldom leaves and lives with its head at the base of a head shaft, and tail towards the tail shaft. To feed, it engulfs soft sand above its head and extracts the edible, causing the level above to sink and soften, creating the saucer-shaped pond depression at the surface. The worm moves back up the tail shaft using its bristles to grip and deposits indigestible sand casts in a neat pile at the surface, then returns to base. Oxygen is absorbed by external feathery gills, visibly red with haemoglobin-based blood like ours. Inside the burrow, keeping oxygen concentration up and waste levels down within sustainable limits is critical. The worm ventilates its home by performing squirming contractions along its length, pumping water through and refreshing the burrow. It does this cyclically with a meticulous regularity. One might imagine that the periodicity of the animal's movements would be determined by the state of its burrow, such as the amount of oxygen in the water, or hunger. Surprisingly this is not the case: it is controlled with the regularity of clockwork – in fact by a complex internal 'biological clock'. One rhythm seems to be sited in the upper part of the animal's gut – even the dissected part in isolation goes through the movements. It transpires that the clock is even more sophisticated than first imagined; when moved to a laboratory environment, an animal is most active at times corresponding to the tidal rhythms of its home beach.

Surprise beach finds included the joy and dismay of inert remains of civilisation – frequently, old wooden fish boxes ideal for improvised camping furniture. Over the years, the sea's wooden remnants were replaced by objects and pieces of plastic and polystyrene. Recently, seaweed tangles of the upper tide line include myriads of plastic pieces reduced to the smaller and the more dangerous – the size of confetti, fit for further degradation into the Atlantic Garbage Vortex.

On occasion, even non-biodegradable human detritus can deliver a treasure – a surfboard appeared. It had been battered, wedged between rocks, but was retrievable: '*it might be useful…*' either for its original purpose, or another… '*maybe, one day*'. For years it lay dry and useless until that 'one day' arrived with the opportunity to clothe ourselves in insulating blubber, like seals and dolphins – in thick wet suits. The board was recycled into use. Then we were closer than ever to sea creature experience, and both rekindling childhood joy: lying on one's belly, feeling the board skating the breaking crest of the wave, the power from behind and the surge of acceleration, skimming the surface with bouncing sparkling droplets in one's face. To feel the bond with surfing dolphins and sea lions indulging in such wave antics was a delight yet to come.

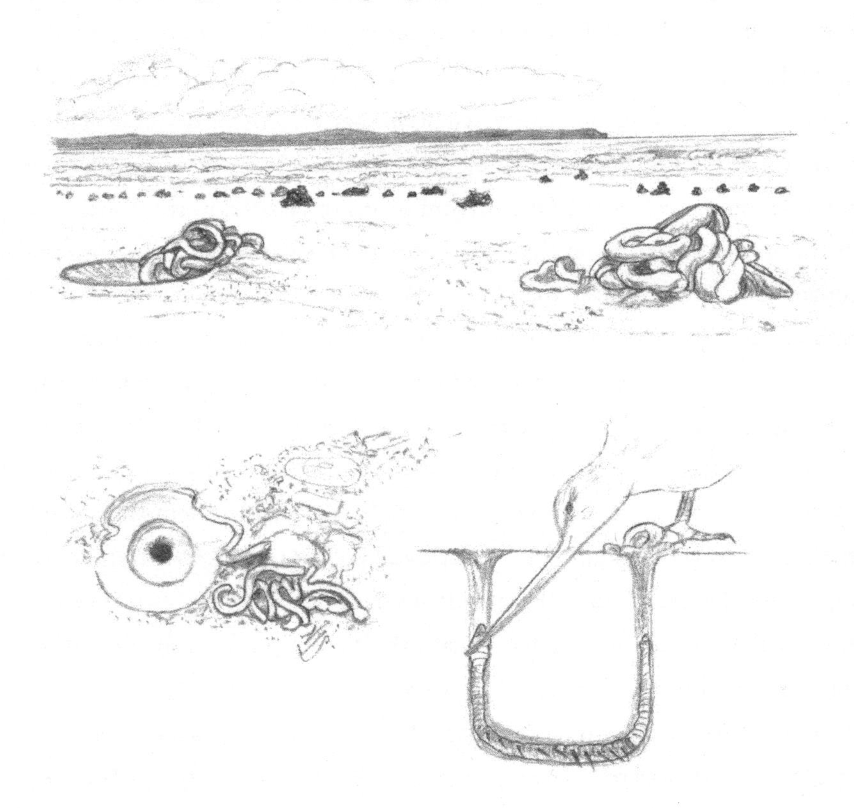

A bird's eye-view. Top: A feast from afar – ground level view of lugworm (lobworm) 'sand castles' down the beach to the water's edge. Left: Clues of a burrow beneath- a pool and a neat pile of sand. Right: A bird finds its goal. The worm's retractable bristles on the middle section allow anchorage and movement within the burrow.

ABOVE AND BELOW

CLIFFS AND BIRDS

Higher up the beach, there was the inanimate underlay of this shore, indicative of its past. Large striped pebbles were relics of the slow build-up of different coloured sands and silts on the floor of an ancient lake. Deep, dark and tropical, it once covered this part of Scotland – the dinosaurs came and went but the muddy floor remained undisturbed. Today one can pick up pieces of sand ripples which patterned its shallows, 385 million years old – frozen motion in time and stone. The layers accumulated, like flaky pastry in stone, and in between lie the perfect, crisply detailed remains of primitive armour-plated fish which swam in the shallows. As a student, I had met some of these – as plaster models and exquisite delicate fossils in museum display cases. The naturally thin plates of this stone are perfect as traditional local building materials: beautifully regular dry stone walls, roof tiles and flat flagstone floors. In the nineteenth century, the Caithness flagstone industry paved the city streets of the British Empire. Unknowingly I had already stepped on this ancient bed of Lake Orcadie – as a child walking on Sydney's old pavements.

Today some of the ancient silts now stand as cliffs bordering the sea which partly replaces the lake – the Pentland Firth. The high sheer cliffs of Duncansby Head stand like a gatepost at the corner of the mainland. As the sea rounds into the Firth the waves crash, roll up and cascade down in waterfalls. Weathering of the layered silts creates stone shelves and ledges, ideal for nesting seabirds. In early summer these cliffs resemble avian tower blocks, overcrowded, rowdy and raucous. The air is crowded with outspread wings, squeals, squawks and action. Jostling on ledges there are outstretched necks, upward pointing beaks, pecking, tender meetings of bill stroking and precision feeding of young birds. Guillemots, be-spectacled 'Bridled', and Black with vivid scarlet legs, stand on high narrow sills, probably the smallest territories of any bird. Their very pointed eggs are laid directly on to the rock, poised ready to fall from these natural skyscrapers. Somehow, in spite of the melee, their shape rolls them round in a tight circle and they remain aloft. Above the slatted rock towers there are dark openings of deep burrows in the turf where Puffins sit squat and sheltered. In shallower recesses Fulmars nest quietly, able to float out and over the sea with ease, gliding free, on stiff horizontal wings. Returning from feeding, they wheel in circles, banking round steeply to alight gracefully on their nests. On the sea below them, foraging Guillemots and Puffins gather in large rafts of bobbing black and white on the surface, diving for fish, using powerful wings for underwater diving.

At the base of the cliffs, tilted plates of stone form outlying rocky reefs, convenient rest points for shags and cormorants to groom between dives. At times they stand like heraldic phoenixes, with wings half extended. It was variously thought that their pose was a means of keeping their balance, a signal of a successful food forage or an aid to swallowing fish, but intense studies have shown it is the means of drying wings and general plumage. They shudder and flutter intermittently and gently vibrate the long flight feathers, then abruptly stop still – allowing maximum drying effect for minimum effort. Their untidy nests are secreted low down on rock shelves in deep cut narrow clefts in the cliff or 'geos', from Old Norse. Here, crystal clear green water surges just below, welling up and falling against red and golden stone. Occasionally individual shags nest under rock overhangs at the mouth of sea caves shining with green velvet growth above the water. Beneath the surface diminutive fish dart past pale opaque shapes which pulsate into recognition as jellyfish. Vivid pink and blue Squat Lobsters lie low, bright blue starfish creep and white crabs teeter across slanting rock shelves. These and the cave walls are encrusted pink, mauve, blue, yellow and beige – meadows of tight packed seaweed threads and tiny sessile animals. Within the geos and caves life is diverse and relatively protected; tiny fish fry cruise and shelter out of sight of the masses of sea birds outside in the open. Some of the fish around these shores are as irresistible to land-based birds as the sea birds. In this remote part of the country there was always the possibility of the unusual and spectacular animal encounter, the privileged optimism of 'when' rather than 'if'... as long as there was time in hand. There was, behind the pebble beach at Berriedale, a magic river wound round the base of a sheltering cliff. Magic, because here were the migrating fish of student lectures, which, amazingly, change their body chemistry between salt water and fresh. There were multitudes of salmon, newly arrived from far away in the North Atlantic, forming a dense mass loitering in the shadows, waiting for rain to swell the river's flow so they could continue their heroic swim back to the small burns on the high moorlands where they had hatched. Their predators were in attendance too – fishermen wading and ospreys circling and scanning the water. Sparse sightings of past decades have increased in recent years to the excitement of six hovering birds at a time.

Between fishing sorties, shags stand and groom on rocky reefs.

SLEEK HUNTERS

Larger fish hunters are paradoxically the most elusive, glimpsed rarely and unpredictably. Steady drizzle and mist are frequent on these exposed coasts. It can be a scene of uninviting grey: low, dark clouds with wafts and shreds dangling down, shrouding shore, rocks and slopes in wet. These are the times to watch: wild animals continue to go about life undeterred.

Opposite me, a seal had surfaced briefly and dived. Trying to track it, I idly made a binocular sweep along the shimmering seaweed and grey ripples. A small brown ginger body, matching the weed, was writhing and scrabbling out of the surface. Ears, and long tail appeared. The otter turned its pug-like face and slithered fast, merging onto moving seaweed. Radiating ripple rings moved and it reappeared, dancing lightly along the weed, arching body, trailing tail tapered to a sharp point. It dipped down again out of sight. Four times it materialised, apparently out of nowhere, body low to the rocks, treading with a fluid grace, face in the weed, rummaging and chewing – a crab's legs flashed in and out of view. Then it swam shallow, trailing wake ripples of shadows and light, to a place where water cascaded over rocks into the sea. Intermittently we caught sight of an arching back, a tail twirling and twisting as it darted and rolled in the splash. If it had been a child one would have said it was revelling in the movement and play. Again, it ran up the rocks, with its characteristic undulating lollop as if swimming on land, bounding through non-existent waves – a being as used to water as gravity. Under the shelter of an overhanging rock, it tossed its head, juggling and balancing an immense unwieldy plate-like fish in its mouth, maybe a flatfish. It rolled like an indulgent dog, one might say happily languishing, kicking its legs in the air, squirming and rubbing its back either on the prey or the seaweed. Finally, it returned to hunting, and as the rain fell heavier and the light dimmed its brown body became barely distinguishable. Finally the otter dipped and was gone. But beneath the surface it had entered the abundant realm of sinuous waving kelp, where brown fronds could transform to burnished bronze splashed with green in a trick of light and swell. Here, anchored to the seaweed and drifting, crawling and swimming through it, there was another world in miniature – of eat or be eaten- providing food for fish and ultimately the otter.

After decades of looking, and occasional enticing glimpses of otter heads surfacing out of the kelp or the sea, the incident was another example of the best encounters being those totally unplanned and unexpected. Perhaps more extraordinary was the sight of the familiar profile in the field outside our gate as we emerged early one morning. The long body was crouching, facing the other way. The rounded head turned and looked at us. We froze still and looked in disbelief. So did the animal. The set of its shining dark eyes, shape of the head, no ears visible and wet, smooth fur suggested a first thought – what was a seal doing three miles from the sea? The animal turned. Little ears showed and a powerful tail followed the undulations of a bounding body. This was no seal, but an otter leaving the rain-swollen river en route to moorland burns or the sea.

The similarity of otter face and seal face is no accident. Both are sleek and streamlined for fast underwater expertise in hunting down their prey. In the Pentland Firth their fish are abundant. Views of seal torsos lying on shores and heads above the waves were common, but seeing their fishing skills in action was an unusual treat. Near Duncansby Head seals regularly lolled in Sannick Bay – these are Grey, or Atlantic, Seals and this group of around sixty is relatively undeterred by humans as there is a constant summer tourist presence en route to the tip of mainland Britain and the famous Stacks.

These animals do not land here in daylight; they cruise and drift about in the clear pale water of the calm bay while the Firth just beyond is rough and intensely dark blue. Watching them bobbing and lolling in the sea, with their distinctive long Roman noses pointing skywards, they looked the part depicted by their scientific name – 'sea-pig with a hooked nose'. Mothers and juveniles played, cavorting and twisting, tail flippers out of the water splashing, and pale bellies gyrating. As two animals somersaulted, one opened its pink mouth and showed its teeth. A large 'old man' seal was the closest in, keeping a watchful eye on the beach, his breathing snorts audible. A fish leapt out in front of a line of six lolling seals; they all turned and dived as one. Above them, gannets and terns caught the light, glinting white as they circled, hovered and dived. Both species swoop with wings folded back, dive bombing vertically down, gannets accelerating further into the water, sharp beaks ready to grab and impale careless fish. Their water entry was so fast as to be invisible in the real time of the human eye – only a camera can catch the moment. The force of impact is colossal and neck and other injuries are frequent. It seemed miraculous they avoided spiking the seals and cormorants, all aiming for the same feast – large numbers of fish were sheltering from the rough sea beyond and the seals were herding them together for the big catch. An Arctic Skua suddenly flew across, fast and swooping, with distinctive black wings and pointed tail streamer. Its flight was the epitome of the sophisticated predatory pirate. There had been two Great Skuas flying earlier in the afternoon, but these now seemed like amateurs by comparison. As the Arctic Skua zoomed in, fulmars, gulls and terns evaporated. No doubt the seals continued feasting below.

An otter pauses as it twists and scrabbles, its front paws searching amongst seaweed. This multi-tasking limb bounds on land, grapples slippery fish and steers and paddles underwater.

WINGS, PADDLES AND PAWS FOR THE HUNT – VARIATIONS ON A THEME

These fish hunters share more than their prey – a design template. The underlying pattern of their limbs is the same; a two-part arm or leg ending in hand or foot with five digits. It is the basis, a theme waiting for variations – the pentadactyl limb. Our agile otter's limb was not far from our own basic arrangement of a limb with a hand of five – the multi-purpose tool for running, bounding and sliding across land, handling slippery fish as well as manoeuvring water, paddle-like, when swimming using webbed paws. The basic limb plan may be heavily deformed and disguised by extreme demands, but it is always there in essence: an indelible stamp, a similarity of structure rather like an evolutionary brand name in each of these hunting birds and mammals. There is a delight in playing detective and tracking and unravelling the theme and variations which have come about for a particular purpose – a unity and order in the jigsaw. It was a puzzle that delighted Charles Darwin when he considered the fore limbs of man, moles, horses, porpoises and bats.

The remnant bird wing amongst the beachcombing finds has a familiarity, a design similar but somehow different – fragments of evidence lying on the sand. The clue is the pattern of exposed bones which have some resemblance to the human arm which reached out and grasped them. Both have a thick upper arm and two thinner bones of the fore arm. From there the differences of use and emphasis become apparent; my hand has a group of wrist bones enabling me to twist my hand and use my five fingers independently to curve round and close into a tight hold. By contrast, the design of the flying bird is governed by flight in air, needing an extended, light arm in order to remain airborne, to glide and the ability to flap. The bird's wrist and hand have reduced to slender essentials – wrist and hand articulate just two or three extremely extended fingers. What is not visible is yet further sophistication within – the arm bones have hollowed out air sacs to reduce weight and which are also involved in the animal's breathing.

Diving Guillemots, Puffins and Razorbills need stronger wings, designed not for flying through air but shifting through heavy dense water. In order to make any progress, fore arm bones are shortened and fingers are stocky to withstand the force. Such short 'flipper' wings have to flap very fast when the bird flies in air, using up a disproportionate amount of energy compared to those designed to be airborne. Inevitably, the requirements for flight and swimming come into competition.

The seals face a similar dilemma – their finely controlled swimming is at the cost of cumbersome movement ashore. Twisting and turning with incredible speed, accuracy and extreme efficiency, their graceful swimming is achieved by undulating sideways movements of the whole body. For a fast swim the backwards-facing hind limbs serve as a powerful flipper while the fore limbs are held close to the body. During a slow swim the front flippers stabilise, steer and paddle. Upper and lower arm bones are short and strong and with a very elongated hand with five webbed fingers with long claws – ideal for paddling and steering but unable to carry weight. Unsupported by water the animals become heavy, awkward and vulnerable. They move by wriggling their bodies inefficiently, using abdominal and back muscles to squeeze themselves over rocks and sand, intermittently gripping with their claws.

Animal movement creates some strange extremes and beachcombing sometimes produces the unexpected evidence from land as well as sea. A deer lying half submerged in sand with legs outstretched 'mid-leap' was a spectacular example of the basic limb design taken to a very different extreme. Here the fast running fore leg is lengthened by extraordinary means. All the body weight is carried vertically on just two finger tips – an apparently ludicrous idea to a human equipped with wide hand and stable foot. En route to developing into such an unlikely final product, embryos often demonstrate their unexpected ancestry. Darwin's horse example is the most extreme, running on one elongated finger; in the womb its embryo passes through a five-digit stage before a remaining one gives rise to the single extended hoof.

In a fanciful way, all of these clever limb modifications are something like variations on a musical theme: the basic melody changes speed and emphasis, slowing and quickening so it re-emerges afresh. In this mechanical melody, different body movements have called the tunes – wading, waddling, bounding, jumping, running, flying, swimming, diving and grasping. But the theme remains the same.

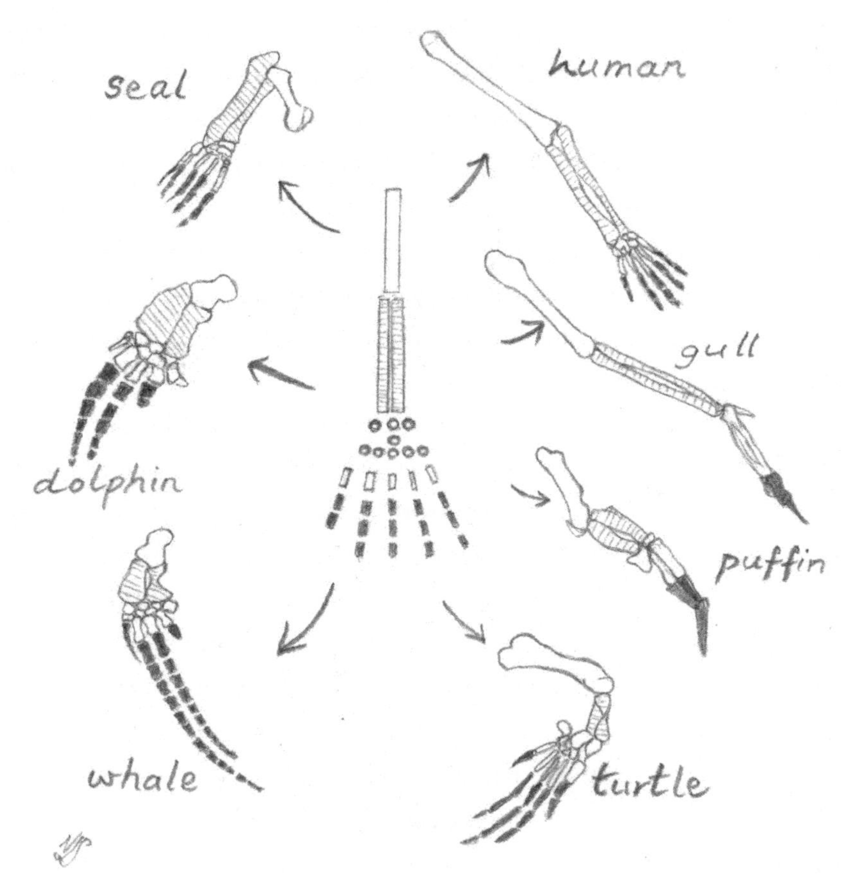

A flexible design. Changing the proportions of the basic limb bones (central) offers a variety of uses. Clockwise: human arm and hand manipulates; slim gull wing flies efficiently in air; sturdy puffin flipper/wing flies well underwater but less efficiently in air; turtle flipper paddles and moves laboriously across sand; whale and dolphin flippers steer and stabilise; as does the seal flipper which can also act as a cumbersome lever on shore. All forearm bones are shown with horizontal hatching and 'finger' bones shaded dark for comparison.

'SELKIES'

There was a remote place where we spent hours watching swimming in action – mesmerised by the comings and goings of Common (Harbour) Seals. We followed a sheep track maze along the top of moorland cliffs carpeted with heather and fluffy white heads of Bog Cotton Grass. Eventually, there was a sudden sheer drop to a deep scooped bay – not a place to approach in thick mist or grey rain gloom. A safer option was to crawl the last stretch to the cliff overhang which (we thought) also allowed us to remain hidden from seals below. Here, life for all land mammals was, literally, on the edge; we had found the dead deer, half submerged in tide and sand beneath cliffs close by. The sea facing gullies and steep slopes offer lush vegetation for grazing invisibly. On one occasion, as we crawled back from the edge and stood up, a young deer leapt into the air only a few feet away. Both wide eyed, animal and humans were as startled as each other. With ears high pricked, it bounded away across the cliff tops.

We lay on our stomachs, heads raised enough to peer over cropped heather shoots at the edge of the cliff. Far below everything was quiet – silent in terms of human noise, just timeless wind and distant waves, almost indistinguishable from an occasional low moan of a seal. In the past, we had been told you could mimic their moans and call them in from the sea to a particular special place. We had tried on many occasions with voices and recorder, our small son solemnly piping to empty rocks and sea, but in the wrong place. This natural seal haven is difficult to find; no seal-lover was too specific about such locations when animals are sensitive to disturbance and we had seen them shot during salmon netting days in the past.

Now in the right place, the water below was transparent over pale rocks and pebbles. Seals lolled, leaning back like slanting logs, 'bottling', eyes shut, asleep or vaguely dozing, noses just out of the water or bobbing just below. In this state, one half of the seal's brain sleeps while the other half is awake, like dolphins. When on land, seals sleep like humans. We could see nostrils opening and shutting and sensitive whiskers quivering – each hair can move independently, tracking the vibrations of prey moving underwater. It was an opportunity to admire the spotted patterns of their fur – each animal has a unique signature skin pattern, like tigers, zebras, leopards, frogs and others. Common Seals can be mottled with spots or rings, an overall pale-grey to dark brown, often darker on the back, paler on the belly – less visible to a predator looking from below up to a paler background of sky above the sea surface.

A few individuals lay on small exposed rocks out in the bay, one per rock. These were obviously prime sites, as there was immediate irritable bickering if another tried to clamber aboard. Sometimes these confrontations escalated towards territorial dispute but stopped short, succumbing to the lazy warmth of the day. The seals then relapsed into relaxed drapes, sprawling flat out, mottled grey blubber bodies almost inseparable from grey rock. Some perched motionless, seemingly tense, like beached bananas impaled on narrow sculpture plinths, tightly closed tail flippers and faces stiffly poised skywards, a characteristic posture of Common Seals. Lone animals in the middle of the bay, lying 'head up tail up' on rocks hidden just beneath the surface, looked as if levitated by miraculous means, balancing on the water.

There was the soft sound of ripples as a young seal stirred, see-sawed precariously and slowly slid into the water. Others followed suit: they began to play. As they swam together they steered precisely in tight turns and U-bends. They seemed to be sparring like puppies, or, like all young and adolescent carnivores at play, experimenting, learning, practising and testing their hunting and social skills of aiming, grabbing and coming out on top. They snaked their bodies round and twisted with ultimate ease and grace, with sinuously curving spines, chasing, gliding close, suddenly veering away. They rolled and somersaulted over each other such that it was impossible to differentiate one animal from the other. This rolling behaviour is not limited to young or courtship; it is part of their rich social life: mothers play with their young, pups with pups, and pairs of juveniles.

Others just swam about slowly, apparently just cruising – I recalled a lecturer who pointed out that far from being 'red in tooth and claw', most animals spent most of their time doing nothing in particular. As we and the seals lay at our separate vantage points – doing nothing in particular – the other creatures of the shore went about the business of catching food. A Herring Gull glided across the watery weed as if driven by clockwork. It occasionally dipped its head under the surface into the brown fronds below and shattered the silence with spraying droplets. Then, a splash. It emerged, beak clamped on a large straggling dark clump. Binoculars resolved the strands into segmented legs waving energetically – a crab as large as the gull's head. The gull wrestled it into a new position. The crab fell, a quick head dip retrieved it and four pairs of legs were firmly locked, forcibly thrashing wide each side of the tight shut beak. A renewed hold, another drop, another grab, and the prize was won, as the mandibles crunched together. How would the bird swallow such a width of sharp appendages? The head tilted and with a stupendous gulp, the crab was a large lump halfway down the throat, the last leg tips protruding at an angle. With a head toss and a neck twist it disappeared, and the gull continued on its searches.

On a windy day we had watched a similar performance by a Hoodie Crow. It tilted, apparently precariously, tipping wings against a strong wind. It hung in mid-air, wings balancing and splaying tail feathers. A dark round object dropped from its beak; it dived down after it and disappeared behind rocks. This was obviously a tried and tested procedure – the bird reappeared, rising effortlessly with wings spread, head to the wind, expertly angling and adjusting to every gust. The head arched down purposefully and the projectile was dropped again, not an accident, but carefully tracked by the crow as it fell. The bird lurched down, compensating against wind and alighted on its fallen prize, efficiently split, open and available.

The seals ignored such domestic scenes. They seemed to ignore us too – we had thought we were utterly quiet and invisible, but faces occasionally looked round at us. This species regularly scan for danger, even if none is present. Their alternative name, Harbour Seal, reflects their preferred features for an ideal haul-out site: shelter from land predators (here, a horse-shoe of cliff), shelter from strong winds and waves and direct access to deep water with plentiful fish and shellfish resources. In such ideal conditions groups can moult, rest and females give birth – and this was such a place. When animals emerged from the water on to land they lurched and lolloped like bouncing caterpillars. The more we looked the more animals we saw, resting and sleeping, well camouflaged against sand and rock. About fifty individuals lay on the beach, inert but for an occasional prod from a neighbour, or the awkward wave of a front flipper to fan off irritating insects.

Two left the group on shore. They squirmed down the pebbles, slithered, submerged and their metamorphosis was immediate. Awkward postures, making the best of improvisation for land travel, were transformed into elegant movement, flowing like the water all around the undulating torsos. They were back in their element. They porpoised very slowly across the bay, their streamlined bodies rising and falling smoothly through the still mirror surface, each making just two circles of perfect concentric ripples as they swam. We could follow the action of muscles moving beneath the sleek fur of curving backs and arching heads. Their hind legs which had been such a hindrance on land now transformed to a sinuous rear flipper. Eventually distance obscured them as they dived towards the narrow protected opening, towards the fishy haunt of speed diving gannets and terns out in the Firth. They could have been off on a foraging trip lasting several days, possibly travelling 50km (30miles) on their search. The seals could swim between the islands and could dive deep, 60 m (200 ft), to hunt. Only 16 km (10 miles) away, there were the artificial reefs of Scapa Flow's wrecks, now softened with living colour - wafting fronds and threads, grasping tentacles, tentative antennae, beating bristles, legs crawling and creeping. There would be fish hiding, drifting and hunting. Seal shapes could glide unnoticed amongst the metal hulks and loom out of the gloom, their stiff flared whiskers and staring dark intelligent eyes seeking out every movement.

The waters of the Pentland Firth live up to their reputation visibly and frequently. Along this short stretch of coast we had seen two great waves appear out of nowhere, like an outsize stylised wave design in strict sequence – lines of bulging, pregnant menace. They turned into two angry high walls of water, crossing outside the wide mouth of a bay from east to west. Each body of water looked stationary, keeping their distance, two moving as one as if manipulated by some powerful remote controlling force. Their tops were breaking and frothing along their whole length; they gained height and became gigantic. When they had passed, in their wake there was a regular sequence of equally spaced, smaller waves – paradoxically running in the opposite direction, from west to east. Three days later, just before high tide there was a similar distinct line of water moving from east to west in an arc, and another moving from west to north towards Stroma – as if the Atlantic Ocean was visibly moving across the Firth towards Orkney.

The sea here is deep, but not for seals. Humans can only take a few deep breaths, slow their breathing and exhale a little to reduce buoyancy and dive… not too far for not too long. Even with diving equipment we soon enter the realm of physiological complications: water pressure and increased nitrogen intake while down, or nitrogen bubbles forming during too rapid an ascent back up. Marine animals and seals in particular have special adaptations for coping with these problems and for conserving oxygen when underwater. Before a deep dive, a Harbour Seal exhales to reduce the amount of air in its lungs. Instead, the oxygen is stored in blood and muscles – in these seals the amount of oxygen-binding protein available for this job is ten times greater than in us. There is also a greater volume of blood available for retaining oxygen as compared to an equivalent sized land mammal. This large blood volume is used strategically, the bulk being shifted to the most vital organs – heart, lungs and brain – and for further efficiency the heart beat slows to a staggering low level.

Top: A Common (Harbour) Seal lying on a submerged rock in 'banana posture' - hind flippers are held tightly together and short fore flipper held close, ideal for scratching or a steering paddle, but unable to take weight on land. Below: 'Sea-pig with a hooked nose' - Grey (Atlantic) Seals. A 'bottling' seal sleeps and two alert animals have nostrils wide open, then tightly closed. Prominent stiff whiskers of seals detect minute disturbances in surrounding water. The seal ear, without ear flaps, is usually hidden beneath fur, but visible in the sketch below right.

POST SCRIPT – 'SELKIES' AND HUMANS

Seal faces and inquisitive eyes are reminiscent of their look-alike distant carnivore relatives, dogs. Humans have had such close relationships with dogs through eye contact it seems little wonder that seals' soulful eyes and allure have infiltrated human awareness and cultures – assuming near human roles as mermaids and beings with strange powers, as well as the selkie tales. The Grey Seals of Sannick Bay took enormous interest in their surroundings. In such sheltered water they were free to turn their attention to intently view the passing humans – sometimes it was questionable as to who was watching whom. They watched as a horse and rider crossed the beach or children played at trying to dam the burn on the beach. They habitually stared with rapt attention at the dogs chasing sticks and playing.

Years before, at Sinclair's Bay we had experienced a lone seal swimming beside us, keeping level with us, close in, along half of the length of the long beach, its eyes following our dog's every move. We turned to leave, put the dog on her lead and looked back along the dune path. The seal was out of the water, following in our footsteps up the sand, 'chasing' after us. In teleological terms it seemed to be trying to catch up with us, almost as if it wanted something. We viewed it from across the beach; it did not seem to be injured so we continued on our path and left it to return to the sea undisturbed. It was a strange and touching 'near communication' between three species.

West along the coast we had another encounter with a lone seal, injured and lying on a sand bank across a narrow, deep, fast-flowing estuary. It was a Common or Harbour Seal, with a double collar of dried blood. It dozed, head up, lying on its side a few feet above the water line where river met sea waves. I scrutinised its wound through powerful binoculars and the cause was obviously fishing line – a straight-edged cut stretching round a third or half of its neck, raw-edged at the bottom and quite a chunk of flesh missing. Smooth fur and blubber undercoat were tightly squeezed so that it was impossible to see if the line remained or had made the indented cuts and tears as it was wrenched out. I rang the number for sea wildlife injuries and strandings. Raising a team of volunteers for a rescue on a shore without any easy access is a far reaching operation, illustrated by the seal expert on the other end of the phone dangling at that moment somewhere further along the coast near the foot of a dangerous cliff. He asked for more details: did it have tears? Mucous continually washes over their large eyes to protect them, and as they lack a duct for draining eye fluids down into the nose, the ring of mucous round the eyes gives them their familiar sad look of brimming over with tears. If there were no tears it would be a sign of dehydration and the animal not having fed for at least twenty-four hours. I tried hard to decipher through my binoculars but could not see obvious mucous. It is at such moments that one realises how little detail one usually sees, and how small and shaky is one's baseline of knowledge for a meaningful comparison. The detailed state of the seal was essential for judging if it would heal satisfactorily on its own, or if it would be necessary to anaesthetise the animal in order to catch it and tend the wound. The immediate decision was for the local warden to come and take photographs as, infuriatingly, our pocket-sized camera did not have high enough definition for the experts to inspect the wound's severity. Meanwhile, we returned every day and updated the volunteers. The next day the animal was there, in the same spot. It was looking perkier, changing position frequently, and seemingly unable to settle for any long period – I recalled the itching of deep wounds healing and hoped this may be the cause. In between it rested and seemed not to be deteriorating, but there was still concern from the experts as to whether it might be dehydrating. Was it leaving its safe haven to fish in between our visits? On day four it had gone. We were left with the hope it might regain strength, heal further, and would survive the big predators of the turbulent waters beyond the bay.

A WHALE AND TALES

DOLPHINS AND A MINKE WHALE

Bordered by sea on two sides, this northerly triangle of land is a realm of unpredictable extremes. There are days of four seasons, paradoxical cold winter squalls, even snow flurries succumb to dazzling summer postcard sun. This was one of those: a bright sun was shining, the sky was blue, the sea brighter, but covered with high, white, frothing waves all the way to the horizon. Sinclair's Bay, normally vacant except for the birds and an occasional seal, was full of ships and boats. The wind was wild; the gale's force had driven them to run for shelter to wait before sailing north and through the challenging Pentland Firth. We sat on the dunes scanning the birds and ships with binoculars. Suddenly, out of the surf sprang three Bottlenose Dolphins; they leapt high, bouncing from wave to wave. Their energy radiated; it was as if they delighted in dancing amidst the power of the raging sea. Then, suddenly they were gone. In subsequent years of tracking dolphins, we have never seen such a sight again – waves, leaping dolphins, crowded ships and boats.

In a different mood, dolphins surfaced on a very unusual day of flat calm in the Firth itself. There was no wind and an unreal distant clarity. Intoxicated with the light, we scanned the cliffs and the sea. Below us a few Puffins waddled and clowned in the clefts. Gannets were skimming and diving very close to the cliffs; a Great Skua was attacking. Way out in the direction of South Ronaldsay, there were splashes. Dolphins were leaping and spouting – they had struck a shoal of fish. Eager to grab the bounty, gannets and birds flew and swooped above them. We shared our binoculars and the experience with a young family, including two children, one on a towbike; they had cycled to this extreme place from Glasgow. In common with every sighting of dolphins at various world locations, everyone was smiling, sharing the experience, talking, and there was a mood of joy and expansive optimism.

Dolphin relatives were more elusive: our sighting of a porpoise was a dead one. It was a surprisingly little creature, quite rubbery in appearance, with white flank and belly, perfect black leathery flippers, small dorsal fin and a very small tail. Its body was strangely and deeply 'scrawled'. Newly washed up, it was the target of a voracious Great Skua and fighting gulls.

The largest dolphin relatives, the whales, were also elusive – evident but absent. Their bones have become part of the locality. Approaching the northerly cliffs of Dunnet Head, there are old cottages with gates arched over with small whale bones. They are untouched by weather: tamed under layers of white paint and neatly pristine. Down the east coast, at Latheronwheel, there is an arch which does justice to the mighty whale. It is the tallest and looks to be the oldest in the county. A simple arch of just two whale ribs topped by a vertebra, it stands incongruously at the entrance of a field. We have been watching the grey tufts of lichens gradually growing over it for more than forty years. The east wind blowing in over the sea cliff and time have skewed it, but it still stands, now guyed up with metal stays. To stand under it is to feel like Jonah. Maybe it is the ribs of one of 104 whales which passed through the Firth in 1899; they were driven into the shallows of Thurso Bay and speared. Latheronwheel is a tiny, quiet village with echoes of lives linked with the sea; vestigial walls and heaps of stones are reminders of past prosperity and a herring boom supporting fifty boats.

Orcas – Killer Whales – frequent this waterway between the mainland and the islands. They are tracked by researchers as they pass the jutting projection of Strathy Point, which they appear to use as a navigational aid. There are other regular travellers, Minke whales, one of which was our one whale sighting, unfortunately a beachcombing find – dead on a beach.

The whale, a single isolated object, lay atop a muddle of rocks high above the water's edge. It was a long, uniform shore of awkward grey lumps and bumps all the way to its final headland blockade, barring the view up the east coast to the Firth. The body was lying half on its side, a marooned wasted hulk of a wreck, like a ship out of water. Its sheer size was impressive, its length about four times Peter's height. The image of a whale seen from the sea's surface is that of an incomplete jigsaw – bits appear and disappear – a grey spread of whale back, a sporadic tail fluke, a briefly waving flipper, and a glimpse of a segment of belly rolling over. The shape, depth and curvature of the body remain beyond view and comprehension. Here we saw it all. The all-powerful tail seemed incongruously small. The bulk was dominated by its white and black striated throat, stretching half its length, packed with the baleen 'sieve' of its filter feeding system. Now fallen back slack, caved in and discolouring to rusty brown, the long strips gave the impression of the broken planks of a once majestic wooden hull.

Its flippers were like sleek oars, suited to steering and stabilising, like a submarine's hydroplanes. If the structure inside had been visible, it would have been very similar to that of a seal, but it has even longer spreading fingers holding the stiff flipper shape – achieving a similar function to webbing. Whale structure and skeletons have always had a fascination, particularly the giants – maybe thoughts of Jonah. In 1883, public attention was riveted by a Humpback Whale's anatomy as entertainment. A 12.2 m (40 ft) male had entered the Firth of Tay, further south. It was harpooned, struggled all night towing two rowing boats and two steam boats south along the coast down to the Firth of Forth before breaking free, only to be found, a week later, dead floating at sea. Thousands paid to view the landed carcass until its decomposition was deemed too unpleasant – except for the Professor of Anatomy at Aberdeen University who was permitted to dissect and investigate its muscle and bone structure. But this was still a unique entrepreneurial opportunity; people paid to view the scientific investigation which was accompanied by stirring music played by a military band.

BY THE PILOT'S HOUSE

It was appropriate that the wrecked Minke whale should have washed up in this place, as the stone house on the shore behind had been the old pilot's house, sturdy and full-square to the sea. For centuries, ships sailing north past Wick, desperate to avoid shipwreck in the treacherous waters ahead, had picked up a local pilot with a lifetime's fishing experience in the Firth. Many ship owners and captains even preferred to avoid the dangers of these currents by making a long detour north of Orkney or sail south and round via the English Channel. From several tiny harbours, havens and slipways watchful pilots would cast off and race out, rowing or sailing, to the distant ship – the first aboard had the best chance of hire and a good price. The pilot's race against his competitors then turned into the bigger race against this part of the sea where twice daily, surges of tide ran through the bottleneck of the Pentland Firth, some of the fastest in the world – in one place up to16 knots (30 kph). Sometimes the ship's captain, either unhappy with the deal or apprehensive of time and tide on this wild, accelerating rollercoaster, would not – or could not – stop to drop off the pilot. In the nineteenth century, at a peak of shipping traffic, individual pilots found themselves in Ireland, the Faroes, Quebec, and America, having to return somehow.

Now the sea seemed quiet, ideal for the old pilots who would have rowed out from this small stone jetty. In the garden of the pilot's house a tall, weather-bronzed man was working. He was digging potatoes with the ease of one who is fit and constantly gardening big scale through seasons of damp bitter cold. With bare shoulders and arms, he was wearing one thin layer: a garb appropriate to the local greeting in this part of the world: 'Och, it's a lovely day', which extends to the grey and drizzling. We were dressed in pullovers and fleece jackets appropriate to the cold sea air. His vegetable garden edges the sea. It seems to grow out of it – the only cultivated patch in a wide view stretching across empty sea and vacant cliffs and moorland far beyond. It is protected from the searing winds by thick buttress walls, made of large, smooth oblong beach pebbles, each brought up from the shore and carefully placed, without mortar, one against the other. The soil is dark, almost black, pliable and rich with years of seaweed compost, carefully gathered. The impeccable lines of peas, leeks, onions, kale, and all manner of nurtured edibles are lush and interspersed with bright stripes of sea blue Cornflowers and Borage, and pink Godetias. Elsewhere grassy areas are edged with gold and orange – Pot Marigolds, Montbretias, Alstromeiras – and pink pompoms of Opium Poppies and Clarkias. The flowers seem more intensely bright than anywhere else, being an isolated oasis of vivid earth colours against such a backdrop of blue and greys. In a sheltered nook there is quiet grassy space with a wooden seat and a silent statue of a heron and a Bhudda. It is the man and his garden we have actually come to see; the whale was unexpected. For a decade or more we have made this little pilgrimage for its rare meeting of connections – this place, far places, far peoples and living history. To him we are passers-by.

We talked of the Minke whale, which had been washed ashore, dead, in a gale. It had been there a while, and would be something of a saga for the local authorities to remove. He was soft spoken and his accented voice rose and fell with a musical lilt. I was fascinated by his delightful Scottish old-world vocabulary and turn of phrase, now sadly disappeared from colloquial English, such as 'good' mother and 'good' father (mother and father-in-law) and shopping 'messages'. Equally, we were both enthralled by his lapses into the Occitan dialect of Provence interspersed with French with a fine accent. He also spoke Malay and Tamil; languages 'took his fancy' as he put it, and he had learnt cant from a Gitane who refused to be called a gypsy. In 2009, at the age of 80, he described himself as 'an old man sitting in the sun blethering at passers-by'. The only true part of the statement was the sun and 'passers-by'; he was (and is still, I hope) a fine storyteller with natural timing and a delivery such as would charm the birds from the trees. And we were always compulsive listeners. Through all these linguistic and actual adventures, he had absorbed and understood much history, culture and soul of each people. He had spent long periods in Provence, picking the grape harvest, and with a natural aptitude for language and getting on well with people, he had absorbed its complex ancient ethnicity and rural customs. Listening and translating (intermittently) as he talked in patois of Cathars and vineyards and swimming, it slowly dawned on me that this was a moment of déja vu. Many years previously during our first years visiting Caithness, I had repeatedly seen a swimmer taking to the waves on a nearby beach, an unusual sight in these latitudes, so I had struck up conversation. He had told me how he swam every day of the year, regardless of rain, gale or snow: he did not 'feel alive' until he immersed himself in the sea. He had also spoken of whole summers spent grape-picking in Provence. Other details fitted the profile exactly; I tentatively presented my case. The answer was yes – our conversations were continuing after thirty-four years.

His tales always enthralled and surprised. Apparently there were a few local people nearby descended from French prisoners of war brought back from the Napoleonic Wars. Their ancestors were the three 'free' slaves promised by the English as bribes in order to get as many Scottish fighters as they needed for their army.

Many more were of Viking descent. At the head of the bay we had been aware of an archaeological dig some years previously which had uncovered a dune midden of shells and a longhouse. We had often marvelled at the layered lines of exposed shells exposed as the sand slipped and the dunes eroded. Just visible beyond the bay there was a castle built by a Viking about 900 years ago. It stood on a narrow geo, which was the right size to shelter his longboats with immediate access to the open sea, and was almost wholly surrounded by a natural moat. Building stones and strata beneath have become almost indistinguishable; its remaining walls grow tall out of the rock, eroded by wind, shaped by wild times and weather. Its position was vulnerable to being starved out, which, according to our storyteller, it had been, and the inmates had escaped through a secret underground passage, and disappeared in their longboats to one of their other castles near Dublin. Their year had apparently followed a seasonal pattern of raiding and feasting between their venues in Ireland, the Scottish west coast and Orkney. On one of their Irish raids a vessel carrying silk had been seized. With flamboyant swank, the returning longboat was borne through the Pentland Firth on sails made of the finest silk. We mused over the surreal possibility of this particular sight being seen from the shore by the Norse shellfish traders near John o' Groats. Another homecoming had been less joyful: the castle was on fire and mother and siblings had been murdered, so escape to the safe hiding place of the Island of Stroma had been the only course open. Revenge was cruel and torturing; culprits were tied down by hands and feet, slit open and left alive for the skuas and gulls to eat out their insides, just like the little corpse of the porpoise we had seen recently.

There were tales and exchanges of wildlife sightings too. He always knew when a pod of Orcas was approaching the bay as all the seals disappeared, as if by magic. These killer whales were quite frequent visitors; we thought of the possible fate of our injured seal with apprehension. He too had noticed that dolphins were less common than the other creatures of the bay.

A dead Minke Whale washed ashore and wedged among rocks gives a view of an oar-like flipper, huge mouth and throat folds. Skuas, gulls and crows have been feeding on the remains.

RUINS AND FUTURES ON FOREIGN SHORES

This pilot's vantage point is a scoop out of the coast, its water calmed by protecting long fingers of rock and strands of land, green and verdant in summer. The tiny harbour is a single groin of beautifully mitred stone slabs extending out beyond the slipway, still offering shelter to two small wooden clinker boats tied alongside their lobster pots. It was here that the old pilot's boat would have stood at the ready. Old crofter's fields nearby remain, small, some edged with floppy wild Scottish roses and yellow Corn Marigolds, ancient remnant weeds, lost elsewhere. Behind low walls and extreme wind-shaped hedges crofters' but 'n' ben cottages sit low and a few taller modern ones defy past custom and the elements.

Evocative cottage ruins remain, acting as humble sentinels on the approach to the Viking castle. A few ghost shapes of abandoned but 'n' bens still stand in Caithness and Sutherland, scattered in fields and moorland and nestled into hills or cliffs. Time has reduced them to a low rectangle of thick walls, sometimes with two small window spaces like dark eye sockets staring out from each side of an empty front door frame. Stark chimney ears stick up each end of a roof long gone. In forty years many have disappeared; some of those in hamlets and fertile valleys have metamorphosed into modern bungalows or improvised kennels. The ruined walls of these tiny two-room cottages are skilful dry stone jigsaws of different sized squares and rectangles, packed level with stacked strips of the fine layered flagstone. Some, even more skilful, appear to be ad hoc jumbles of found stones, but they have retained their strength and integrity for centuries. The chimney and its wide fireplace with a massive stone lintel is usually the last structure to succumb, sometimes with a grate flanked by rusted remnants of extended side surfaces for pans and a resting kettle for constant hot water. Stray dangles of rusting chain, once long and strong, suspended cooking pots over smouldering peats. Occasionally, at shoulder height, a wall recess remains, shelved with simple plates of stone – the salt shelf, a feature unchanged since the ancient days of Skara Brae. Early on in our northern pilgrimages we sought out such a cottage and salvaged it as a camping cottage. Having staggered with buckets – water up from a river and down from the sky into straight chimneys – we had fellow feeling for the tenacity of a past tenant who had reared seven children within its two rooms. We found time clues. A scrap of paper from 1937 surfaced under rotting lino as we dug through the generous topping of cattle manure; old 1927 newspapers emerged from wall cavities and a traditional flat-iron and medicine phials from the earth. Like all crofters, she was a tough lady. Winds from the surrounding seas dominated even modern luxuries: our propped mattress was blown, still vertical, down the hill, and a modern car door was blown out of alignment and useless.

Isolated cottage ruins of the estuaries and coasts do not share any aura of a cosy past; they have witnessed cruel and bitter times. South, down the coast from the pilot's house, at the extremity of disappearing pale blue headlands, there are remnants of Badbea, a village perched above a cliff edge. A few stone walls emerge from a harsh, infertile terrain battered by continual winds, wild seas and unpredictable weather. Children and chickens were tethered to the rocks lest the wind blew them over the cliff edge. When the sun shines beneath wisps of high cirrus clouds the sky is balmy and the sea lies as flat as a silver pond – it becomes a beautiful place. Changing light plays tricks and lends a sense of unreality and fantasy in the drifting sea mists and enveloping haars. Unlike us, these people had no energy or time to stand and stare. Theirs was a desolate life of grinding survival out of this precarious place. They were not here by choice. Like other tenant crofting communities of the far north at the end of the eighteenth century, they had been forcibly resettled. They had been evicted from lush valley pastures to make way for the higher profits of grazing sheep. Here, a high dry stone wall defined the land for sheep and the remaining strip edging the cliff – for families, their few cows, family pig and potato patch. Of necessity, farming men turned to the herring fishing boats running from Berriedale to the north and the women turned to fish gutting. Around the 1870s, fish stocks fell with natural variations in herring shoal habits and overfishing by local boats as well as Norwegian, Swedish, Dutch and, according to a local enquiry, the distant Spanish. Their primitive life became harder, with only one horse and no plough in the village.

'Starve or emigrate' – New Zealand, Australia and North America offered hope and optimism. Alexander Robert Sutherland, born in Badbea in 1806 left for Wairarapa in New Zealand in 1838. His journey into the unfamiliar was a common one: in the same year over 2,000 Scots had taken advantage of the offer of a free passage to Australia. Their resilience and courage had been finely honed by hardship and survival. They embarked on new lives with bountiful seas, unexpected challenges of different climate, enormous distances, land and resource disputes, alien plants and extraordinary wildlife including venomous species.

Antipodean shores are vast, seas range from tropical to cold, and the ocean to the south can be the most treacherous: the planet's biggest, coldest and wildest, with wildlife diversity to match. The land, sea and sky scapes of north-east Scotland and its islands have a certain resemblance to these southern shores. There is a similar sense of space and wilderness, big undulating landscapes under wide skies, sparsely populated, a place where animals and their worlds can be an integral part of everyday existence. This was the magnet which had first attracted us to Scotland's north and it had gradually come to possess us. We had discovered we were wilderness and sea creatures, and subliminally I was on familiar territory again – on empty sandy shores battered by powerful waves. For Peter it was a paradise of wildlife and fishing and maybe distant subliminal rapport with his

Viking genes; he knew nothing of remoteness on an Antipodean scale. It was time to introduce him, and to follow the Badbea travellers to southern seas and shores. It is a place of abundance of different animal diversity – sea lions, fur seals, dolphins, whales, Manta Rays, crocodiles, coral reef fish in multitudes, Whale Sharks, turtles, penguins, eagles, shearwaters and albatross... and some extraordinarily committed people. The southern part of our odyssey had begun… down under…

At a field entrance – an ancient arch of whale ribs, topped with a vertebra.

Acknowledgements

Gratitude for an early passion for nature must go to my mother who brought me up to look carefully at the sky and clouds each day and to colour them accurately. Ahead of her time, she designated part of our suburban garden for wild Australian bush species, largely reviled at that time. Most of all, when I was paralysed by polio she introduced me to the potential of swimming. My father, dedicated to chemistry research, unintentionally intensified my school focus on biology by relegating it to the status of only meriting study before breakfast as it was a mere 'pseudoscience', but along with particular teachers, lecturers and my research supervisor, he taught me to ask questions and to think.

In writing this book I am indebted to the eight friends who gave me their time to read and criticise the manuscript at various stages and I am particularly grateful to James Scourse for his input on the longest lived animal on the planet, the Icelandic Clam. Special thanks are due to my son, Andrew Scourse, for sharing his unique diary of life in the raw, surviving on a tiny island in the vastness of the Pacific Ocean, and for the use of his fine photographs as the basis for sketches of shared underwater happenings.

Wild quests spanning many years, through trials and disappointments as well as joys, can only come to fruition through support, encouragement and shared hope and enthusiasm. This vital and constant companionship has come from my husband, Peter, who has also on a practical level kept me out of trouble in the sea and on land. Most of all, he shared whole-hearted commitment and the demanding and disciplined task of reading and re-reading the manuscript in all its stages, and contributed many improvements.

I must also thank each of those whom we met along the way who shared their enthusiasm and knowledge and became a treasured part of the identity of time and place. Most important to the future of these wild shores and their seas are the dedicated individuals and organisations who protect and maintain them.

About the author

Nicolette Scourse was brought up in Australia where wildlife and beaches became part of her life; ever since she has passed on her passion for animals and plants in wild places through lecturing, teaching, writing and creating ceramics. She is the author of *The Victorians and their Flowers*. For nineteen years she was a children's Wildlife Watch Leader. Her mobility on land was impaired by childhood polio, but her late discovery of the wet suit and snorkel brought the opportunity for animal encounters in the one place where wild creatures remain largely unafraid of humans - the sea.

She studied Zoology at Nottingham and has a Cambridge PhD in Animal Behaviour.

INDEX OF ANIMALS AND PLANTS

Illustrations in italics

INDEX OF PLACES